THE
APOSTOLIC
FATHERS

AND THE NEW TESTAMENT

THE APOSTOLIC FATHERS

AND THE NEW TESTAMENT

Clayton N. Jefford

The Apostolic Fathers and the New Testament
© 2006 by Hendrickson Publishers, Inc.
P. O. Box 3473
Peabody, Massachusetts 01961-3473

ISBN-13: 978-1-56563-425-1
ISBN-10: 1-56563-425-X

Printed in the United States of America

First Printing —July 2006

Except where otherwise noted, Scripture quotations are from the New
Revised Standard Version of the Bible, copyright © 1989 by the Divi-
sion of Christian Education of the National Council of the Churches of
Christ in the United States of America, and are used by permission.

Cover Art: Ivory casket known as the "Brescia Lipsanotheca" with me-
dallion portraits of Christ and Apostles, and scenes from the story of
Jonah, Christ teaching, Christ entering a sheepfold, and the story of
Susannah. Syrian-Alexandrine, 4th century C.E. Located in the Museo
Civico dell'Eta Cristiana, Brescia, Italy.
Photo Credit : Scala / Art Resource, N.Y. Used with permission.

Library of Congress Cataloging-in-Publication Data

Jefford, Clayton N.
    The Apostolic Fathers and the New Testament / Clayton N. Jefford.
      p. cm.
    Includes bibliographical references and indexes.
    ISBN-13: 978-1-56563-425-1 (alk. paper)
    ISBN-10: 1-56563-425-X (alk. paper)
    1. Apostolic Fathers. 2. Theology—History—Early church,
  ca. 30–600. 3. Bible—Criticism, interpretation, etc. I. Title.
    BR60.A65J43 2006
    270.1—dc22
                       2006006413

For Valiant Warrior, Ash Tree Meadow, and Deep Waters,
my heroes and heroine

Table of Contents

Abbreviations

ANCIENT SOURCES

Barn.	*Barnabas*
1–2 Clem.	*1–2 Clement*
Clement, *Protr.*	Clement of Alexandria, *Protrepticus* (*Exhortation to the Greeks*)
Clement, *Strom.*	Clement of Alexandria, *Stromata* (*Miscellanies*)
Col	Colossians
1–2 Cor	1–2 Corinthians
Dan	Daniel
Deut	Deuteronomy
Did.	*Didache*
Diogn.	*Epistle to Diognetus*
Eph	Ephesians
Eusebius, *Hist. eccl.*	Eusebius, *Historia ecclesiastica* (*Ecclesiastical History*)
Exod	Exodus
Ezek	Ezekiel
Gal	Galatians
Gen	Genesis
Gos. Thom.	*Gospel of Thomas*
Heb	Hebrews
Herm.	*Shepherd of Hermas*
Hippolytus, *Haer.*	Hippolytus, *Refutatio omnium haeresium* (*Refutation of All Heresies*)

Ign. *Eph.*	Ignatius, *To the Ephesians*
Ign. *Magn.*	Ignatius, *To the Magnesians*
Ign. *Phld.*	Ignatius, *To the Philadelphians*
Ign. *Pol.*	Ignatius, *To Polycarp*
Ign. *Rom.*	Ignatius, *To the Romans*
Ign. *Smyrn.*	Ignatius, *To the Smyrnaeans*
Ign. *Trall.*	Ignatius, *To the Trallians*
Irenaeus, *Haer.*	Irenaeus, *Adversus haereses* (*Against Heresies*)
Isa	Isaiah
Jas	James
Jer	Jeremiah
Jerome, *Vir. ill.*	Jerome, *De viris illustribus* (*On the Lives of Illustrious Men*)
Lev	Leviticus
LXX	Septuagint
2 Macc	2 Maccabees
4 Macc	4 Maccabees
Mal	Malachi
Mart. Pol.	*Martyrdom of Polycarp*
Matt	Gospel of Matthew
Num	Numbers
Origen, *Cels.*	Origen, *Contra Celsum* (*Against Celsus*)
Origen, *Princ.*	Origen, *De principiis* (*On First Principles*)
1–2 Pet	1–2 Peter
Phil	Philippians
Pliny, *Ep. Tra.*	Pliny the Younger, *Epistulae ad Trajanum* (*Letters to Trajan*)
Pol. *Phil.*	Polycarp, *To the Philippians*
Prov	Proverbs
Ps/Pss	Psalm/Psalms
Rev	Revelation
Rom	Romans
Sir	Sirach (or Ecclesiasticus)
Tertullian, *Praescr.*	Tertullian, *De praescriptione haereticorum* (*Prescription against Heretics*)

1–2 Thess   1–2 Thessalonians
1–2 Tim   1–2 Timothy

MODERN SOURCES

AF	Apostolic Fathers
AGJU	Arbeiten zur Geschichte des antiken Judentums und des Urchristentums
ANRW	*Aufstieg und Niedergang der römischen Welt*
AUS	American University Studies
BETL	Bibliotheca ephemeridum theologicarum lovaniensium
CBQ	*Catholic Biblical Quarterly*
CRINT	Compendia rerum iudaicarum ad Novum Testamentum
CS	Coptic Studies
CSHJ	Chicago Studies in the History of Judaism
FF	Foundations and Facets
HDR	Harvard Dissertations in Religion
HNT	Handbuch zum Neuen Testament
JBL	*Journal of Biblical Literature*
JECS	*Journal of Early Christian Studies*
JSNTSup	Journal for the Study of the New Testament: Supplement Series
JTS	*Journal of Theological Studies*
KAV	Kommentar zu den apostolischen Vätern
LCC	Library of Christian Classics
LD	Lectio divina
NGS	New Gospel Studies
NovT	*Novum Testamentum*
NovTSup	Supplements to Novum Testamentum
RevScRel	*Revue des sciences religieuses*
RivAC	*Rivista di archeologia cristiana*
RSR	Recherches de science religieuse

SBLSBS	Society of Biblical Literature Sources for Biblical Study
SEÅ	*Svensk exegetisk årsbok*
SJC	Studies in Judaism and Christianity
SJT	*Scottish Journal of Theology*
SNTSMS	Society for New Testament Studies Monograph Series
SNTW	Studies of the New Testament and Its World
StPatr	*Studia patristica*
TUGAL	Texte und Untersuchungen zur Geschichte der altchristlichen Literatur
VCSup	Supplements to Vigiliae christianae
WUNT	Wissenschaftliche Untersuchungen zum Neuen Testament
ZNW	*Zeitschrift für die neutestamentliche Wissenschaft und die Kunde der älteren Kirche*

Introduction

How to Talk about the Apostolic Fathers?

I am especially grateful to have the opportunity to produce this volume. And yet, there is a real sense in which the writing of this book has been an unexpectedly difficult task for me. I may perhaps best illustrate my point with the following scenario:

Imagine a scene in which a mother takes her child into a large candy store. At the door the child is told that whatever he or she desires is available for the taking—everything is up for grabs, so to speak. The choices are endless, and it would be almost too much for a youngster to imagine! Thrown into such a world of choices, most children could be placed into one of several categories. Those who are aggressive and of single purpose undoubtedly would launch immediately into the task at hand—grabbing and eating, or choosing and hoarding. Those who are more cautious might freeze in their tracks, hardly able to make that most basic of decisions when faced with such a marvelous opportunity. But a third option is also possible, the gathering of what seems to be the most attractive options, followed by the abandonment of those choices in favor of yet other possibilities. A person's first task, then, must be to decide where to begin and exactly how to proceed.

This book has been, in many respects, my own personal candy-store hell. The opportunity to explore together the two subjects that intrigue me the most in a professional sense—the New Testament and the apostolic fathers—is very much in my case what might be aptly described by the popular phrase "death by chocolate." Where can I, and where should we, begin the whole discussion of the apostolic fathers and their relationship to the world of New Testament literature? What must be said, and what is probably best left for another occasion?

Frankly, there seems to be no good way to describe the relationship between these two collections of early Christian literature in twenty-five words or less. In the same way that both apples and oranges are representatives of the fruit category, both of these literary collections are a secondary grouping of the same type of materials that were produced by the early church. The ancient formation of the New Testament canon eventually produced a body of (more or less) diverse texts that came to assume the status of "Scripture" for the Christian tradition. By a completely different avenue, the modern assemblage of the apostolic fathers ultimately linked (more or less) diverse texts that had previously become the "also-rans" of that same tradition. Early bishops and church councils made the watershed choices about which texts were to be included in the canon and which simply "need not apply." Of course, the assurance of apostolic authorship and the common usage of a particular text among scattered congregations came into consideration during such decisions. But ultimately, the distinctions between the writings of the fathers and the discourses of Christian Scripture are few. So, where are we to begin and what are we to say?

From the outset the reader should be aware that the treatment in the following pages is not arranged according to systematic and separate discussions of how the individual writings of Scripture and the fathers are related. I have decided that to begin with each of the fathers in order to compare individual writings to relevant New Testament texts would be both boring and tedious for most readers. Throughout the secondary literature one is able to find scattered commentaries on the fathers (though virtually none on the New Testament) that offer such attempts. Also, I have made a very brief and general effort myself in my student's introduction to this collection of literature.[1]

Further, and undoubtedly a surprise to many readers, I have not chosen to place my primary focus upon the common and important themes that each set of literature possesses. To be sure, such themes invariably are raised and addressed throughout the following pages.

---

[1] See Clayton N. Jefford, with Kenneth J. Harder and Louis D. Amezaga Jr., *Reading the Apostolic Fathers: An Introduction* (Peabody, Mass.: Hendrickson, 1996); and more recently, Clayton N. Jefford, *The Apostolic Fathers: An Essential Guide* (Nashville: Abingdon, 2005).

However, it seems better to me to discuss issues that tend to plague any student of Christian antiquity who attempts to read the Scriptures with a broader understanding of historical and literary background and who, at the same time, wishes to make some effort to inform that scriptural knowledge with the insights of other contemporary Christian voices. I chose, then, to address issues through a comparison of texts and not, vice versa, to address texts through a comparison of issues.

Finally, this volume is not designed to be a methodical, text-critical comparison of New Testament texts with parallels from the apostolic fathers, focusing upon the variations in manuscripts and sources. In that vein, several worthy efforts have already been made to cover the entire corpus of the apostolic fathers in the past, including the early work of the Oxford Society of Historical Theology in 1905[2] and, of course, the landmark Marburg dissertation of Helmut Koester, published in 1957, which was directed by Rudolf Bultmann.[3] Apart from these volumes, other scholars have undertaken more restrictive research into individual writings within the corpus on the question of biblical parallels, many of which are both thorough and convincing. But beyond this reason, the current volume was never envisioned as an attempt to undertake such a broad academic effort, particularly in the light of contemporary scholarship. Instead, we must be content here to work with broader themes and selected illustrations from relevant comparisons of intertextual parallels.

Of course, some time and effort are necessary in order to engage our current task. For some students, the endeavor is a candy-store delight—the rewards are both engaging and intoxicating. For other students, the restrictions of some "sugar intolerance" may make the entire project unpalatable and not worth the effort. The following materials are designed to make the rewards more immediate and intense for the first group of students and perhaps more encouraging for the second. Chapters are divided according to issues, not texts. They appear as follows:

---

[2] A Committee of the Oxford Society of Historical Theology, *The New Testament in the Apostolic Fathers* (Oxford: Clarendon, 1905). An academic conference at Lincoln College in Oxford, held in April 2004, was conceived as an opportunity to celebrate the research efforts of this particular volume. It was anticipated that two volumes of papers from the conference would appear in 2005 to mark the one hundredth anniversary of that original publication.

[3] Helmut Koester, *Synoptische Überlieferung bei den apostolischen Vätern* (TUGAL 65; Berlin: Akademie-Verlag, 1957).

In chapter 1 ("Finding a Time and Place for the Texts") we begin where, I believe, the most challenging snare of our study lies in wait: the question of when and where our texts were written. This is a problem both for the corpus of the apostolic fathers and (in a lesser way) for the New Testament. Within each field of study some broad consensus of opinion has been formed in recent years, sometimes achieved with the advantage of recent archaeological data and secondary estimations, but all too often from the larger void of limited information and sheer guesswork, which now have become accepted opinions. For those who want the ultimate answer to such questions (and I happily include myself here), I offer nothing to shake the world of early Christian studies. For those who could stand to have the questions more clearly identified, perhaps I will provide at least a surface map for further investigation. My primary concern in either case, however, is to inform the reader with respect to my own starting points and assumptions.

Chapter 2 ("The Authority of Texts and Traditions") provides some focus to the written and oral sources that now lie behind the apostolic fathers. This is a broad category of materials, naturally, a subject whose more intricate details already have been the subject of numerous studies in books and journals. My goals are not so ambitious. I hope simply to identify the types of materials that are shared among our texts, to isolate some of the forms that seem to serve as common links between the fathers and the New Testament, and to suggest some general trends that may help to shed some light upon our general knowledge of early Christian literature.

Chapter 3 ("Codes of Conduct and Christian Thinking") takes a quick look at one of early Christianity's most important issues: the regulation of the ethical lifestyle. Already an issue among Paul's earliest contacts, by the end of the first century specific codes and regulations had become foundational for the Christian life. There is a curious regularity about these codes, whose use and abuse continued to dominate the attention of later church leadership. Such codes never stood alone, but were offered both as support and justification within countless ecclesiastical debates.

A typical concern of those who study the rise of early Christian communities is addressed in chapter 4 ("Imagery of the New Testament Faith"). This section is a sweep through the apostolic fathers in a survey of New Testament imagery that appears there. The focus of this review is to offer a synopsis of ideas and motifs that the authors of the fathers found to be useful, either having borrowed them from the texts of Scripture themselves or having drawn them from the common materials of early Christian faith. Although some reference is made here to specific quotations that the fathers have drawn from Scripture, the primary focus is upon the use of broader images and ideas.

The next two chapters represent opposite sides of a coin, and perhaps should be considered as an extended unit. Chapter 5 ("The Question of Christians as Jews") seeks to review the struggle of the rising church consciousness concerning the role of Judaism in the midst of the fledgling Christian faith. The New Testament is a clear witness to this evolution, as has long been recognized. At the same time, the apostolic fathers offer further reflection on the theme as experienced by second-century church communities. In chapter 6 ("The Question of Christians as Citizens") I consider the result of the so-called Jewish question as the church of the fathers gradually came to define itself according to the parameters of Roman society. This evolution was by no means complete by the latest text of the apostolic fathers, but a clear transition is evident.

The final chapter, chapter 7 ("How Persons and Places Influence History"), is a brief survey of historical personalities and locales that influenced the thoughts and theology behind the apostolic fathers. Although much of what appears here is modeled upon New Testament paradigms, at the same time a momentous transition occurred between the first and second centuries. Old ideas were expanded, and new possibilities were envisioned. In many cases, the transition represents the work of specific leaders who have responded to various problems and ecclesiastical issues, particularly as those concerns characterized specific church communities.

Finally, I have appended a short section entitled "The Significance of the Apostolic Fathers for New Testament Study." It is my hope that the present volume will serve as a worthy example of how the apostolic fathers may serve to underpin our further investigations into early Christian Scripture.

As a standard throughout the following pages I have employed the translations of the New Revised Standard Version for the scriptural references. For the apostolic fathers I have typically used the translations of Michael W. Holmes's most recent revision of J. B. Lightfoot and J. R.

Harmer's *The Apostolic Fathers*.[4] One will find here those texts that are most often included among the fathers: *Epistle of Barnabas, 1–2 Clement, Didache, Epistle to Diognetus, Shepherd of Hermas*,[5] the seven letters of Ignatius (*To the Ephesians, To the Magnesians, To the Philadelphians, To Polycarp, To the Romans, To the Smyrnaeans,* and *To the Trallians*), *Martyrdom of Polycarp, Epistle of Polycarp to the Philippians,* and the Fragments of Papias. As directly indicated when relevant, I occasionally offer my own translation of texts when I believe that some specific issue or rendition is desirable for the context of the discussion. No foreign words or phrases appear here without an accompanying English translation.

Let us begin!

---

[4] Michael W. Holmes, ed., *The Apostolic Fathers* (2d ed.; Grand Rapids: Baker, 1999). A third edition was due late in 2005.

[5] Two different systems, one older and one newer, are commonly used to cite the text of the *Shepherd of Hermas*. The present volume uses the newer system. For a helpful chart that compares the two systems see Holmes, *The Apostolic Fathers,* 333.

Chapter 1

Finding a Time and Place for the Texts

Those who read secondary literature on the apostolic fathers encounter a variety of perspectives and arguments with respect to the provenance and date for many of the texts. A typical introduction to any commentary on the literature will provide some survey of opinions for the text in question. A traditional patrology, most often within its section on the Christian literature of the second century, will provide a similar review of positions on the collected corpus. With more general investigations on the apostolic fathers, however, writers rarely offer much information by which to orient the reader toward his or her presuppositions. On the one hand, this approach gives the author a certain freedom to move between texts without the need to engage in the technical difficulties that arise with the critical issues behind the foundation of individual texts, or to address those scholars who debate such issues. On the other hand, the reader is less apt to discern any inconsistencies of logic that arise when an author holds certain views about one text that are not clearly compatible with views about another.

The present chapter is offered as a means by which to differentiate where and when the texts of the apostolic fathers were penned, at least as I understand the situation. I am fully aware that a variety of views may be found within the secondary literature. Speculation on these issues sometimes seems endless, though in most cases it may actually be culled into several dominant schools of thought. Some of these approaches are well reasoned and researched, while others are primarily speculative and intuitive. For certain texts the questions of time and place are relatively assured, and for others no answer seems possible.

I freely acknowledge that my own research into the fathers is not balanced. My personal interests and research needs have often found me at labor among the longer and better-known works within the collection rather than among the lesser-known pieces. At the same time, however, I have tried to pay attention to the total corpus of materials on a regular basis in order to gain a more rounded feel for the assumptions that lie behind the writings as a whole. In certain cases my judgments concerning place and date are motivated by the findings of patristic scholars and historians who are far more experienced with a particular writing. In other instances I find that I am comfortable working from my own personal intuition and private guesses.

As those who work in the field are fully aware, to some extent the determination of place and date may be argued according to the known authority behind the writings, as with the cases of Ignatius of Antioch or Polycarp of Smyrna. But in most instances the authors behind our texts are either assumed through the culmination of oral tradition or are lost to the annals of history. Historians generally acknowledge that the final form of the entire corpus of the apostolic fathers falls within roughly one hundred years, oriented primarily around the end of the first century until the latter half of the second century. At the same time, the location of the texts may span as wide a geographical range as from Rome to Egypt, incorporating important centers of early Christian faith and culture that arose within Palestine, Syria, Asia Minor, and Greece.

If students of second-century literature were honestly to confront the paucity of evidence concerning the origins of the apostolic fathers, there would be precious little that could be said with certainty. The difficulty with this reality, of course, is that it makes it particularly difficult to talk about these texts without the working framework of time and history. This becomes especially important when we discuss the apostolic fathers with respect to the collected literature of the New Testament, much of which itself is only assumed with respect to its specific historical circumstances. In other words, we know little more about the composition of New Testament texts such as the Gospel of Mark and the letters of Colossians, Hebrews, James, or Titus than we do about noncanonical works such as *2 Clement,* the *Shepherd of Hermas,* the *Didache,* the *Epistle of Barnabas,* and the *Epistle to Diognetus.* The primary difference is that scholars have researched and discussed the New Testament literature in a continuous stream of inquiry since its inception. No such history lies behind the apostolic fathers, however. These writings were composed early and, for the most part, were rediscovered by scholars only within more recent days.

The following pages are thus designed to provide the reader with my own position on the individual roots of the apostolic fathers, especially in the light of my understanding of New Testament texts. I am fully aware that many readers will not be in agreement with certain views that I hold either for the fathers or for Scripture. I am also painfully aware that my perspectives may ultimately be incorrect, either in small part or to some greater extent. Furthermore, I hold the inalienable human right endowed by ignorance to advise the reader that I am entirely likely to change my mind on specific texts as I become aware of new information and ideas, or simply because I acquire a different feeling for certain literary situations. In any case, the following is a brief presentation of my current views on the origins of the apostolic fathers. The writings are reviewed in order of my own certainty about specific texts, a certainty that wanes quickly as we move through the collection.

THE LETTERS OF IGNATIUS

As stated above, there are two individuals with whom certain of our texts may be clearly associated: the famous Ignatius, bishop of Antioch in Syria, and Polycarp, bishop of Smyrna in Asia Minor. I begin my review with Ignatius because what remains of his writings is more easily restricted in terms of a historical framework and timeline.

Ignatius was the second bishop of Syrian Antioch (or perhaps third, depending upon how one reads the evidence of the episcopal succession of that city)[1] until shortly after the beginning of the second century. At that time he was arrested by governmental authorities and taken to Rome for trial and, presumably, execution. The last indication

---

[1] Eusebius says that Ignatius was the second bishop after Evodius in one reference (*Hist. eccl.* 3.22.1), but second after Peter (presumably the apostle) in another (*Hist. eccl.* 3.36.2). One might thus infer that if Peter may be counted as the first bishop of Antioch, then the actual sequence may have been Peter, Evodius, Ignatius.

of the bishop's anticipated travel plans as known from his own hand appears in his comment that he would soon travel from Troas to Neapolis as he progressed toward Rome (Ign. *Pol.* 8.1). Not much beyond this is known. The bishop Polycarp, who clearly had close ties to Ignatius, indicated in later correspondence that he himself remained confused as to the fate of his friend (Pol. *Phil.* 13.2). No specific reliable record of the ultimate fate of Ignatius remains, with the exception of the ancient *Martyrium Ignatii*, which purportedly is an eyewitness record of the trial and execution of the bishop as reported by Philo, a deacon at Tarsus, and the Syrian Rheus Agathopus.[2] This text seeks to confirm the common tradition that Ignatius was martyred in Rome, but its authenticity has been questioned. Ultimately, the historical record preserves no reliable information for the modern researcher.

What remains from the pen of Ignatius comes to us only in the form of letters that he wrote during his forced march westward. From these texts we gain some knowledge of his personal concerns and ecclesiastical anxieties. It is indeed unfortunate that we have nothing from the bishop that was written prior to the time of his arrest, since what remains is primarily a testament to his thoughts while under duress. All the same, those letters that are preserved for us offer some feel for his place and time of writing.

There were two primary routes from eastern Syria across Asia Minor to Greece, the so-called northern and southern routes.[3] If one can accept the authenticity of the middle recension of the Ignatian correspondence,[4] which remains the most widely endorsed collection of letters attributed to the bishop, then it is possible to gain a reasonable reconstruction of his journey, at least across Asia Minor. It is unknown whether he traveled first from Antioch to Asia Minor by land

---

[2] The final, most reliable form of this document, the so-called *Martyrium Colbertinum,* is preserved in a heavily interpolated form within the tenth-century manuscript Codex Colbertinum in Paris. It derives from several recensions and surely was written after the second century, perhaps as recently as the fifth. Eusebius does not seem to have known the text himself.

[3] The description of these routes as a primer for the discussion of Paul's letter to the Galatians was admirably described over a century ago by W. M. Ramsay in *The Church in the Roman Empire before* A.D. *170* (London: G. P. Putnam's Sons, 1893) and *A Historical Commentary on St. Paul's Epistle to the Galatians* (London: G. P. Putnam's Sons, 1889).

[4] Namely, the letters to Ephesus, Magnesia, Tralles, Rome, Philadelphia, Smyrna, and Polycarp.

or sea.[5] From that point forward, in either instance, it seems that he was taken to Smyrna by an avenue that did not include the cities of Magnesia, Tralles, or Ephesus. His letters to these churches were written from Smyrna and clearly acknowledge that he was in contact with them through their own messengers. Presumably, these delegates were sent to the bishop precisely because he had been unable to visit the congregations himself while en route. The letters to the churches at Smyrna and Philadelphia were penned in Troas before Ignatius crossed the Aegean Sea to Neapolis in Macedonia. The letter to Polycarp appears to have been written in Neapolis, or at least it indicates that Ignatius had reached that port. Polycarp's own letter to the church at Philippi sometime later offers the strong suggestion that Ignatius had passed through that city along his way. From this point further the journey of Ignatius is unknown.[6] Thus, the authentic letters of Ignatius ultimately may be localized to the settings of only a few cities: Smyrna, Troas, and probably Neapolis. His letter to Rome gives no clue as to its place of origin, though clearly it was written along this same route.

Our second concern is the date of composition that is to be associated with the Ignatian correspondence. The letters undoubtedly were written within a short span of time, but those specific years are not quite clear. Three possibilities come to mind. The first is that Ignatius was arrested as an individual either for civil or religious reasons, and that considerations of widespread harassment of Christians remain irrelevant for consideration. Though this is possible, there is no evidence

---

[5] Several letters that are generally considered to be spurious must be taken into consideration here, including the letters to Tarsus, Antioch, the deacon Hero in Antioch (who followed Ignatius as bishop there), Philippi, the proselyte Mary of Cassobelae (location uncertain), and two to the presbyter John, as well as a letter sent to Ignatius by the same Mary. The first three letters (to Tarsus, Antioch, and Hero) claim to have been written in Philippi in Macedonia, a natural point along the bishop's route. These include greetings to the church of Tarsus and Laodicea, but they do not indicate whether Ignatius passed through those cities. Laodicea undoubtedly would have lay on his way regardless of which route he followed, while Tarsus would have been known to him simply because it lay within the relative proximity of his home at Antioch. The letter to the church at Philippi indicates that Ignatius employed an acquaintance, Euphanius, whom he met at Rhegium in southern Italy, to serve as his courier.

[6] See the reconstruction in William R. Schoedel, *Ignatius of Antioch: A Commentary on the Letters of Ignatius of Antioch* (ed. H. Koester; Hermeneia; Philadelphia: Fortress, 1985), 11–12.

to suggest its merit. Scholars traditionally have pointed instead to some period of more general Christian persecution for the arrest of the bishop, as has been suggested by ancient authors such as Eusebius.

Two successive imperial reigns have been the focus of the debate: the reign of Trajan (98–117) and the reign of Hadrian (117–138). The later reign of Hadrian has received some limited endorsement,[7] but the majority of scholars have supported the Trajan persecution as the most likely time of arrest. The early church historian Eusebius listed the presence of Ignatius within the Antiochean church during the reign of Trajan, yet he understood the arrest of the bishop to have occurred prior to Trajan's arrival in the city in the tenth year of his reign, around 108.[8] Otherwise, the specific years of the arrest and subsequent trip to Rome are not so clear. There does not seem to be any particularly good reason to focus on any specific year, and the span of a mere twenty years does not seem to be such a significant period of time that it ultimately makes much difference for the modern researcher. Though numerous scholars have argued for a date late in the reign of Trajan, I am content to support the traditional view that the arrest occurred sometime during the years 107–109.

This brings us to the question of which New Testament texts were known to Ignatius. It is clear that the bishop falls well within the influence of the letters of Paul, particularly since his letters to Ephesus and Rome are so closely modeled upon those of the apostle. Ignatius indicates only a slight awareness of the Gospels of Mark and Luke, and he seems familiar with Johannine themes, if not John's Gospel itself. It is clear, however, that the Gospel of Matthew is his preferred text, a gospel upon which he is dependent for many of his arguments. Though Matthew was the most widely preferred gospel text throughout the early Christian world, I am compelled to place its origin, or at least its earliest usage, within the Antiochean community. The use of Matthew's Gospel by Ignatius is only one of several components that lead me to this conclusion, some of which will arise in the discussion about the *Didache* below.

---

[7] To some extent this is based upon the variant reading of *Martyrium Colbertinum* that the arrest of Ignatius was in the nineteenth (not ninth) year after the start of Trajan's reign, thus the year 117.

[8] Eusebius, *Hist. eccl.* 3.21–22. The *Martyrium Colbertinum* supports this view with the added note that Trajan himself arrested Ignatius in the ninth year of the emperor's reign. This would place the arrest, and possibly the execution, sometime around the years 107–108. Jerome places the date as 109.

THE *LETTER OF POLYCARP TO THE PHILIPPIANS*

The next writing for consideration is easily attributed to the author Polycarp, bishop of Smyrna.[9] To my knowledge, the authenticity of this text has never been questioned. The text represents the only communication that we have from the venerable Polycarp, and it reveals some important insight into his view of the nascent Christian situation.

Polycarp is widely known to have served the church as an important leader over numerous decades. The age at which he came into a position of prominence in the church is uncertain, but early authorities observed that he lived a full life, dying at the age of eighty-six.[10] The year of his death by martyrdom is likewise uncertain, but typically it is placed around one of two dates. The primary witness to the death of Polycarp is the *Martyrdom of Polycarp,* a text that is poorly preserved and much edited. The meager evidence that the *Martyrdom* offers includes the following single reference:

> Now the blessed Polycarp was martyred on the second day of the first part of the month Xanthicus, seven days before the kalends of March, on a great Sabbath, about two o'clock P.M. He was arrested by Herod, when Philip of Tralles was high priest during the proconsulship of Statius Quadratus, but while Jesus Christ was reigning as King forever. (*Mart. Pol.* 21.1)

It appears that most patristic scholars work with this testimony as evidence that the bishop's death occurred sometime during the years 155–160 (most often given as 156). If one follows the testimony of the early church historian Eusebius, the martyrdom took place a decade later at the time of Marcus Aurelius, who reigned during the years 161–180 (most often given as 167). If we accept the later date of death, it would place Polycarp in the important ecclesiastical role of bishop at a very young age, since, as argued above, he corresponded with Ignatius "bishop to bishop" shortly before or around the year 108, thus making Polycarp roughly twenty-seven years of age. This is not impossible, of course, and it has been accepted by some as sufficient reason to date the martyrdom of Ignatius to the latter days of Trajan's reign.[11] If one were

---

[9] Early on, the letter is attributed to the bishop by Irenaeus, *Haer.* 3.3.4; see also Eusebius, *Hist. eccl.* 4.14.8.

[10] So *Mart. Pol.* 9.3; Eusebius, *Hist. eccl.* 4.15.20.

[11] See, for example, Helmut Koester, *History and Literature of Early Christianity* (vol. 2 of *Introduction to the New Testament;* 2d ed.; FF; Philadelphia: Fortress; New York: de Gruyter, 1982), 281.

to accept the earlier date of death, however, then Polycarp would have been roughly thirty-eight years of age at the time of his correspondence with Ignatius. This, to me, seems a more likely scenario and is the assumption that I hold throughout the following pages.[12]

In the final analysis, of course, none of this information provides us with a specific date for the writing of Polycarp's letter to the church at Philippi. Instead, we are dependent upon the internal data of the text for clues. Specific references to Ignatius within the letter (Pol. *Phil.* 1.1; 9.1; 13.2) often are cited as evidence that the bishop of Antioch most likely had already reached his end at Rome. Polycarp seems to have heard this news yet eagerly sought to gain further details concerning the event and its aftermath. The resulting date of the text might thus be attributed to a time of several weeks to several months after the death of Ignatius around the year 108. Indeed, this is the assumption of many scholars.

This solution naturally assumes that our letter was composed as a single piece. The challenge to textual unity, and thus to such an early date, offers an argument that would place a portion of the letter (chapters 1–12) several years later than the original text (chapters 13–14). The proposed date for the later letter would be 135–137, according to this argument, based upon perceived anti-Marcionite aspects that come through, especially in chapter 7.[13] This hypothesis has received detailed consideration and offers some intriguing possibilities with respect to our understanding of the date for the correspondence, but it has not been universally accepted among scholars. Subsequently, I, too,

---

[12] Others who support an earlier date for Polycarp's death include Johannes Quasten, *The Beginnings of Patristic Literature* (vol. 1 of *Patrology;* Utrecht: Spectrum, 1950; repr., Westminster, Md.: Christian Classics, 1990), 77; Paul Hartog, *Polycarp and the New Testament: The Occasion, Rhetoric, Theme, and Unity of the Epistle to the Philippians and Its Allusions to New Testament Literature* (WUNT 2/134; Tübingen: Mohr, 2002), 31; Kenneth Berding, *Polycarp and Paul: An Analysis of Their Literary and Theological Relationship in Light of Polycarp's Use of Biblical and Extra-Biblical Literature* (VCSup 62; Leiden: Brill, 2002), 11 n. 32. For further discussion about the issues involved with the history of interpretation of Polycarp's death see Boudewijn Dehandschutter, "The Martyrium Polycarpi: A Century of Research," in *ANRW* (ed. Hildegard Temporini and Wolfgang Haase; Part 2: *Principat,* 27.1; Berlin: de Gruyter, 1993), 485–522.

[13] This view was first proposed by P. N. Harrison, *Polycarp's Two Epistles to the Philippians* (Cambridge: Cambridge University Press, 1936).

follow the traditional understanding for the unity of the letter and thus assign the writing of the text to the years 108–109.[14]

The next question is that of provenance. There is no particular reason to argue that Polycarp's letter was written from any place other than his home community at Smyrna. This is the general assumption of those who have worked with the letter, and it is mine as well.

Of more curious consideration is the matter of which of the early Christian literary resources were available to Polycarp. Comparisons of language and style would seem to indicate a close association between Polycarp and the Pastoral Epistles of the New Testament.[15] To this end, Polycarp is very much in the Pauline tradition that Ignatius likewise endorsed. One discovers in Polycarp's letter a similar consideration for church order that dominated the time of ecclesiastical leaders throughout the second century. With respect to other scriptural sources behind Polycarp's work, his single correspondence provides precious few clues. It appears that he was aware of 1 Peter and 1 John, and made some limited use of the Gospel of Matthew. Otherwise, he has left us no further evidence of gospel traditions and their usage among the churches of second-century Asia Minor. We must assume from his status as a prominent bishop for a prestigious Christian community such as that at Smyrna, that he had access to various early traditions. Unfortunately, the textual evidence to support further speculation is meager.[16]

THE LETTER OF THE ROMANS TO THE CORINTHIANS (*1 CLEMENT*)

The letter that we know as *1 Clement* purportedly was written by the church at Rome to the church at Corinth in response to problems that had arisen among the Corinthian Christians. As the letter states,

---

[14] However, a strong case may be made for the later date of 115; see Hartog, *Polycarp and the New Testament,* 169.

[15] See Clayton N. Jefford, "Household Codes and Conflict in the Early Church," *StPatr* 31 (1997): 121–27. Though I find von Campenhausen's suggestion that Polycarp may actually have edited the Pastoral Epistles intriguing, I do not find it ultimately conclusive; see Hans von Campenhausen, *Aus der Frühzeit des Christentums: Studien zur Kirchengeschichte des ersten und zweiten Jahrhunderts* (Tübingen: Mohr, 1963), 197–252.

[16] Most helpful here is the survey of New Testament sources offered in Hartog, *Polycarp and the New Testament,* 170–71.

the issue in question revolved around certain Corinthian presbyters who had been expelled from their positions of leadership. The ultimate concern of our author was for community harmony and the need to re-establish order and peace within the divided church.

No specific author is named for the text; merely the context of the church at Rome (proem) is given. In a certain sense this is both helpful and distracting. On the one hand, we can feel reasonably certain that the text was written in Rome. On the other hand, this insight combines the answer of location with the less clear question of authorship, which itself ultimately raises the more provocative issue of date.

No real effort has ever been undertaken to deny a Roman locale for the origin of the text. The issues of church hierarchy and apostolic succession seem well suited to the concerns of a context such as that at Rome (though other domains need not be excluded). As many authors have argued, it seems appropriate that the church at Corinth would appeal to Rome for leadership and guidance on the question of displaced presbyters. The capital of the empire would be a natural direction for citizens within the Mediterranean world to look, the appeal of a provincial community to the central government. Here, we can imagine the truism that "all roads lead to Rome."

At the same time, we should not be misled by more modern constructions of ecclesiastical power, since the Christian situation in antiquity was not as clearly defined with respect to avenues of influence as were the economic and political states of affairs. For example, one might easily argue that the Corinthians may well have asked for help from the Roman church because of collegial ties, not because of Rome's perceived dominance.[17] This perspective is supported by the observation that *1 Clement* makes no reference to the authority of any local bishop.[18] Presumably, if a single authority such as a bishop had pre-

---

[17] So James S. Jeffers, *Conflict at Rome: Social Order and Hierarchy in Early Christianity* (Minneapolis: Fortress, 1991), 95. As W. H. C. Frend indicates, the tradition that a single monarchical bishop "had always been the form of church government cannot be traced beyond Hegesippus (c. 175)" (*The Rise of Christianity* [Philadelphia: Fortress, 1984], 130).

[18] Ignatius himself may have penned his letter to Rome because he anticipated it as a site where he held little actual influence, not because he considered it a superior center of faith. This is the foundation of my suggestion elsewhere that the bishop's letter was more of a subtle plea for assistance than, as is traditionally assumed, a bald declaration on behalf of a desire for martyrdom; see Clayton N. Jefford, "Ignatius of Antioch and the Rhetoric of Christian Free-

sided over the Roman church, the power of his authority would have been readily accessed for the author's argument. It would appear, instead, that the correspondence of *1 Clement* involved advice from a college of ruling presbyters to yet another group of presbyters. The advice given throughout is pastoral and pleading, never authoritative.

This leads us to the question of authorship behind the letter. The situation of *1 Clement* strongly suggests the collective voice of many persons, as is suggested by the consistent use of "we" throughout the text. Undoubtedly, this multiple voice was expressed through the hand of a single individual, perhaps the secretary of church rulers or a leader among leaders. The letter gives no indication as to the specific identity of this person, but later authorities have made clear suggestions that should be given serious consideration.

It was not until the late second century that Christian writers began to connect the name of Clement with our text. The *Shepherd of Hermas* (early second century) already had mentioned a certain Clement as a Christian of Rome, a person who may have served some secretarial or administrative function within the church there.[19] Yet the author of the *Shepherd of Hermas* never made any specific association between this person and the writer of *1 Clement*. Indeed, the *Shepherd* made no use of the text of *1 Clement* at all, which is a curious omission because the two writings presumably came from the same locale. Various other Christian authorities, writing later in the century, made a more exact association of the letter with the name of Clement. In a letter to the bishop Soter of Rome (ca. 166–ca. 174), the bishop Dionysius of Corinth referred to two previous letters that had been sent to the Corinthian church from Rome. Soter had written the first one; the second, earlier text was from the hand of Clement, an individual who received no further description.[20] Irenaeus made a more specific connection between the text of *1 Clement* and the third bishop of Roman succession named Clement. The details of the letter that is ascribed to the bishop are clearly those of our *1 Clement*.[21] Finally, Clement of Alexandria

---

dom," in *Christian Freedom: Essays by the Faculty of the Saint Meinrad School of Theology* (ed. C. N. Jefford; AUS 7/144; New York: Lang, 1993), 25–39.

[19] So *Herm.* 8.3: "Therefore you will write two little books, and you will send one to Clement and one to Grapte. Then Clement will send it to the cities abroad, because that is his job."

[20] As preserved by Eusebius, *Hist. eccl.* 4.23.11.

[21] Irenaeus, *Haer.* 3.3.3; see also Eusebius, *Hist. eccl.* 3.15.1.

attributed the text of *1 Clement* to the "apostle Clement" and quoted freely from scattered portions of the letter.[22]

The quantity of ancient testimony for someone named Clement as the author of our text seems convincing, but the uncertainty of who this individual may have been—apostle, bishop, administrator—is not comforting. Such titles and roles are not mutually exclusive, of course, but they yield little specific idea as to the author's exact identity. The question of authorship thus leads us into the issue of the date of the writing. I am convinced that a decision on the time of composition is inextricably interwoven with some decision about the author.

A standard school of thought has come into existence among scholars that the text belongs sometime toward the end of the reign of the emperor Domitian (81–96) or perhaps at the beginning of the reign of the emperor Nerva (96–98).[23] As argued, this would explain the persecution that faced the church in Rome according to the author (*1 Clem.* 1.1), the reference to the Christians who had lived blamelessly within the community "from youth to old age" (*1 Clem.* 63.3), and the suggested reference to the deaths of Peter and Paul (*1 Clem.* 5.3–6.1) in past days, presumably during the reign of the emperor Nero (54–68). This would also be in accord with the rule of Clement as the bishop of Rome from 92–101, as indicated by Eusebius.

Of course, not everyone agrees with this dating, and I myself am not completely satisfied. Some have argued for a later time, but many prefer something earlier. Clearly, the best arguments for an earlier date include the following:[24] (1) Even if Clement is considered the author of the text, the suggestion that he was some type of secretary might argue that he was not yet bishop. (2) The discussion of the temple in chapters 40–41 seems to assume that the temple is still standing and liturgically active. (3) An argument based upon any reference to the temple would have been seen as counterproductive among the anti-Jewish tendencies of the church at the end of the first century. (4) The reference to chaos

---

[22] Clement, *Strom.* 4.17.

[23] See Frend, *Rise of Christianity*, 97, 120; Quasten, *Beginnings of Patristic Literature*, 42–43; John Dominic Crossan, *The Birth of Christianity: Discovering What Happened in the Years Immediately after the Execution of Jesus* (San Francisco: HarperSanFrancisco, 1998), 511.

[24] I am dependent here upon the brilliant analysis by Thomas J. Herron, "The Most Probable Date of the First Epistle of Clement to the Corinthians," *StPatr* 21 (1989): 106–21.

and problems in *1 Clem.* 1.1 may be less a reference to an imperial persecution than a reference to troubles throughout the empire in general, or even within the local church community in specific. (5) The recognition of Peter and Paul as those who "belong to our own generation" (chapter 5) may mean more specifically in recent years, rather than simply "of our time." (6) The author uses the motifs of the suffering servant of Isa 53 and Ps 22 that were likewise employed by the New Testament gospels but does not cite the gospels themselves. (7) The single-bishop system that Ignatius envisioned after the beginning of the second century does not seem evident in *1 Clement,* thus suggesting an earlier date than the end of the century. Indeed, we perhaps should assume that the rise of an established bishop in Rome took more than the decade of time often suggested between the writing of *1 Clement* and Ignatius. I am ultimately content, therefore, to place *1 Clement* in Rome, written by the hand of someone named Clement (perhaps eventually to become Pope Clement) after the deaths of Paul and Peter (by tradition during the reign of Nero) but before the fall of the temple in the year 70.

THE TEACHING OF THE TWELVE APOSTLES (THE *DIDACHE*)

Those who know my work are well aware that the *Didache* is the text to which I have devoted the majority of my research interests. It is an ancient Christian source that has provoked considerable debate and controversy over the roughly 125 years since its rediscovery. Discussion about the time and place of the *Didache* tends to fall into either of two vaguely defined approaches: that of students who believe that the text was written after the composition of the New Testament gospels, and that of students who are committed to the belief that the materials within the *Didache* are preserved from earlier traditions. There are numerous variations on these themes, of course, some of which perhaps may be classified into schools of thought. As I read through secondary literature on the subject, I discover that even I seem to have been classified into a certain school,[25] though this may be a school of only a

---

[25] Thus, I am defined as a "fourth opinion" by Crossan, *Birth of Christianity,* 384 (see the entire helpful survey on pp. 383–87). Though I have refined my

single student! In any case, literature on the *Didache* is extensive, as are the views concerning its origins and development within early Christianity.[26]

The reader should thus be aware that the views I offer here, while in partial agreement with a wide array of scholars, are primarily of my own device. Though I am happy with my own position on issues related to the *Didache,* I remain fully conscious of the reality that my conclusions are based in part upon a mass of confusing evidence and in part upon the "feeling" that I have gleaned from the text itself.

Unlike the literature discussed thus far, the *Didache* clearly is the product of several writings and revisions. This suggests to me that portions of the text may be quite old (perhaps among the earliest traditions of early Christian literature), while others probably benefit from the experiences of a later editor (or editors) who saw the Christian tradition as it came together into a more uniform understanding of the faith. A parallel situation undoubtedly existed with the formation of the New Testament gospels, especially in the case of the Gospel of John, and many of the materials within the *Didache* are comparable to those gospel traditions either in form or application.

With this understanding of an "evolved literature" in mind, I consider a date of composition for the *Didache* to be a complex issue. In the first instance, I believe that the traditions that are found within the *Didache* are precisely of a "remaining" nature; that is, they are preserved materials. They probably are every bit as old as the traditions with which the apostle Paul worked as he visited early Christian communities around the Mediterranean and encountered their idiosyncratic beliefs and liturgies. I am not sure how to put a date on such texts except to say that they precede the work of Paul in their origin.

---

views over the years, I still hold to the basic outline of the origins of the *Didache* that I offered in my published dissertation; see Clayton N. Jefford, *The Sayings of Jesus in the Teaching of the Twelve Apostles* (VCSup 11; Leiden: Brill, 1989), 142–45.

[26] For an excellent review of arguments and issues see Jonathan A. Draper, "The *Didache* in Modern Research: An Overview," in *The Didache in Modern Research* (ed. J. A. Draper; AGJU 37; Leiden: Brill, 1996), 1–42; see also the bibliography available in Kenneth J. Harder and Clayton N. Jefford, "A Bibliography of Literature on the *Didache*," in *The Didache in Context: Essays on Its Text, History, and Transmission* (ed. C. N. Jefford; NovTSup 77; Leiden: Brill, 1995), 368–82.

At the other end of the time line, it is extremely difficult to know at what point the final editor of the *Didache* last contributed to the text. Even those scholars who treat the *Didache* with a conservative eye tend to place the composition of the writing no later than around the year 120. There does not seem to be any particular reason for this date except that it permits time for the prior development of all or most of the New Testament literature and explains why other Christian authors from the early part of the second century do not use the text. I, too, find no reason to reject this time as the probable terminal date.

The real issue remains to explain how the basic elements of the *Didache* came together as an editorial process between the middle of the first century and the early decades of the second century. This brings me to the question of location. Scholars have offered numerous sites over the years, mostly based upon a paucity of evidence and limited hunches. I personally favor the city of Antioch in Syria as the home of the *Didache* for several reasons: (1) Antioch supported a large Jewish community that found itself in continuing turmoil and struggle during the first century. This is admittedly true for numerous cities around the empire, including Alexandria and Rome itself. The issues that arise in the *Didache*, however, have secondary testimony from the New Testament book of Acts, which places them squarely in Antioch. They are to some large extent concerned with the same type of struggles between Judaism and Christianity, especially the debate about the need to employ Jewish perspectives within a Christian faith that was expanding rapidly through non-Jewish converts. (2) There is a strong Matthean angle to the *Didache*. I believe that the author of our text not only knew much of the specifically Matthean materials that now appear in the gospel before they were actually part of the gospel, but also was aware of the Gospel of Matthew as it was being composed.[27] As mentioned above, I would place the writing of Matthew in Antioch, and thus I am comfortable placing the *Didache* there as well. (3) Though scholars have occasionally objected to Antioch because Ignatius, who lived there early in the second century, did not use the *Didache* in his letters, it does in fact seem that he was aware of the traditions that were used by the

---

[27] I, therefore, am willing to accept the Didachist's references to "the gospel" (*Did.* 8.2; 11.3; 15.3, 4) as actual references to a written gospel, the Gospel of Matthew, and not to the gospel as some general understanding of faith and principles.

Didachist (i.e., either the collector of the materials or editor of that collection).[28] Of course, the approaches to community and doctrinal issues that Ignatius and the *Didache* assume would appear to be diametrically opposed, which may explain why the bishop never chose to employ the text in his arguments. Ultimately, I believe that the city of Antioch is as likely a context for the development of the *Didache* as any site that may be suggested. Arguments that seek to place the *Didache* within some isolated area because of the relatively cryptic or unique elements that appear in the text do not quite address what I see to be a very important issue. The issue, as I see it, is the clear tension of an active Christian community that is caught in a transitional moment between its Jewish roots and its developing Hellenistic consciousness, a concern that we find in the *Didache* and that perhaps was better reflected in a busy urban area than in an isolated town or rural setting.

This raises the issue of which New Testament materials were known by the author and editors of the *Didache*. I am convinced that the author knew materials that were often incorporated into the Gospel of Matthew (now commonly known as "special M" texts), though the extent of that collection is now lost to us.[29] There is clearly a Pauline consciousness in the text as well, as is seen in comments about prophets being worthy of their food (*Did.* 13.1; cf. 2 Thess 3:7–9) and warnings about the end times (*Did.* 16.5–6; cf. Gal 3:13; 1 Thess 4:16), though the Jewish concerns of the author are not those of Paul. Finally, the editor of the text, whether the same as the previous author (collector of traditions) or perhaps more than one person, had come to know at least the Gospel of Luke or some version of its materials (see *Did.* 1.3b–2.1).

---

[28] See the argument in Clayton N. Jefford, "Did Ignatius of Antioch Know the *Didache*?" in Jefford, *The Didache in Context*, 330–51. To some extent, this seems a natural conclusion to be drawn from the observations of Streeter that both Ignatius and the *Didache* are deeply steeped in the text of Matthew; see Burnett Hillman Streeter, *The Four Gospels: A Study of Origins* (London: Macmillan, 1936), 504–11.

[29] See the intriguing analysis by Stephenson H. Brooks, *Matthew's Community: The Evidence of His Special Sayings Material* (JSNTSup 16; Sheffield: Sheffield Academic Press, 1987). The question of whether the *Didache* and Matthew have actually used common sources or, instead, whether Matthew has used the *Didache* itself, has been admirably addressed in recent research by Alan J. P. Garrow, *The Gospel of Matthew's Dependence on the Didache* (JSNTSup 254; London: T&T Clark, 2004).

THE *MARTYRDOM OF POLYCARP*

The writing that purports to be an eyewitness account of the death of Polycarp, bishop of Smyrna, contains characteristics that are paralleled both in the letters of Ignatius and Polycarp and in the text of the *Didache*. By this I mean to say that we have a text that is framed as a letter, and presumably was circulated in Christian antiquity in that very format, yet that originally may have been a simple, early account of Polycarp's martyrdom that eventually was handed forward through the agency of several Christian editors.

As mentioned earlier in the section on Polycarp's letter to Philippi, textual sources indicate that Polycarp was martyred either in the year 167[30] or, as I and many others believe, a decade earlier during the years 155–160. The church at Smyrna presumably was a well-established and thriving community. The loss of its bishop does not appear to have been an isolated event, at least as noted by the church historian Eusebius, who places the martyrdoms of Carpus, Papylas, and Agathonice, all from nearby Pergamum, during this same period.[31] It seems reasonable that those members of the church at Smyrna who witnessed the bishop's death would have recorded the event as a means by which to glorify Polycarp. The distribution of the account of the martyrdom by means of a letter to the church at Philomelium, and perhaps elsewhere throughout Asia Minor, may well have been a secondary adaptation of the martyrdom story.

What this tells us is that the text of the *Martyrdom* was written in Smyrna by the faithful followers of Polycarp who lived as a part of his church community. The date of the writing is unknown, but most likely it should be placed within a short period of time after the bishop's death during the years 155–160. We cannot be certain whether the record of the event was made within a few weeks or a few years after the event, but clearly it derived during the living memory of those who were witnesses.

According to chapter 20 of the *Martyrdom,* someone named Evarestus is identified as the author of the text—that is, the person who

---

[30] So Eusebius (*Hist. eccl.* 4.14.10), who places the death of Polycarp within the reign of the emperor Marcus Aurelius (ruled 161–180).

[31] Eusebius, *Hist. eccl.* 4.15.48.

penned the work in response to the queries of the church at Philo-melium. There is some question concerning whether this is the author of the original account or, instead, a later hand in the transmission of the report of the bishop's death. My assumption is that Evarestus is the author of the letter format of the text, not necessarily the person who recorded the actual event. I hold this belief in the light of the numerous parallels to the passion narratives of the New Testament gospels that baldly shine throughout the *Martyrdom*. These are parallels to the trial and death of Jesus that I take to be later reflections upon the death of Polycarp, elements that were designed to bring his martyrdom into fa-vorable comparison with the death of Jesus. Clearly they are secondary to the account, and it seems as plausible to attribute them to the person named Evarestus as to any other unknown editor.

The other names that appear at the end of the text—Gaius, Irenaeus, Socrates, Pionius—tell us nothing about the origins of the text specifically. The name of Pionius traditionally has been associated with a later presbyter of the church of Smyrna who himself was eventu-ally martyred in the year 250. It is unknown whether this is the same person who penned the later *A Life of Polycarp*, but in all probability this text comes from an even later hand.

Apart from these general considerations, little else can be known about the origins of the *Martyrdom of Polycarp*. Smyrna would seem to be a logical location for the composition of the text. One can easily imagine that it derives from a member of the church at Smyrna who lived during the life of Polycarp and witnessed the martyr's horrifying death. The otherwise unknown Evarestus may indeed have been the au-thor of the original account of the martyrdom, but it seems more likely to me that he should be associated with the letter form of the text and the secondary embellishment of the account along the lines of the New Testament gospel passion narratives. In either case, nothing certain is known about this person other than his association with the text as briefly stated in chapter 20.

THE *SHEPHERD OF HERMAS*

The *Shepherd of Hermas,* somewhat like the *Didache,* is, in my opinion, very much the product of the compilation of sources. This is immediately evident (if perhaps unintentionally) from the traditional way in which the text has been divided: the *Visions,* the *Mandates* (or *Commandments*), and the *Similitudes* (or *Parables*). The only hint to authorship and location that is offered by the *Shepherd* appears in the first section, the *Visions.* In these opening chapters various elements are offered with respect to the narrator of the story. The hero of the tale is a slave named Hermas (*Herm.* 1.5), the property of a wealthy woman named Rhoda, who was a citizen in Rome (*Herm.* 1.1). In due course the reader discovers that Hermas has received his freedom, raised a family, and lives as a Christian, presumably in Rome or its environs. Questions naturally arise as to whether we are to understand Hermas, the narrator, actually to be the name of the author of the text as well. Further, if it is fair to make this assumption (as most scholars do), must we assume as well that the entire work of the *Shepherd,* the lengthiest writing among the apostolic fathers, is also to be attributed to this author of the *Visions?* Or, instead, should the remaining materials, the *Mandates* and *Similitudes,* be understood as the contribution of a later editor? Speculation among researchers naturally divides on this very question: single authorship or multiple authorship.

My impression concerning the *Shepherd* is that it surely must be placed within Rome or the surrounding community. The story line claims the vicinity of Rome for the plot, and there is no particular reason to think that the composition of the text does not belong there as well. As best as we can determine, it seems that all early Christian authors made the same assumption about this location, and the text of the *Shepherd* was widely known and used by variously scattered church authors.

With respect to authorship, I am not convinced that a single hand is responsible for the composition of the text in its entirety.[32] The nature of the *Mandates* and *Similitudes* argues for an entirely different authorial concern than that of the *Visions.* The *Mandates* and the *Similitudes* focus upon traditional teachings and moral instruction, while the *Visions* primarily provides the plot that holds the work together. Admittedly, the three units have been tied together admirably, as is evidenced by the return of characters within the story and by the

---

[32] My own view probably falls somewhere into this general observation on authorship offered by Carolyn Osiek: "Most scholars today have returned to the single author hypothesis, though not without some hedging about 'multiple sources' or 'multiple redactions'" (*Shepherd of Hermas: A Commentary* [ed. H. Koester; Hermeneia; Minneapolis: Fortress, 1999], 10).

revisiting of themes and ideas. This, however, merely suggests the hand of a practiced editor. Thus, my position concerning authorship reveals my preference to combine several suggestions that have received consideration over the course of the last century.

Numerous suggestions have been made concerning the identity of the original author of the *Shepherd*. Some scholars have suggested that the author was the apostle Paul, based upon the New Testament allusion to the Christians of Lystra who had dubbed him with the name "Hermes" (so Acts 14:12). Origen of Alexandria believed that the author of the text was none other than the first-century Roman Christian to whom Paul himself made reference in his letter to the Romans (Rom 16:14).[33] The agreement with this opinion that was expressed both by Eusebius and Jerome suggests either that Origen had a marked influence on subsequent interpreters of the *Shepherd* or that the idea already was in general circulation in Christian antiquity.[34] Finally, the Muratorian Canon lists the author as the brother of the bishop Pius of Rome during the years 140–154.

The difficulty for any attempt to assign a date to the *Shepherd* is the determination both of its earliest components and of its earliest author. As is argued by many scholars, the text appears to represent the work of multiple redactions, perhaps by several hands. We can be certain that its final composition occurred prior to the date of Irenaeus's *Against Heresies* (written during the 180s), since scattered portions of the *Shepherd* are cited and used throughout that particular work. At the same time, however, it is perhaps impossible to know the antiquity of the earliest forms of the text and its sources. I have argued elsewhere that the composition of the *Shepherd,* from its original form through its ultimate editions, perhaps occurred during the years 90–150.[35] I continue to remain in agreement with this view, though, admittedly, it is vague with respect to details and does little to clarify either the date of the first form of the text or the various stages that scholars often identify throughout the work. Though the seemingly apocalyptic imagery of the *Visions* and

---

[33] Origen, *Princ.* 1.3.3; 4.1.11. Interestingly, Origen does not offer any argument to justify the claim that this Hermas is the same person to whom Paul wrote. Instead, Origen simply works with this assumption as fact.

[34] Eusebius, *Hist. eccl.* 3.3.6; Jerome, *Vir. ill.* 10.

[35] See Clayton N. Jefford, with Kenneth J. Harder and Louis D. Amezaga Jr., *Reading the Apostolic Fathers: An Introduction* (Peabody, Mass.: Hendrickson, 1996), 139–41.

the brief allusion to coming persecutions (*Herm.* 6.7) are seen by some to reflect a setting of trouble as the background for the earliest form of the text, it is virtually impossible to be more precise concerning the date of such an event. Are we to envision the rule of the emperor Nero (54–68) or, instead, a period of travail under the emperor Domitian (81–96)? Or, could such a reference indicate some other limited external event that has since been forgotten by history? Or, indeed, must the persecution have even been external to the church community at all and not, instead, some internal ecclesiastical matter? I find it impossible to decide on a more specific date with the limited evidence at hand.

With respect to sources, I remain likewise puzzled. The materials of the *Mandates* clearly have parallels elsewhere in ancient literature, including the *Didache* and the *Epistle of Barnabas*. One could hardly argue that the *Shepherd* has been influenced by either of these sources, or vice versa. At the same time, with respect to the *Similitudes,* one hardly finds materials here that even remotely parallel those of the teachings of Jesus in the New Testament gospels. In other words, these are not materials that are dependent upon the writings of the New Testament gospels or even upon their sources, at least to the extent that we can know them. The images are much more detailed in form and function, more along the lines of the well-known fables of Greek antiquity. The elements involved perhaps have been drawn from an oral storehouse of common images that early storytellers used to explain morality and faith. They are inherently allegorical. And to that end, it is difficult to distinguish the antiquity of the story from the antiquity of its inclusion into the *Shepherd*. So for these materials—that is, those that have been incorporated into both the *Mandates* and the *Similitudes*—I can only guess that in some instances they predate the first composition of the *Shepherd*, and in others they are the work of a contemporary hand.

In the final analysis, then, I take the position that the elements of the *Shepherd's* story line are indeed to be assumed as reflective of the original author's situation. I place the text in or around Rome. The original author, who remains unknown, recorded *Visions* 1–4 sometime at the end of the first century, presumably during the reign of Domitian, which, as noted above, is somewhat after the composition of *1 Clement*. The remaining materials of the work—*Vision* 5, the *Mandates,* the *Similitudes*—were assembled subsequent to these opening materials, either by the original author, a different editor, or a combination of both. The distinction cannot be made. These materials probably predate the opening materials in origin or are drawn from some specific source in part. The final editing of the work must fall sometime during the first half of the second century, though speculation on a more precise date seems unjustified.

AN ANCIENT CHRISTIAN SERMON (*2 CLEMENT*)

As with the *Shepherd,* the date and location of *2 Clement* are uncertain. The few manuscripts that preserve this text place it immediately after *1 Clement,* thus justifying in part the early tradition that named the text and sought to link the two documents. In fact, the essence of *2 Clement* provides no reflection of *1 Clement* in any true sense. It is not offered as a letter, nor does it address the particular concerns of a community, unlike the interests stated by the author of *1 Clement.* No location is provided, either for the author or for the intended audience. The text is essentially an early homily or sermon whose occasion has since been forgotten and whose context was never preserved.

Suggestions for the location of the text invariably are tied to the question of authorship. Presumably, some aspect of ancient convention understood the two texts of *1 Clement* and *2 Clement* to be related in a certain sense. If this association may be assumed as the product of an original setting that was shared by the texts, then one might speculate that the works were preserved together at Corinth, the ultimate destination for *1 Clement,* of course. Either *2 Clement* was a homily that likewise was sent by the Roman church to Corinth, or it was preached in Corinth some short time after the arrival of *1 Clement* at the city.[36]

Of course, it is entirely possible that both texts were written in Rome and were preserved together because of their Roman connection, not because of any particular Corinthian association.[37] This leads us to the early suggestion that *2 Clement* was the work of the bishop Soter of Rome (ca. 166–ca. 174). As was observed above, Eusebius recorded that the bishop Dionysius of Corinth had made explicit reference to a letter

---

[36] For the latter option see Karl Paul Donfried, *The Setting of Second Clement in Early Christianity* (NovTSup 38; Leiden: Brill, 1974), 1.

[37] Frend, *Rise of Christianity,* 146–47. Frend places these texts together with the *Shepherd* in Rome as evidence of the diverse nature of the church there. Jeffers (*Conflict at Rome*) offers a more developed view of the Roman church, though without any inclusion of *2 Clement* within his considerations.

that he had received from Soter.[38] Eusebius himself held little regard for the authenticity of the letter that we now call *2 Clement*, however, having noted that it was not known among the ancient Christians.[39] What he meant by "authenticity" is not certain, of course. Presumably he simply did not consider it to be a text that should be associated with the name of Clement.

A noteworthy third option is that of Alexandria, Egypt.[40] Arguments for an Egyptian setting are based primarily on the observation that the text contains words and phrases that have a certain gnostic tone (or, perhaps, anti-gnostic), on the one hand, and that the author apparently had knowledge of the *Gospel of the Egyptians,* on the other hand.[41] Such arguments are perhaps slippery at best, naturally, since Gnosticism was hardly restricted to Egypt, and ancient texts often circulated widely apart from their site of origin. All the same, the possibility of Egypt should be given serious consideration.

As for my own perspective on the issues of place and date, I remain uncertain. I am greatly troubled that *2 Clement* does not seem to be known among the ancient writers of Christian literature. It is true that Eusebius mentioned the text, but whatever evidence may have once existed that the writing circulated in antiquity is now lost to us. If *2 Clement* had been written in Alexandria or elsewhere in Egypt, one might expect to find some reference to the materials in the writings of Clement of Alexandria or Origen, two scholars who made wide use of available materials. If *2 Clement* was produced in or around Rome, much as seems certain for *1 Clement* and highly probable for the *Shepherd,* one might also expect some wider circulation of the text, at least among western church communities.

In addition to the question of use and distribution of the text in antiquity, one must also consider the nature of the text itself. The author of *2 Clement* seems primarily concerned with speculating upon the nature of the church's view of Christ with respect to God: "Brothers, we ought to think of Jesus Christ, as we do of God, as 'Judge of the living and the dead'" (*2 Clem.* 1.1). This observation does not require a late

---

[38] Eusebius, *Hist. eccl.* 4.23.11.

[39] Eusebius, *Hist. eccl.* 3.38.4.

[40] For examples of the argument see Cyril C. Richardson, trans. and ed., *Early Christian Fathers* (LCC 1; Philadelphia: Westminster, 1953), 186–87; Koester, *History and Literature,* 233–36.

[41] See *1 Clem.* 4.5; 5.4; 8.5; 12.2.

date for the text, especially since such themes are abundant throughout the New Testament and early Christian literature, but I find it significant that this topic is the primary focus of the homily from beginning to end. Such sustained christological speculation seems more representative of mid- to late-second-century Christian theology than of earlier writings.

At the same time, it seems somewhat telling that the author of *2 Clement* makes significant use of specific New Testament sources. This suggests to some extent that the writing is somewhat later than the text of the *Didache* and the letters of Ignatius and *1 Clement.* It also suggests that our author is in a location that has access to numerous writings and is not restricted by an isolated setting.

It is true, of course, that a majority of the scriptural focus is on the Old Testament, much like the concerns of the late-first-century church. So too, the question of christological speculation is tightly interwoven with themes and language that traditionally are associated with a somewhat monotheistic understanding of God. To some scholars this has suggested the presence of a community that is primarily Jewish in its understanding of what it means to be Christian. It would be difficult to identify such a setting in the second century, especially since the late first century saw the rise of a competitive and often violent separation of Christian theology from its Jewish roots.[42]

In the final analysis, I place the text within a Corinthian setting. Whatever the connection that early Christians understood this writing to have had with *1 Clement,* it seems that the options for that explanation are more plentiful in the location of Corinth than elsewhere. This does not dismiss the possibility of other settings, naturally, but there seems no particularly strong reason to reject Corinth. Further, because of the author's knowledge of numerous New Testament writings and the focus upon christological speculation, I choose not to place the text either in the first century or early in the second. Instead, though the range of years is wide, I can imagine the composition of the work somewhere during the years 120–150.[43] Perhaps the most difficult question

---

[42] Having stated this widely recognized generalization, I am not convinced that it held true everywhere within the church, of course.

[43] With respect to Corinth as the location and the years 120–150, I find myself in basic agreement with the arguments of J. B. Lightfoot, *The Apostolic Fathers* (5 vols.; New York: Macmillan, 1889–1890; repr., Peabody, Mass.: Hendrickson, 1989), 1.1:201–4.

in this explanation is the strong sense of monotheism that shines throughout the text. Christology is not so clearly distinguished from the dominance of God as a father image here. I imagine that this focus, whether a reflection of any particular concern for the Jewish roots of Christian theology or otherwise, is designed to thwart the threat of gnostic inclinations. As is well known, such concerns existed in Corinth from the foundation of the church there.[44] There is some sense, therefore, in which the author of *2 Clement* has confronted a threat that the bishop Ignatius already had encountered at Antioch and that, as indicated by the limited evidence that remains from that city in the second century, continued into the fourth century.

THE *EPISTLE OF BARNABAS*

Though I tend to work with a very specific understanding of how the *Epistle of Barnabas* came into existence, I have left it toward the end of this review as an admission of the fact that my understanding is based primarily upon hearsay and the lack of irrefutable evidence in any particular direction. Furthermore, though my perspective is specific to a certain setting and date, it is hardly certain. The arguments for possible dates and locations are limited and narrow, and in my review of positions on the text I have not found the weight of any one approach to be ultimately conclusive.[45]

Let us first consider the issue of location. Perhaps the most widely espoused view for the provenance of *Barnabas* is that of Egypt, specifically Alexandria. Several observations traditionally are raised in support of this location. The text was known and used by Clement of Alexandria in the early third century, as well as by Origen and Didymus the Blind in subsequent years. Further, there is a strong association between Alexandria and the tradition of the first-century Christian

---

[44] As is noted by Theissen, Gnosticism often seemed to be a concern of Christians with an elevated social status, a sizable faction within the Corinthian church; see Gerd Theissen, *The Social Setting of Pauline Christianity: Essays on Corinth* (trans. J. H. Schütz; SNTW; Philadelphia: Fortress, 1982), 132–37.

[45] There is perhaps no better and more easily grasped review of perspectives to date than that provided in James Carleton Paget, *The Epistle of Barnabas: Outlook and Background* (WUNT 2/64; Tübingen: Mohr, 1994), 9–42.

Barnabas in early church history.[46] Finally, the allegorical style that the author of *Barnabas* employs was a well-used approach to scriptural interpretation in Alexandrian Christianity, and is broadly acknowledged as a virtual truism by scholars of early church history. These three categories of evidence are general and hardly conclusive to be certain, but together they offer a healthy argument.

There are foils to these suggestions, of course. First, the scholars of Alexandria had a wealth of literary sources available to them by virtue of the famous catechetical school of the city and the famous library that resided there. The simple fact that they knew the text does not comprise a compelling argument that it was written in their midst. Second, the traditional connection between Barnabas and Alexandria provides no worthy comment on the historical reliability of that connection. Furthermore, few scholars would make the argument that the apostle Barnabas of the New Testament book of Acts actually was the author of our work. Instead, the name of our current text may have been provided to the work at any time under any set of circumstances. Third, the allegorical method was used far and wide in the Mediterranean world and can hardly be restricted to the region of Egypt.[47] Though Alexandria was a noteworthy center of this method, it hardly had a lock on such interpretation. In addition to these arguments scholars occasionally raise the objection that the author of *Barnabas* did not utilize the "Logos Christology" that was so famous within Alexandrian theology and appears so typically among Christian authors of the locale.

Alternative locations have been proposed. As is usual for such discussions, the region of Syria or Palestine has been suggested, primarily based upon the argument that the author clearly was familiar with

---

[46] Indeed, it is perhaps not accidental that the New Testament book of Acts does not treat Egyptian Christianity and offers precious little about the character of Barnabas other than his association with the apostolic hero Paul. Perhaps the author either knew little about the church in this region or preferred not to pursue the form of Christian faith that arose there.

[47] This observation, which I believe to be both fair and correct, was raised against my position on Alexandria as the provenance of *Barnabas* in a review of one of my recent books. This was perhaps the single worthy critique in a review that otherwise showed little indication that the reviewer had bothered to read the book much beyond the introduction; see Roger S. Evans, review of Clayton N. Jefford, with Kenneth J. Harder and Louis D. Amezaga Jr., *Reading the Apostolic Fathers, JECS* 5 (1997): 607–8.

and employed rabbinic approaches to scriptural interpretation.[48] This theory is heavily dependent upon the assumption that rabbinic approaches were predominant in this particular region, of course, and stand as testimony to a particular locality.[49] Though the first point undoubtedly was true and the second is possible, it gives little credit to the existence of a large Jewish community and well-known cluster of rabbinic scholars who lived in ancient Alexandria.

A second option for consideration is the region of Asia Minor, with particular reference to the area of Philadelphia. This proposal has been offered primarily with the recognition that *Barnabas* appears to be a typical example of the approach to faith that was represented by those whom the bishop Ignatius opposed in his letter to the church at Philadelphia (see specifically Ign. *Phld.* 8.2). These Christians were highly devoted to the witness of Scripture alone, and they accepted no admission to faith that was not based on scriptural evidence.[50] It would be truly unique to have such a text preserved for us by a specific group that had received the witness of yet another ancient witness. Yet, though possible, the evidence is not sufficiently strong to be convincing to me in the face of other possible alternatives.

With regard to the issue of date, two primary arguments traditionally are raised: conflict and temple. The issue of conflict is a reflection of the fact that the author of *Barnabas* seems predisposed toward a specific understanding of persecution and violence, somewhat in the eschatological framework that exists in the book of Revelation. In chapter 4 references to present "works of lawlessness" ($\tau\grave{\alpha}$ $\check{\epsilon}\rho\gamma\alpha$ $\tau\hat{\eta}\varsigma$ $\grave{\alpha}\nu o\mu\acute{\iota}\alpha\varsigma$), "ten kingdoms" ($\beta\alpha\sigma\iota\lambda\epsilon\hat{\iota}\alpha\iota$ $\delta\acute{\epsilon}\kappa\alpha$) that are to rule the earth, and life in "the last days" ($\tau\alpha\hat{\iota}\varsigma$ $\grave{\epsilon}\sigma\chi\acute{\alpha}\tau\alpha\iota\varsigma$ $\acute{\eta}\mu\acute{\epsilon}\rho\alpha\iota\varsigma$) suggest the existence, threat, or potential threat of persecution for Christians. The issue of the temple is oriented toward the author's understanding of the temple in Jerusalem, which had been destroyed by the time of the composition of the text (see chapter 16). The question has been raised as to whether our author intends this discussion as a reference to the actual physical

---

[48] So M. B. Shukster and P. Richardson, "Barnabas, Nerva and the Yavnean Rabbis," *JTS* N.S. 33 (1983): 31–55.

[49] Much like the argument concerning allegorical interpretation, I suppose.

[50] So Klaus Wengst, trans. and ed., *Didache (Apostellehre); Barnabasbrief; Zweiter Klemensbrief; Schrift an Diognet* (Schriften des Urchristentums 2; Munich: Kösel, 1984), 114–18.

temple or, instead, to some metaphorical spiritual temple. I am convinced that it is to the physical structure that our author refers.

Thus, with conflict seen as imminent and the destruction of the temple as complete, we are left with three options: (1) the years 70–79, a time when Rome was seen as the tenth kingdom and the destruction of the temple was fresh in the mind of Jews and Christians; (2) the years 96–117, the reign of the emperor Nerva (96–98) or the emperor Trajan (98–117), a time when Christianity had grown particularly hostile to its Jewish roots; (3) the years 132–135, the time of the Jewish call to rebuild the temple and the resulting hostility of Rome's response (see *Barn.* 16.3–4). The majority of scholarship tends to favor the middle choice, with a preference for the years 96–100, and I am in agreement. This does not mean that the other options can be ruled out, but the tone of anti-Jewish hostility that pervades the work seems appropriate for a date at the turn of the century.

In conclusion, I hold to an Alexandrian provenance and a date around the turn of the century. Though I have espoused elsewhere that the author of *Barnabas* was not Jewish,[51] I now believe the opposite to be true. In my opinion, the work seems to be too steeped in Jewish tradition and exegesis to be the work of someone outside of the tradition. The author may in fact have been a Christian convert from a Jewish background who had written the work in the enthusiasm of conversion. This holds no specific comment on the date or provenance of the text, of course, but likewise it offers no argument against Alexandria at the turn of the century.[52]

THE *EPISTLE TO DIOGNETUS*

There is little question that the *Epistle to Diognetus* is a text that only barely qualifies to be included within the apostolic fathers, though the parameters of that artificial collection are broad and relatively undefined. Its inclusion into the corpus was made under the assumption that it could have been a text that was more ancient than most scholars

---

[51] Jefford, *Reading the Apostolic Fathers,* 11, 14–16.

[52] At the same time, if someone could demonstrate conclusively that the author was a non-Jewish Christian from Greece in the middle of the second century, I would not be particularly surprised either!

now believe. This, of course, defines the very problem of modern attempts to date and place the writing. The work is less of a letter than an apology, and in that sense it parallels admirably with writings such as *2 Clement* and *Barnabas,* neither of which appears to have actually been a letter in its original form.

An interesting difficulty in any attempt to determine the time and place of the text comes with the recognition that the work bears no testimony to authorship. Even the secondary title that the work now bears suggests only an audience—the unknown Diognetus—not an author. Given the nature of apologies in the second century, the writing theoretically could be located anywhere within the Mediterranean world and could be attributed to any time from the late first century through the third century.

This reality notwithstanding, scholars have offered numerous suggestions with regard to authorship. Names that are commonly suggested include Pantaenus of Alexandria (founder of the famous catechetical school), Hippolytus of Rome, Theophilus of Antioch, Quadratus,[53] or some unknown instructor to the emperor Marcus Aurelius. Most of these suggestions require that the text be placed either in the latter half of the second century or in the early part of the third. Most scholars, some of whom would like to assign the text to an earlier period within the second century, are hard-pressed to identify any specific author.[54]

An important issue in this discussion, of course, is the question of whether the name "Diognetus" should be taken as a reference to a specific historical figure or simply to any official of the Roman Empire to whom an early Christian apology might be deemed necessary. If the latter case is to be maintained, then most likely we can turn to an earlier example known from both the Gospel of Luke and the book of Acts, texts that are directed toward an otherwise unknown figure with the

---

[53] This author is known to us only from the so-called lost apology of Quadratus as mentioned by Eusebius, *Hist. eccl.* 4.3.1–2.

[54] So, for example, the date of ca. 150 offered by Frend (*Rise of Christianity,* 236) as an early compromise within the range of 130–190. Frend here follows the now classic study of the text by H. G. Meecham, *The Epistle to Diognetus: The Greet Text with Introduction, Translation and Notes* (Publications of the University of Manchester 305, Theological Series 7; Manchester: Manchester University Press, 1949). In contrast, we might consider the work of Johannes Quasten, who presents an admirable survey of possibilities. Ultimately, Quasten (*Beginnings of Patristic Literature,* 248–53) defers, but clearly he is attracted to the possibility that the work should be attributed to Quadratus.

name "Theophilus" ("Lover of God"). As with the *Epistle to Diognetus,* the identification of this individual remains uncertain among New Testament scholars. I personally am persuaded by the very nature of the name that we have only an imaginary figure in Luke and Acts. The name undoubtedly is a moniker that any early Christian reader could have used in self-identification. This may hold true with the name "Diognetus" as well, though the meaning of the name in Greek remains unclear, apart from the possibility that it served as a form of "Diogenēs" ("Ordained by God"). The conscious application of such a title, which would have held a natural appeal to those in authority, may have been the intent of the author. But if this is indeed a nonspecific label or is intended simply to indicate a certain stock figure for the common reader, then it does little to help place the text.

The other possibility, of course, is that the name actually represents a historical figure. This line of approach leads us to the one person whom scholars occasionally have suggested, Claudius Diogenes, a procurator of Alexandria at the end of the second century. Known from papyri that date from this period,[55] this figure is referred to within the papyri both as "procurator of Augustus and interim high priest" and "the most excellent Diognetus." The possibility that this person is the same as that to whom the title of our text refers is intriguing. On the one hand, the late date would explain why the *Epistle to Diognetus* does not seem to be known among second-century Christian authors. On the other hand, the location would explain why Clement of Alexandria was passing familiar with the text.

This is the assumption that I hold throughout the present volume, that the text of our epistle is directed toward Claudius Diogenes of Alexandria. At the same time, I am not entirely comfortable with this easy solution to a slippery text that otherwise reveals little specific evidence for either date or place. A skeptical element in my personality finds the quick-and-easy answer to such a vexing question to be rather suspicious. But what is more, this resolution to the problem of where and when still does not address the issue of who wrote the apology, an issue that may never be resolved to the satisfaction of those who research the history of early Christianity.

---

[55] See Robert M. Grant, *Greek Apologists of the Second Century* (Philadelphia: Westminster, 1988), 179.

THE FRAGMENTS OF PAPIAS

One last collection of material has been reserved for final discussion, the so-called Fragments of Papias. This assemblage of materials has been placed at the conclusion of this review because of the nature of the texts, not because I have some uncertainty either about the date of the author or his works or about the place where he wrote. Unlike our other writings, what remain in this particular category are simply fragments of the works of Papias or reports about him. None of these texts have been preserved within the context of any single document from him, but rather they survive as segments that have been embedded in the works of others.

The author of our fragments was the well-respected presbyter Papias of Asia Minor, who ultimately acquired the post of bishop of Hierapolis. Because there are various collections of the fragments of the writings and traditions of Papias, it is impossible to assign any particular date to the materials. It must be sufficient to note only that the bishop was active during the early second century, and that it was during these years that he penned his famous, though now lost, *Expositions of the Oracles of the Lord* (ca. 130). A well-known voice among early Christians, Papias led a Christian community that undoubtedly rose to some prominence within the early church because of the close proximity of Hierapolis to the important cities of Laodicea and Colossae. There is no particular reason to think that those materials preserved from Papias derive from any location other than the region of Asia Minor itself. Subsequently, I follow most scholars in the assumption that our materials, at least those traditions authentic to Papias, come from second-century Asia Minor.

FOR FURTHER READING

For modern authors who address the issues of setting, date, author, and audience with respect to the majority of texts in the apostolic fathers, see the following:

- Grant, Robert M., ed. *The Apostolic Fathers: A New Translation and Commentary.* 6 vols. New York: Thomas Nelson & Sons, 1965.

- Jefford, Clayton N., with Kenneth J. Harder and Louis D. Amezaga Jr. *Reading the Apostolic Fathers: An Introduction.* Peabody, Mass.: Hendrickson, 1996.
- Tugwell, Simon. *The Apostolic Fathers.* Outstanding Christian Thinkers. London: Geoffrey Chapman, 1989.

Other helpful introductory materials may be found in these volumes:

- Ehrman, Bart D., trans. and ed. *The Apostolic Fathers.* 2 vols. Loeb Classical Library 24–25. Cambridge, Mass.: Harvard University Press, 2003.
- Holmes, Michael W., ed. *The Apostolic Fathers.* 2d ed. Grand Rapids: Baker, 1999.
- Quasten, Johannes. *The Beginnings of Patristic Literature.* Vol. 1 of *Patrology.* Utrecht: Spectrum, 1950. Repr., Westminster, Md.: Christian Classics, 1990.
- Staniforth, Maxwell. *Early Christian Writings: The Apostolic Fathers.* London: Penguin, 1968.

Chapter 2

The Authority of Texts
and Traditions

As with most materials from antiquity, both the New Testament and the apostolic fathers are the production of two basic elements: tradition and innovation. The category of "innovation," or the ways by which an author or editor shaped materials, is the natural focus for most of the present volume. As one would expect, the process by which this was achieved followed what now are considered to be typical patterns of the period for both sets of texts. The category of "tradition," or the sources from which an author or editor drew specific materials, is the primary concern of the present chapter. As with innovation, the processes of tradition were similar for both sets of texts—that is, for the New Testament and for the fathers. Unquestionably, however, the single, best-known, and most widely debated caveat to the processes of tradition building lies within the question of the degree to which the authors of the apostolic fathers may have known and used the materials of the New Testament itself.

Students of early Christian literature are quite familiar with the numerous genres of tradition that appear throughout our texts: sayings, parables, miracle stories, and narratives; homilies, letters, liturgical directives, and martyrologies; hymns, prayers, creeds, and ethical codes—to name but a few. Many of these genres will serve as the specific subject matter of later chapters. The present chapter is intended to serve as a general review of the more prevalent genres and the possible links that they form between the apostolic fathers and the New Testament.

LETTERS

A considerable amount of ink has been devoted to the nature of letters and epistolography in antiquity, both Christian and non-Christian.[1] The categories into which the correspondence of ancient writers may be divided range from the casual notes that appear in various papyrological evidence to the classic royal letters between lesser and greater government officials. The letters of the New Testament, to the extent that they were actual letters and not merely works that have been forced into an epistolary style or have been mislabeled by later tradents, serve as the typical models of our literature.

The natural point of departure, of course, must be the writings of Paul.[2] The works of the apostle, whether from his own hand or that of an amanuensis, are at once both typical of Hellenistic literary style and unique to it. Here one finds the usual formulas for greetings and closings, as well as a distinctive body of content. Such elements are customary of any letter (whether ancient or modern), and they may be found even in the ancient papyri. At the same time, Paul tended to include elements that directly reflected the structure of more formal correspondence. These elements, though paralleled in the official letters of government figures, commonly assumed specific Christian nuances and forms. For example, the traditional opening of praise directed toward higher figures of authority in royal correspondence became the model for Paul's opening thanksgiving section, materials directed toward the praise of God and appreciation for the faith of his readers. Likewise, a closing benediction commonly falls toward the end of each of Paul's letters precisely where another author might have offered some parting good wishes to a reader of superior status.

Perhaps the single major contribution of Paul to the ancient letter form is his paraenesis section—that is, that part of the letter body that falls between the body proper and the closing materials. Here one dis-

---

[1] The most convenient introduction to early Christian letter forms may still be found in William G. Doty, *Letters in Primitive Christianity* (ed. D. O. Via Jr.; Guides to Biblical Scholarship; Philadelphia: Fortress, 1973).

[2] Here I will focus on the more commonly accepted authentic Pauline texts, though I realize that there is some dispute on the matter. The Pastoral Epistles, Colossians, and Ephesians are not included, except as representatives of the Pauline school. Hebrews is rejected.

covers what might be called Paul's "imperative" to his previously stated "indicative." It is his command to the reader to observe what he already has affirmed to be true.[3] Similar materials are found scattered among ancient letters, but most scholars have identified this feature specifically with Pauline writings. What is perhaps most interesting among the apostolic fathers is that the use of the paraenesis section was not continued among subsequent Christian authors.

Perhaps the primary imitator of Pauline style was the bishop Ignatius. His letters are replete with Pauline ideas and letter structure. The most obvious example of this may be found in a comparison of the bishop's letter to the Ephesians with the Pauline letter of Ephesians, which I assume to be a product of the Pauline school and not of Paul himself.[4] The elaborate greeting that Ignatius offers to the Ephesians, which is typical of his other letters as well, undoubtedly has been modeled upon similar Pauline forms. Numerous terms and phrases that Ignatius has employed in this greeting bear striking similarity to those that appear in the Pauline salutation (Eph 1:3–14).[5] The themes and movement of ideas that follow throughout the bishop's letter show further parallels.

Of course, we must ask what this means for the modern student of early Christian literature. One certainly may argue that Ignatius was a devoted follower of a certain Pauline school of thought and action. To that end we may assert that his work was highly influenced by the reverence for Paul that remained in the city of Antioch for several centuries after the apostle's departure. More importantly, however, it seems likely that we discover here a certain acknowledgment by the bishop that the church at Ephesus knew and revered Paul as well. The book of Acts

---

[3] C. H. Dodd set the earlier academic trend to make a clear distinction between what was kerygma and what was paraenesis within each letter (the difference between the body and the paraenetic section), but it seems instead that the paraenetic sections were actually intended to be a restatement of the main theme of the apostle's thought; see C. H. Dodd, *The Apostolic Preaching and Its Developments* (London: Hodder & Stoughton, 1936); *Gospel and Law: The Relation of Faith and Ethics in Early Christianity* (Cambridge: Cambridge University Press, 1951).

[4] For a helpful comparison of elements throughout his discussion of this letter see William R. Schoedel, *Ignatius of Antioch: A Commentary on the Letters of Ignatius of Antioch* (ed. H. Koester; Hermeneia; Philadelphia: Fortress, 1985), 35–99.

[5] See ibid., 37.

clearly provides good reason to believe that Paul was in close contact with the Christians of the city, regardless of whether the scriptural letter to the Ephesians actually came from Paul's hand.[6] The fact that Ignatius had modeled his own letter to the Ephesians so closely upon the pseudo-Pauline letter to Ephesus suggests that this form would have gained a happy reception by the Christians there.

One might expect that Ignatius's apparent infatuation with the Pauline approach to Christian faith would have led him to pen all of his correspondence along the Pauline model. And this indeed appears to be the case. There is a special instance of this devotion that appears in the bishop's letter to Rome, however, and it is to that missive that we now briefly turn.

The letter to Rome from Ignatius clearly is unique when compared to the pattern of his remaining works. As has been noted elsewhere, the tone of the letter is more like that of royal correspondence, in the form of a minor official who would make a request of an official of greater rank or status. This seems a reasonable move on the part of the bishop. In the first instance, his movement from Antioch to Rome was a forced march, so to speak. He was in chains, dragged against his will to an unknown and surely undesirable fate. At the same time, he recognized that he was a stranger to the Roman situation. He was a person of no particular influence or standing west of Asia Minor. His only real hope to be heard among the Roman Christians was to put himself into a position of inferiority. His language is that of submission and the desire of martyrdom for the glory of Christ. To some extent, he specifically patterned his letter upon Paul's own letter to Rome. A quick comparison of the two letters clearly indicates this to be true, even though the language is not the same. Nonetheless, it is clear here that, in the same way that Paul adapted his usual letter style to appeal specifically to the Roman situation,[7] so too Ignatius imitated Paul in this endeavor.

---

[6] See, for example, Acts 18:18–21; 19:1–20.

[7] For example, note Paul's deference to Rome in terms of the opening greeting, as well as his extended thanksgiving, which here takes the form of a creed more than simply a hearty blessing upon the congregation. This undoubtedly is Paul's attempt to show Rome, a community to which he has not yet traveled, that his faith is their faith. We must assume that Ignatius, realizing his own situation to be a parallel to that of Paul, has chosen to approach Rome through something of the same logic.

Apart from the works of Ignatius, only two true letters remain among the texts of the apostolic fathers:[8] *1 Clement* and Polycarp's *Letter to the Philippians.* In the case of the latter, it is clear that Polycarp, like Ignatius, has been highly influenced by the Pauline letter style. The traditional greeting, thanksgiving, letter body, concluding prayers, and closing found in Paul's letters appear in Polycarp's text as well.[9]

A slightly different situation exists with *1 Clement.* Like those New Testament letters that are clearly "letter-like" in format, but not so closely patterned according to Pauline guidelines, the author of *1 Clement* has written to the Corinthian church in an acceptable style of ancient epistolography, but has not chosen to use any particular Pauline features beyond the required greeting and concluding blessing. The sheer length of *1 Clement* makes the epistolary nature of the text somewhat suspicious, often leading commentators to comment on the homiletic or diatribe style of the work. It is perhaps better to discuss this work in the following section on homilies.

HOMILIES

There are no writings in the New Testament that can be clearly distinguished as homilies or early sermons in their entirety. It is true that the Gospels are to some extent designed homiletically, or are at least structured to proclaim the "good news" message. So too, either a work such as Revelation or Hebrews certainly was intended to preach a very specific understanding of early Christian faith. Nonetheless, the final form of these texts is clearly not that of a sermon, nor should we assume that anyone might be expected to sit through a reading of either text. Within the book of Hebrews there are materials clearly designed to function as a homily. Most obvious of these is Heb 8:1–10:17, which probably is a complex homily designed to model the death of Jesus

---

[8] The so-called *Letter of Barnabas* is anything but a letter, having been only slightly adapted to epistolary form by some secondary hand. So too is the case with *2 Clement,* which reveals no indication of ever having been conceived as a letter.

[9] For a specific comparison of Polycarp's dependence upon Pauline style and language see Paul Hartog, *Polycarp and the New Testament: The Occasion, Rhetoric, Theme, and Unity of the Epistle to the Philippians and Its Allusions to New Testament Literature* (WUNT 2/134; Tübingen: Mohr, 2002), 109–20, 170–79, 216–35.

upon the actions of a high priest on the Day of Atonement.[10] Otherwise, the closest thing to a homily that we have from the New Testament appears in the form of the speeches or preaching episodes scattered throughout the book of Acts. Even here, however, the amount of material that can be clearly accepted as evidence of early Christian homilies is minimal.[11]

It is perhaps only in the fathers that we find our first true "preaching" texts. The most obvious of these is *2 Clement*. As secondary possibilities we might include the texts of *Barnabas* and *1 Clement*. Whether other writings among the fathers were originally composed to serve the purpose of a homily is unclear. Most scholars assume, for example, that the concluding portion of the *Epistle to Diognetus* (chapters 11–12) preserves some portion of an ancient homily. Certainly the tone of the work finds an abrupt change in this concluding section, in terms of both theological emphasis and terminology. However, the uncertain provenance of the work and the added difficulty in any attempt to date these latter chapters apart from the text as a whole leave little room for discussion of their possible role as a homily fragment. Let us move, then, to what is clearly an early Christian homily, the text of *2 Clement*.

The author of *2 Clement* remains unidentified, of course, but the aims of his preaching ring true and clear. The basic elements of "church building" are to be discovered here. First, there is a call for the believer's recognition that Jesus as the Christ is essential for salvation. This call is offered at the very beginning of the homily, without introduction and preface, as a bold declaration of who Jesus Christ is and what his role is for Christians everywhere. It is Jesus who stands to judge the living and the dead (*2 Clem.* 1.1). In response to this declaration, the author issues an appeal for those who accept this premise to respond in obedience. The church community to which our author makes this plea seems to stand in the midst of some struggle, either internal or from outside the walls. In either case, this community is charged to remember its

---

[10] So identified and discussed by Harold W. Attridge, *The Epistle to the Hebrews: A Commentary on the Epistle to the Hebrews* (ed. H. Koester; Hermeneia; Philadelphia: Fortress, 1989), 18.

[11] The classic study of such materials is Dodd, *Apostolic Preaching*. Dodd concluded from collections of materials in the book of Acts that the earliest form of sermon in the ancient church included a recollection of three elements: the baptism of John, the ministry of Jesus, and the remembrance of the crucifixion.

makeup as the body of Christ, and to accept its responsibility for such an important role. Finally, the element of immediacy is introduced. While the church must respond in obedience to its faith, the time is now, and the response must be one of righteousness and holiness (*2 Clem.* 5.6; 15.3). Repentance is expected from all who listen to this message (*2 Clem.* 8.1). An act of genuine faith is demanded—and immediately!

One can hardly argue that such a message, delivered in three basic points of emphasis, directed toward an essential article of faith and the appropriate Christian response to that statement, spurred by a call for a timely decision and response, does not reflect a typical homiletic style that has been perpetuated by the preachers of divergent Christian churches and denominations ever since. Included here are warnings against idolatry (*2 Clem.* 3.1), encouragement to preserve the sanctity of baptism[12] and a pure heart (*2 Clem.* 17.1), pleas to think of treasures to be gained in future days, and appeals to the authority of Scripture and the promises of the Lord. The themes of *2 Clement* might serve a modern preacher well in many contemporary pulpits.

We must ask, then, whether the texts of *1 Clement* and *Barnabas* lend themselves to this same kind of analysis. With *1 Clement,* the answer clearly is mixed. As noted above, *1 Clement* offers itself in a clear letter format. And yet, the primary issue that the author addresses—the question of disorder within the hierarchy of the church community—is raised primarily in the opening chapters (chapters 1–3) and basically resolved in the latter chapters (chapters 40–65). What remains in the middle (chapters 4–39) are, as many scholars have noted, materials that appear to be couched within an early homiletic style, perhaps even reminiscent of practices that were followed in early synagogue services.[13] There is no question that the themes confronted within this middle section serve as an added repertoire of support for the Roman

---

[12] In some sense, perhaps, a conscious reflection of 1 Peter.

[13] See L. Lemarchand, "La composition de l'épître de saint Clément aux Corinthiens," *RevScRel* 18 (1938): 448–87; Johannes Quasten, *The Beginnings of Patristic Literature* (vol. 1 of *Patrology;* Utrecht: Spectrum, 1950; repr., Westminster, Md.: Christian Classics, 1990), 50; Philipp Vielhauer, *Geschichte der urchristlichen Literatur: Einleitung in das Neue Testament, die Apokryphen und die Apotolischen Väter* (de Gruyter Lehrbuch; Berlin: de Gruyter, 1975), 532–35; Dominique Bertrand, *Les écrits des pères apostoliques: Texte intégral* (Paris: Cerf, 2001), 67.

response to the Corinthian dilemma. At the same time, however, such themes look suspiciously like many that one finds in the clearly homiletic work of *2 Clement.*

The themes of *1 Clem.* 4–39 are related specifically with the elements of a solid Christian lifestyle, an existence to which Christians are called by the author of *2 Clement* as well. Warnings against jealousy and its consequences are issued (*1 Clem.* 4.1–6.4). The need for repentance is emphasized (*1 Clem.* 7.1–8.5). The benefits of obedience, faith, piety, hospitality, humility, and peace are listed as typical of a virtuous lifestyle (*1 Clem.* 9.1–12.8). God's promises for the future and the obligation of the faithful believer to respond in holiness are recalled (*1 Clem.* 24.1–28.4). Ultimately, then, the hearers of *1 Clement* (and perhaps some local church community that had listened to these materials preached previously) are instructed to fall into order, as soldiers under a commander, and to stand as one body, united as the body of Christ.

Finally, one finds the core of *Barnabas* to reflect a pattern suspiciously like that of *1 Clement.* Couched between the text's opening greeting and thanksgiving (*Barn.* 1.1–5) and its concluding warnings and blessings (*Barn.* 21.1–9)[14] lies a rolling diatribe of doctrinal assurance and the call to respond with a worthy lifestyle (*Barn.* 1.6–17.2). The initial statement of faith (or as the author of *Barnabas* most clearly states, of "dogmas" [δόγματα]) concerning the hope of living in faith, the promise of righteousness in the face of judgment, and the experience of joyful love as a testament to worthiness stands at the beginning of the work as a thematic statement for the entire treatise (*Barn.* 1.6). The hearer is then chided to respond in obedience with a life of virtue, sacrifice, and fasting. Our author is perhaps even more steeped in scriptural images than are the writers of *1–2 Clement,* though one may hardly deny that these texts are likewise oriented toward scriptural themes and supportive proof texts. In the final analysis, and despite the intriguing applications of Scripture to the situation of the epistle's audience,[15] the author of *Barnabas* can offer no ultimate conclusion for

---

[14] I do not include the penultimate materials of chapters 18–20 on the "two ways" theme here, since I believe these materials, though undoubtedly present at the time the text was turned into a pseudo-epistle, to be a secondary addition to the argument of *Barn.* 1.6–17.2.

[15] See the interpretation of the scapegoat and red heifer in chapters 7–8 and of the threat of Amalek and of the serpents in chapter 12, all of which reflect contemporary rabbinic elements of understanding.

understanding the role of Scripture in the early second century, except
to say that the mysteries of salvation ultimately come as in a parable for
those who may understand them (*Barn.* 17.1–2).

At this point we must question whether the original ending to
these materials has been sacrificed to the addition of the concluding
"two ways" section, or perhaps whether the final concluding warnings
of chapter 21 once served as the final words of the homily. In either
case, the sequence of faith statement, call to obedience, and warning of
urgency seems closely aligned with the ancient homily pattern followed
also by the author of *2 Clement*.

MARTYROLOGIES

The matter of martyrologies within early patristic literature is most
interesting in that the roots of this genre surely must lie within late Jewish and early Christian literature. At the same time, however, those
roots are perhaps vague at best. For our present purposes, I will initiate
the discussion of the genre "martyrology" with the works of 2 Maccabees and 4 Maccabees. It seems generally clear that the stories of persecution, torture, and destruction that appear in the materials of
2 Macc 6:18–7:42 are the same as those adopted and adapted for the
purposes of illustration by the author of 4 Maccabees. Of course, what
happens to those stories is decisively distinct in the latter text, since
there they become the illustrative moments of decision through which
the reader may recognize the author's claim that "reason holds more
power of persuasion than passion."

I begin with these texts because it is evident to me that the bishop
Ignatius envisioned himself and his predicament within the borders of
the philosophy of "reason over passion" extolled by the author of 4 Maccabees.[16] The terminology that Ignatius employs in his letters[17] and the

---

[16] I am not alone in this observation; see O. Perler, "Das vierte Makkabäerbuch, Ignatius von Antiochen und die ältesten Märtyrerberichte," *RivAC*
25 (1949): 47–72; W. H. C. Frend, *The Rise of Christianity* (Philadelphia: Fortress, 1984), 124. At the same time, I admit that this view is not universally accepted. So G. W. Bowersock, who argues that Ignatius and the author of
4 Maccabees simply are the common participants of their times (*Martyrdom
and Rome* [Cambridge: Cambridge University Press, 1995], 77–82).

[17] So, for example, Ignatius's word for "ransom" (ἀντίψυχον) in Ign.
Smyrn. 10.2 and Ign. *Eph.* 21.1, though rare in Greek, is the same as that which

position that he assumes with respect to his captors[18] seem to betray his dependence upon the perspective of this text. A similar dependency upon 4 Maccabees may be found in later authors—Ambrose, John Chrysostom, and Gregory of Nyssa—which would support the strong possibility that Ignatius himself already found a model for martyrdom in this particular source.

In light of this, the text of the *Martyrdom of Polycarp,* the only example of a true and complete martyrology within the apostolic fathers, appears all the more surprising. The original form of this writing surely dates to the latter half of the second century, but it shows little sign of dependence upon the Maccabean idea of martyrdom. The death of the bishop Polycarp is instead viewed against the backdrop of the crucifixion of Jesus as portrayed in the New Testament gospels. It is impossible to know how much of this imagery was original to the actual event of the bishop's death and how much is the careful work of the author of the text or one of its editors. Whatever the situation, it is clear that the death of Polycarp, unlike the anticipated death that Ignatius envisions for himself, has been fashioned against the parallels of another "death tradition."

There is, of course, yet a third story to be compared in this analysis: the death of Stephen in Acts 7. This passage, which undoubtedly is our earliest Christian martyrdom according to Christian literary tradition, bears neither the traits of the Maccabean story nor the elements of the death of Jesus himself. It is instead the recollection of a pious Christian witness whose testimony to a view of Jewish history in front of the high priest in Jerusalem leads to his death by stoning. It seems reasonable to argue that the Stephen story does not come to us free of editorial considerations. The author of the Luke-Acts tradition is famous for the manipulation of texts and sources in a quest to present a logical and consistent view of Christian history as a conscious unfolding of the plan of God. All the same, it is perhaps strange that the Stephen episode does not bear the editorial markings of a tradition that was molded either along the witness of the Maccabees or the death of Jesus.

---

appears in the discussion of 4 Macc 6:27–29. Polycarp follows this same usage in Pol. *Phil.* 2.3; 6.1.

[18] For example, Ignatius refers to the soldiers who guard him by the now-famous designation "leopards" (λεόπαρδοι) (Ign. *Rom.* 5.1), which may perhaps be a conscious reference to the "leopard-like" torturers of 4 Macc 9:28 who assaulted the second of the seven brothers.

The story of the stoning of Stephen is instead full of references to Jewish Scriptures as they attest to the history of Israel and its quest to fulfill the desires of God. The intention of Acts seems fairly clear here. Stephen is to be seen in the role of the ancient prophet of Israel, the true spokesperson for God's voice. The role of Stephen in the mind of the author is perhaps not unlike that of John the Baptizer in Luke: he is the forerunner of what is to come. In John's case, what is to come is the long-expected Messiah; in Stephen's case, what is to come is the long-anticipated mission of those who are faithful followers of the Messiah.

Ultimately, then, we are left with three scenes of martyrdom or anticipated martyrdom whose only real item of unification is the death of the martyr himself. Ignatius anticipates a demise that he interprets according to the most faithful advocates of Jewish faith. To some extent, he probably sees himself as a devoted follower of Paul in this scenario. Polycarp is portrayed against the highest model of Christian devotion, the very passion of Jesus himself. Whether Polycarp actually sees his death according to this interpretation is unknown, of course, but the scenario certainly reflects the perspective of the author of the *Martyrdom.* Stephen is painted in the colors of a true prophet of old, perhaps the first of the earliest Christian prophets. His death is an inspiration to what ultimately becomes the conversion of Paul, a part of the divine plan for Christian expansion.

There seems little question that each of these scenes is, either consciously or otherwise, the portrayal of Christianity's earliest heroes according to the classic model of a "noble death"—that is, someone who endures an undeserved end that becomes a means of salvation for the people.[19] There is little question that the earliest interpreters of the death of Jesus were forced to explain the inconceivable situation of the death of their own messiah. This ultimately was achieved through the guidelines of Scripture, of course, with the classic pattern of "prediction and fulfillment" having been fully employed. The basic elements of the gospel passion narrative—the arrest, trial, and crucifixion—were interpreted through the lens of scriptural anticipation.

---

[19] See S. K. Williams, *Jesus' Death as Saving Event: The Origin of a Concept* (HDR 2; Missoula, Mont.: Scholars Press, 1975); David Seeley, *The Noble Death: Graeco-Roman Martyrology and Paul's Concept of Salvation* (JSNTSup 28; Sheffield: Sheffield Academic Press, 1990); Jan Willem van Henten and Friedrich Avemarie, *Martyrdom and Noble Death: Selected Texts from Graeco-Roman, Jewish and Christian Antiquity* (London: Routledge, 2002).

There are various modern theories for exactly how this may have been envisioned within the early church.[20] But whatever the approach that is taken, the historical facts of the death of Jesus were of less concern to the early church than the meaning that should be applied to those facts. What was left, the combined efforts to ascribe meaning to the facts, is what remains for historians and believers alike. By the same token, the deaths of Stephen, Ignatius, and Polycarp reflect that same sort of early Christian need to interpret devastating events. Their stories are the tales of three different avenues by which to explain the noble death of a faith's earliest heroes.

APOCALYPSES

One of the most prominent forms of literature to be found in Scripture is that of the apocalypse. The example of this genre that immediately comes to mind for most students is the New Testament book of Revelation. Elements of apocalyptic material are scattered otherwise throughout the later Old Testament materials, especially in works such as Daniel and Ezekiel. And early Christian narratives include the materials of Mark 13, Matt 24–25, Luke 21, 1 Thess 4, 2 Thess 2, in addition to other scattered sayings. Apocalyptic narrative is replete with warnings about the end times, the nature of the coming Son of Man, signs of the final destruction of the wicked, and promises for the righteous. Most important, however, these are not merely alarms about future events and happenings. They are crafted as quite specific warnings to encourage the ancient listener to pay close attention to the message that is offered, framed by the authority of God and the power of divine justice and punishment.

The apostolic fathers certainly are not distant from apocalyptic concerns, though as with our other genre forms, this emphasis tends to be concentrated among certain specific documents. Two works that are most often considered in this discussion are the *Didache* and the *Shepherd of Hermas*. The nature of apocalyptic in these two works oper-

---

[20] I am convinced that the author of the Gospel of Mark inherited a basic framework much like that now found in chapters 14–15 and expanded it into the longer form of chapters 11–15 according to the text of Pss 41–43.

ates in similar ways and may be easily summarized in a brief review of their function.

The apocalyptic materials of the *Didache* are restricted to the final chapter of the text, chapter 16. As has been long observed by careful students of early Christian literature, the sayings that appear here may be among the oldest segments of the *Didache*. What is contained in this chapter is a collection of images that appear to reflect at once the apocalyptic emphasis of Mark 13, the specific tradition of Matt 24–25, and the individual views of 1–2 Thessalonians. Whether one can ever decide with certainty that the Didachist has borrowed from any of these New Testament sources is difficult to determine. More likely, the author of the *Didache* has tapped into specific early Christian apocalyptic traditions that have been borrowed in turn by the authors of the New Testament writings.[21]

What is most remarkable about the *Didache* in its use of these materials is the function that apocalyptic seems to serve for the writing. If, as some authors have argued, the apocalyptic materials were the original ending of the collected sayings contained within chapters 1–6, then it would seem that chapter 16 was intended to serve as a warning for the reader (or listener) to pay attention to the value of these sayings specifically. Chapters 1–6 are primarily a collection of warnings that counsel the hearer to give strict obedience to the teachings of Jewish Scripture and to avoid any deviant actions that might lead to a dismissal of these instructions. Thus, if the earliest form of the *Didache* included the materials of chapters 1–6 and 16 only, then the closing apocalyptic verses would have served here, as is often the case in Jewish Scripture itself, as a warning (through the threat of future events) to live an ethical lifestyle in the present.

In its present form at the end of the somewhat longer version of the *Didache* that now exists, the apocalyptic materials of chapter 16 may serve as a similar warning to observe and remain faithful to the entire corpus of materials, both the sayings of Jewish ethics and the liturgical regulations of the Christian community. This would represent an interesting shift in intention for early Christian usage of a specifically Jewish tradition. Having moved from the original and ancient function of Jewish apocalyptic—warnings of future retribution to those who do not

---

[21] See John S. Kloppenborg, "Didache 16 6–8 and Special Matthean Tradition," *ZNW* 70 (1979): 54–67.

attend to God's commandments in contemporary life—the Didachist has applied the same set of principles (i.e., future warnings) to something beyond ethics: liturgical and community practice. Nothing quite like this is captured elsewhere in early Christian literature.

When one turns to the *Shepherd of Hermas,* a slightly different understanding of apocalyptic is revealed. The *Shepherd* is, of course, a collection of different types of materials. Here one finds commandments about the Christian lifestyle mixed together with long, illustrative parables about the nature of the church and the value of early Christian theology. It is the beginning of the text, and undoubtedly the earliest materials within the document, that is concerned with the nature of apocalyptic.[22]

In the opening *Visions* section of the *Shepherd* the protagonist of the text (Hermas) is confronted with a number of revelations concerning the construction and nature of the church. These include progressive images of the church as an old woman (chapters 2–4), as a young woman (chapters 5–8), as a youth (chapters 9–21), and as a bride (chapters 22–24). The nature of the church in each form is determined less by the physical age of those believers who compose the body of Christ than by the health of their faith. The application of such visions to the composition of the church in its many stages of existence has, to my knowledge, no parallel in early Christianity.

In the midst of these revelations Hermas confronts an image that does in fact have a familiar Christian parallel: the obstacle of a great beast (chapters 22–23). This beast is listed as a fourth *Vision* (and occurs while the narrator is traveling along a major public road, the Campanian Way. A cloud of dust accompanies the vision of the huge beast, which Hermas describes as roughly one hundred feet long with fiery locusts coming from the mouth of its ceramic head of black, red, gold, and white coloration. Though terrifying in its presentation, this great monster eventually lies down upon the ground and makes no attempt to harm Hermas as he passes by. Hermas soon is greeted by the young lady (= the church) who explains the meaning of the vision as a foreshadowing of the great tribulation that is to come into the world.

One is immediately reminded, of course, of the two great beasts of Rev 13. As with the beast of the *Shepherd,* the vision of two beasts in

---

[22] For an interesting discussion of whether the *Shepherd* is an apocalypse see Carolyn Osiek, *The Shepherd of Hermas: A Commentary* (ed. H. Koester; Hermeneia; Minneapolis: Fortress, 1999), 10–12.

Revelation offers a specific description of the heads. The first has ten horns with ten crowns placed upon seven heads. While some brief description is given to the body of the beast (a leopard with bear's feet), there is a quick return to its mouth, which is like that of a lion. The second beast is envisioned with only two horns, with no other description given. The reader is left to interpret the meaning of these visions, whose numerological significance can be easily equated with the rise of Roman power and abuse.

It is perhaps most interesting to note here that, while the *Didache* clearly has tapped into a tradition of apocalyptic materials known within both the Pauline and gospel traditions, the author of the *Shepherd* has made use of imagery that the author of Revelation knows as well. One might argue that the *Shepherd* is dependent upon Revelation for this imagery, of course, much in the same way that the Didachist may have made use of gospel imagery. It seems the more intriguing, as is suggested here, to consider the ways in which these texts from the fathers may have continued to make use of stock apocalyptic figures that also circulated among the authors of the New Testament.

SAYINGS

We move away from a consideration of literary genres within the fathers and Scripture at this point to engage in a consideration of forms. Perhaps the most common means by which teachings were transmitted in antiquity was through the collection of sayings and teachings. This held true within the writings of ancient Israel and maintained itself in the New Testament literature, particularly with works such as the Gospels and James. By the same token, the apostolic fathers continue the practice of assembling sayings into thematic clusters. With the exception of the "two ways" tradition of *Did.* 1–6 and *Barn.* 18–19, however, these collections typically are not assembled into large blocks of teaching.

Studies of the two ways tradition have indicated that the materials in *Did.* 1–6 and *Barn.* 18–19 are the product of a long heritage by which sayings were assembled by Jewish authors.[23] However, the materials

---

[23] See M. Jack Suggs, "The Christian Two Ways Tradition: Its Antiquity, Form, and Function," in *Studies in New Testament and Early Christian Literature: Essays in Honor of Allen P. Wikgren* (ed. D. E. Aune; NovTSup 33; Leiden:

that appear in these two works are generally not drawn from the teachings of Jesus, contrary to what one would expect. Instead, they are the compilation of random teachings that are typically ethical in nature, oriented toward apocalyptic concerns, or driven by the parameters of ancient wisdom.[24] Such compilations are relatively rare in our literature, however. Much more numerous are individual sayings or small groupings of teachings that are associated with a particular theme or that have been extracted from the general tradition of wisdom in order to prove some argument.

Texts such as *1–2 Clement* are replete with such examples. In certain respects, these texts incorporate individual teachings in the same way that the New Testament letters of Paul and the texts of 1 Peter and Hebrews use sayings. It is not always certain from where such materials derive. Sometimes they are ascribed to the teachings of Jesus. Sometimes, as with Paul, they are credited to "the Lord." No distinction typically is made in such cases as to whether "the Lord" here means the historical Jesus or the risen Christ—that is, whether these words are believed to have been passed down through the tradition of preserved words from the man of Nazareth, or derive instead from the lips of the contemporary Christian prophets who freely spoke "a word of the Lord" within the church communities where they worshipped.[25]

Brill, 1972), 60–74; Robert A. Kraft, *Barnabas and the Didache: A Translation and Commentary* (AF 3; New York: Thomas Nelson & Sons, 1965), 4–16; Huub van de Sandt and David Flusser, *The Didache: Its Jewish Sources and Its Place in Early Judaism and Christianity* (CRINT 3/5; Assen: Royal Van Gorcum; Minneapolis: Fortress, 2002), 55–270.

[24] The materials in *Did.* 1–6, for example, are mostly a compilation and editing of traditional Jewish ethical materials. Some of these undoubtedly have been drawn from the tradition of Judaism, while others may be the work of the Didachist. It is difficult to make a distinction between the two in this case, however. The well-known passage *Did.* 1.3b–2.1, which now is generally accepted as an interpolation at some stage in the tradition, contains traditional "Jesus teachings" that have been borrowed either from the Gospels of Matthew and Luke or from one of their sources. Chapter 16 of the text contains another rudimentary collection of sayings that is apocalyptic in nature. As discussed above, it appears that these materials are drawn from independent sayings of Jesus, some form of the apocalyptic teachings of Mark 13 and Matt 23–25, and the corpus of sayings about the coming of the Son of Man that was incorporated by Paul in 1 Thessalonians.

[25] So M. Eugene Boring, *The Continuing Voice of Jesus: Christian Prophecy and the Gospel Tradition* (Louisville: Westminster/John Knox, 1991).

It is also difficult to determine whether individual sayings have been borrowed from written sources or simply have been drawn from oral tradition. Those who endorse the former view typically argue as a consequence that the authors of the apostolic fathers wrote in a second-century context, fully aware of our New Testament gospels as authoritative sources.[26] This is the more traditional approach to dating the fathers, a schema that prefers to work with the texts as historical successors to the majority of scriptural traditions. Those scholars who want to argue otherwise, whether they place the Gospels in a later context or place individual writings of the fathers earlier with respect to date, typically support the position that sayings circulated in the early church primarily through oral means. Subsequently, evidence that the church fathers knew sayings primarily in their oral form endorses the idea that early Christian editors within the apostolic fathers gleaned individual sayings from divergent circumstances.[27] It is perhaps unwise to assume an "either-or" position here, but rather to accept the likelihood that some authors among the fathers had access to written collections of sayings, while others were dependent primarily upon oral sources; or, even more likely, that authors generally were exposed both to written and oral sources of the traditions in which they worked.

Of course, this review should not exclude the consideration of *testimonia* (collected quotations of Scripture arranged around a single theme). The theory behind the collection of such scriptural sayings as the framework for early preaching and teaching is not easily supported by available manuscript traditions.[28] At the same time, evidence from the Dead Sea Scrolls[29] and the grouping of texts around scriptural themes and sayings, as illustrated by the way that the author of *Barnabas* makes use of numerous passages from Isaiah, would seem to support this idea. It is true, of course, that such *testimonia* typically were

---

[26] See, for example, C. M. Tuckett, "Synoptic Tradition in the Didache," in *The New Testament in Early Christianity* (ed. J.-M. Sevrin; BETL 86; Leuven: Leuven University Press, 1989), 197–230.

[27] So the classic study by Helmut Köster, *Synoptische Überlieferung bei den apostolischen Vätern* (TUGAL 65; Berlin: Akademie-Verlag, 1957).

[28] See the arguments and assumptions of L. W. Barnard, "The Use of Testimonies in the Early Church and in the Epistle of Barnabas," in *Studies in the Apostolic Fathers and Their Background* (New York: Schocken, 1966), 109–35; and more recently, Ferdinand R. Prostmeier, *Der Barnabasbrief* (KAV 8; Göttingen: Vandenhoeck & Ruprecht, 1999), 101–6.

[29] One thinks of texts such as the *Testimonia* and the *Florilegium*.

collections of Jewish Scriptures, not of the words of Jesus. But undoubtedly the early church, if perhaps only through the time of the
apostolic fathers themselves, clearly collected the teachings of Jesus as
the focus of homiletic activity and ecclesiastical teaching. This activity
presumably is prefigured in the work of the Gospel of Matthew, as opposed to the activity of the Gospel of Mark, for example. Certainly such
actions served as the early foundation of later Christian lectionaries.

PARABLES

Readers of the New Testament gospels are well familiar with the
parables of Jesus. Their shape, concerns, and themes have become the
stuff of common reflection for the Christian tradition. As scholars are
well aware, the genre of "parable" within ancient literature was recognized already by early authors as an eclectic assembling of various traditional materials. Included in this category are riddles, prophecies,
illustrative stories, moral tales, fables, elaborated *chreiae*, allegories, and
so forth. Unlike the parables of Jesus for the most part, such parables
can vary in length and often are quite long.

As we look around the New Testament, we see precious little that
may be categorized as a parable, apart from those items associated with
the teachings of Jesus in the Gospels. A similar situation exists within
the apostolic fathers, with the single exception of the final section of the
Shepherd of Hermas (chapters 50–114). The "parables" collected there,
however, are hardly comparable to those in the Gospels. Indeed, these
stories lay no claim to be the teachings of Jesus. They are instead the
teachings of ancient Christian authorities to the church in general, presumably in this case, with the specific church at Rome in mind.

The most noticeable aspect of the parables in the *Shepherd* is that
they are directed toward two basic concerns. On the one hand, their
content tends to be primarily ethical in nature. The concern of the author of these texts, or at least of the editor who compiled them, is the
correct observation of a Christian lifestyle. The reader is chided to live
according to the acceptable precepts of a faithful existence, marked by a
reverence for Christ and a respect for those who compose his church.
As an illustration, the image of the vine and the elm in chapter 51 argues that there is something to be gained in any church congregation in

which the weak draw upon the strong members, and vice versa. A basic lesson about Christian living clearly is to be discerned here.

On the other hand, the parables of the *Shepherd* tap into images that serve to explain the nature of the church in general, the role of the Messiah as the Son of the Father, and the nature of true believers in the church who ultimately are mixed with those whose values and faith are not so pure. These parables differ widely from the parables in the Gospels in that often they are meant to be interpreted strictly on an allegorical level. There is no secret message here that can be determined apart from a simple one-to-one analysis of the elements. Further, they offer the reader broad teachings about the nature of the church and its theological suppositions. The reader is treated to themes about the nature of those believers who compose the church, the role of Christ as an element of church history, and the value of being a believer who produces the fruit of faith.

There are parallel images elsewhere in the apostolic fathers. In both *1 Clem.* 23.4 and its parallel passage *2 Clem.* 11.3, for example, the growth of a Christian is compared to the cycles through which a tree or vine produces leaves, shoots, flowers, sour fruit, and then ripe fruit. As emphasized in each text, God eventually will bring a good reward to those who remain faithful through turmoil and tribulation. However, nothing is quite like this in the parables of the Gospels, except for those instances in which the teachings of Jesus would seem to be directly related to the nature of the kingdom of God.

An essential aspect of the *Shepherd's* parables is that they hold nothing of the enigmatic nature of their New Testament parallels. Though their meaning is not always clear at the beginning, by the end of each parable the message is hardly to be questioned. If for no other reason, the essence of each "parable" is explained to the reader, typically with an allegorical solution. This style of parable telling already had its roots in Mark 4, where we see the author of the Gospel of Mark wrestling with the means by which parables should be transmitted and interpreted. For the Markan author, who appears to be uncomfortable with the use of parables and chooses to include only five within the gospel text, the only solution to a parable's meaning is that which may be gleaned through allegory. This is offered in the first parable that is told, the so-called parable of the Sower (Mark 4:1–9), to which an allegorical explanation is applied (Mark 4:13–20). It is noteworthy that this single illustration of the means by which parables are to be interpreted is surely considered to be programmatic. No other allegorical meanings are attached to the parables.[30] And yet, subsequent Christian interpreters realized that the parables of Jesus were to be understood in just this way, allegorically. It is only in the last few centuries, of course, that this dominant trend of thought has been broken among the students of New Testament literature. Questions of context and historical milieu have become important since the work of C. H. Dodd and Joachim Jeremias. But even more important in recent years are those studies that have focused upon signs and metaphors, and upon the nature of parables as tools toward meaning instead of meanings themselves.

The abandonment of allegory as a primary approach for the interpretation of the parables of Jesus has truly exposed these texts to a new way of understanding, an approach that is perhaps more authentic to their Semitic roots than a reflection of Latin categories. With the parables of the *Shepherd,* however, the abandonment of allegory brings the reader to no solution at all. Clearly, the whole intention of these parables is allegory, a one-to-one equation of the elements of the story with the elements of Christian truth. The basic composition and intention of these parables suggests little similarity to the gospel parables of Jesus.

Of particular interest in the examination of ancient parables is the probability that early authors drew upon a common stock of images and themes to produce their stories.[31] This takes us beyond the usual observation of oral tendencies such as the use of three characters, the single perspective of the narrator throughout the parable, and so forth. Instead, it seems evident from as early as the work of Aesop through the writings of the later church fathers that certain elements were continually utilized in the telling of parables. One finds, for example, the presence of a good element and a bad element, sometimes depicted in

---

[30] There is, of course, the single exception of the parable of the Weeds in Matt 13:24–30, 36–43. I take this second illustration of allegorical interpretation to be the result of the Matthean author's typical desire to provide two examples of any event, witness, or situation, thus to insure the validity of what is offered. The image of the sower remains constant in early Christian parables, of course, as is illustrated by *1 Clem.* 24.5, in which the sowing of seed is compared to God's providential intention for the resurrection of all Christians.

[31] I am greatly indebted to the work of Aimee Bigham Efird, "The *Shepherd of Hermas:* A Critical Introduction" (paper presented for a seminar on the apostolic fathers at Baylor University in Waco, Tex., October 25, 1997), for many of the following observations.

human terms and at others in terms of natural elements such as animals or types of plants. At the same time, the occasions for parable construction often remained consistent. We read of the construction of a building, the tending of a crop in the field, the discovery of a treasure, the relationship of a master and a slave or of a businessperson and a worker. The issues are likewise predictable. The reader is asked to anticipate how one character will respond in reaction to another and is often given various options in terms of those characters who act one way and those who behave another. Always, however, the key element is that of option or choice. We are asked to anticipate how each character will respond.

Ultimately, we might safely argue that both the materials of the parables of Jesus and the examples that may be drawn from the apostolic fathers, not to mention similar materials among the rabbis, are consistent in the elements that they employ. At the same time, the ways in which these materials are utilized indicates a basic divergence in perspective and understanding about the role and function of parables. Most obviously, use of parables by the early church is much more consistent with the traditional approaches of Greek and Roman culture in general.

MIRACLE STORIES

The appearance of miracles in early Christian literature is a curious phenomenon. Students of Christian Scripture typically are quick to point to the New Testament gospels for evidence of such stories among canonical texts. One must include the miracles in Acts with these accounts as well. Of course, it is only natural that miracles would be found within the narratives of the life of Jesus, as well as among those of his followers in Acts. These events were part of the evidence by which those who initiated the faith of the early church were identified as authorities. A primary purpose of miracles, then, was to provide evidence by which those who would believe might find justification for their faith in those who would be believed.

The author of the Gospel of Mark makes clear use of this principle. In those materials that fall shortly after the introductory scenes of John the Baptizer (Mark 1:21–3:35), the reader finds Jesus in a number of settings whereby he performs miracles in the presence of both his disciples and those who are curious about his teachings. Though these scenes appear at first to be a random assortment of activities, their ultimate purpose may be determined by what they say about Jesus' role as the Messiah. He has the authority to call others from their activities, and they come without objection (see Mark 1:16–20; Matt 9:9). He has the authority to cast out demons from those who are sick, and they depart with words of recognition on their lips. He has the authority to do works that are unlawful on the Sabbath, and the priests and Pharisees have no recourse against his actions (see Mark 2:23–3:6; John 5:1–18). The purpose of miracles is to serve as one type of proof among many that Jesus has divine authority as the Son of God.

A similar perspective seems to be evident in the Gospel of John. The author of that text, as is widely recognized, offers seven miraculous acts by Jesus (perhaps eight when chapter 21 is included). However, these actions are never called "miracles." Instead, they are labeled as "signs" (σημεῖα), with the intention that the reader might recognize the validity of who Jesus is without becoming dependent upon what others claim that he did. In other words, the primary focus of the Johannine author is upon the concept of "word" and only secondarily upon that of "deed." It is quite possible, of course, that the telling of the so-called signs of Jesus in this gospel are originally modeled upon miracles that previously had been attributed to John the Baptizer by his own followers. In either case, it seems clear that the presence of miracles in the telling of the narrative serves the express purpose of indicating the authority by which the performer of the miracle, whether John or Jesus, speaks.

Finally, the book of Acts offers a number of miracles that are performed either by the apostles of Jesus or by Paul, the apostle of the risen Christ. As with the Gospel of Luke before it, Acts seeks to portray the followers of Jesus as those who bear the same authority as their master. They baptize and heal "in the name of Jesus Christ," a clear indication that their authority to do so is received directly from God. As with the Gospel of Mark, Acts seeks to portray the validity of the Christian mission by the authority of its adherents when expressed in miraculous deeds.

It is perhaps not surprising, as suggested by this review, to discover that the apostolic fathers offer virtually nothing that looks like a miracle story. The reason for this seems apparent. The New Testament contains two basic types of materials: materials by an author who speaks to the author's own situation (e.g., the letters of Paul), and materials by an author who speaks to another person's situation (e.g., the Gospels). Authors never talk about their own miracles, though authors sometimes speak of the miracles of others. So too, the writings of the fathers fall into similar categories. The great majority of these texts are the composition of authors who speak to their own situations (e.g., the letters of Ignatius and Polycarp, the letter to Diognetus). These works, like their parallels in the New Testament, do not speak of personal miracles. Only one of the remaining writings (the *Martyrdom of Polycarp*) speaks to anything of the miraculous. And even there, what is miraculous, the way in which a pious martyr cannot be consumed by fire, is not so much the work of the martyr himself. Instead, it is a product of his divine protection.

Traditionally, one might be compelled to argue from this lack of "miracles" within the fathers that the authors of these texts already are working within a context that carries an understanding that the period of the founders of the Christian faith had now passed. The duty of the fathers, on the other hand, is to shape that faith into a form that will propel the growth of the church. As an illustration of this principle, the author of *1 Clement* seems to support this view. Aware of the recent deaths of the apostles Peter and Paul (see chapter 5), our author makes no attempt to glorify these apostles through tales of the miraculous. The perspective of our author is that the authority of the apostles need not be established, either because they are so well known within the communities at both Rome and Corinth, or because their reputation is widely respected among all of the churches. If our author had written from some point much later than the death of the apostles, one might expect to see an attempt to establish the reputation of these apostles, especially since this heightening of apostolic authority would have given weight to the argument of the Roman church as it addressed the congregations at Corinth. But in fact, no such attempt is undertaken.

At the same time, two sets of texts offer some secondary consideration of the question of miracles as they appear (or do not appear) within the apostolic fathers. First, as mentioned above, the *Martyrdom of Polycarp* offers the miraculous death of a revered figure of the second century, the bishop Polycarp of Smyrna. It is clear that, though a later hand has edited this text, its original telling was somewhat within the context of the Smyrna church. Whatever miraculous elements were attached to the bishop's death from the first telling clearly were designed to establish the authority of Polycarp, primarily for the original audience of the work (the church at Philomelium), and secondarily for succeeding generations of Christian readers. Thus, unlike the remaining texts of the fathers, the *Martyrdom* is a text that naturally attracts the elements of the miraculous.

Our second set of texts includes writings that were never included in the collection of the apostolic fathers. Works from the same general historical period that actually contain accounts of miracles, writings such as the *Acts of Paul and Thecla* and other "acts" of the apostles, were not widely known or used among the second-century churches. Of course, the exclusion of such writings from our apostolic fathers is the work of secondary considerations—that is, the choice of modern scholars. At the same time, there is some value to the recognition that the absence of miracles in the fathers is not so much a comment upon the views of the early church as it is a bias of modern interpreters.[32] Had the various "acts" of the apostles been included among our writings, rather than assigned to a category of apocryphal writings, then our discussion of miracles in the fathers may have been entirely different.

CREEDS

Creeds are not prevalent either in the New Testament or in the apostolic fathers apart from a few primary exceptions. Most likely the earliest of the Christian creeds is that which is reflected in 2 Cor 4:5: "Jesus is Lord." Similar types of affirmations concerning the nature of who Jesus of Nazareth was believed to be by his earliest followers are found throughout the Scriptures, of course. These are, for the most part, simply titles given to Jesus as the Messiah in one context or another—for example, "Holy One of God" (Mark 1:24); "Son of the Most High God" (Luke 8:28); "King of Israel" (John 12:13).

The most easily identified creeds within the New Testament are those that appear in the letters of Paul. It is at the very beginning of his letter to the Romans that perhaps our most readily apparent creed may be found. Romans 1:2–6 provides several well-defined elements of an

---

[32] For both a Jewish and a Hellenistic background to this tradition, with textual examples through the third century, see van Henten and Avemarie, *Martyrdom and Noble Death*.

early Christian creed: the coming of Jesus was promised by the prophets of Scripture, a historical descendent of the king David whose identity as God's Son was made clear in his resurrection, and who provides the grace necessary for salvation. This creed, which is stated so concisely and yet with the distinct emphasis of faith, is not reflected in a similar way elsewhere in Paul's writings. One is led to believe that the explication of these words by the apostle Paul was intended to serve in some sense as his own introduction to the church at Rome, a city that he had not visited previously. Undoubtedly, he has begun his letter to the Roman congregation with words that they themselves would have recognized as the theology espoused by Roman views of the Christian faith. In essence, then, he has sought to establish his credibility with the great church at Rome through an initial confession of what was believed there.

This leads us immediately to two sets of materials within the apostolic fathers. The first, quite naturally, is the set of letters from the hand of Ignatius. The bishop Ignatius, who clearly was an avid disciple of all things Pauline, has attempted to establish his own understanding of Christian doctrine throughout Asia Minor with the use of quite specific creeds. These appear a number of times in his letters,[33] and they focus upon standard elements of theological concern. By way of example, we may note an emphasis upon several creedal items that become standard in later Christian confessions of faith: Jesus as a true descendent of David; born of Mary and God; crucified under the rule of Pontius Pilate. The focus of these creedal elements, of course, is a rebuttal of docetic interests that seem to have plagued Ignatius in his role as bishop at Antioch.

In addition to these scattered creeds among the writings of Ignatius, we are drawn specifically to his own letter to the church at Rome. In his opening thanksgiving to the church of Rome he offers a virtual confession of faith that is unlike any other opening segment of his remaining letters. Like Paul before him, Ignatius takes the opportunity here to address the Roman Christians, a church in which he presumably is not well known, to establish his own faith and doctrinal beliefs. His words offer an exceptional compliment to the Romans, whom he calls "worthy of God, worthy of honor, worthy of blessing,

---

[33] See, for example, Ign. *Eph.* 7.2; 10.2; Ign. *Magn.* 11.1; Ign. *Trall.* 9.1–2; Ign. *Smyrn.* 1.1–2.

worthy of praise, worthy of success, worthy of sanctification" (Ign. *Rom.* proem). At the same time, however, those doctrinal elements that Ignatius mentions do not closely resemble Paul's own confession to the Romans. The bishop's categories contain elements that are more directly related to an understanding of who Christ is in his actions and relationship to the Father: Jesus is the only Son of the Most High Father; it is through him (though it is not clearly understood whether this refers specifically to the Messiah or to the Father) that all things were called into existence; it is by his commandments that the church in Rome lives.

It is perhaps most significant here that, though Ignatius has chosen to model his thanksgiving to some extent upon the confessional form employed by his hero Paul in the apostle's own letter to the church at Rome, the elements of that confession are not the same. On the one hand, one might argue that Ignatius is not necessarily in agreement with Paul's creedal perspective. But this would generally run counter to most other ways in which Ignatius seems to have imitated Paul's apostolic example. On the other hand, and perhaps a better option, it may be that Ignatius actually understands the theology of the church at Rome better than Paul himself does. This is not to say that Ignatius is a well-known figure in the Roman church. In fact, I think otherwise. Instead, it is to say that Ignatius himself has a good impression of the Roman situation. And his impression of Rome is that it holds the figure of Jesus as the Christ to be an agent of God as the Father, and the commandments of Jesus to serve as the basic structure of the active Christian lifestyle.

One might hope to turn to *1 Clement* for some confirmation of this theology, but unfortunately, this letter from the congregation at Rome contains no creedal formulas to support this view of Roman faith. At the same time, *1 Clem.* 42.2 does in fact acknowledge that the apostles were sent with their gospel message by Christ, who himself was sent from God. In this instance the aspect of agency Christology that Ignatius expects to find in Rome does seem to have substantial support. Further, the author of *1 Clement* notes that the "all-seeing God" actually "chose" or "selected" Jesus as the Christ (*1 Clem.* 64.1). This suggests a theology that may have been somewhat shaped by adoptionism, as is often argued about the Gospel of Mark. The resolution to this matter certainly is not clear from the evidence that appears within the apostolic fathers.

The only other minor creedal formulation that must be addressed in our literature is that of the general confession of Christ having come in the flesh. The goal of this confession is similar to that of Ignatius: the denial of Docetism among the early churches. The most prolific use of this theme in the New Testament is found in the argument of the author of 1 John. This text continually reassures its readers that salvation is only for those who confess that the Christ has come in the flesh. To deny this reality is to assume the role of an antichrist within the community. This very theme is incorporated into the letter of Polycarp to the Philippians in chapter 7. Presumably, the bishop is here heavily dependent upon the very arguments of 1 John, both in the nature of his theology and in terms of how he characterizes his opponents in the church at Philippi.[34] As a creed, this theological strand does not stand as a monolithic confession of faith. At the same time, however, it clearly is a confessional element that found its way into later creeds of the church.

HYMNS AND PRAYERS

It seems appropriate to group two categories together here, not because they are necessarily so similar in form, but because they appear so rarely in the apostolic fathers. At the same time, there is a certain sense in which these two types of materials function together in early Christian liturgy. Thus, it may ultimately be appropriate that the two categories of hymns and prayers should unavoidably be treated together in any survey of materials shared between the Scriptures and the fathers.

In the New Testament we are confronted constantly with the issue of prayer and praying. In the Gospels there is a continuous acknowledgment that Jesus prayed in various circumstances. Most noticeably, he is seen to pray in times of distress or hardship. In nearly every setting in which he does pray, one sees that he does so privately. This is not to deny that he was involved in public prayer, of course. In fact, the Gospels of Matthew (Matt 6:9–13) and Luke (Luke 11:2–4) both preserve

---

[34] Only the Johannine Epistles within the New Testament and Polycarp among the apostolic fathers make use of the term "antichrist" in reference to their opponents. Hartog (*Polycarp and the New Testament,* 186–90) notes the debate on this issue and chooses to support a Johannine connection as well.

what, at least by tradition, is assumed to be the framework of public prayers that were intended for use within the liturgical situation of the early church, especially in the form that appears in Matthew. The Matthean form of the Lord's Prayer is found in an almost exact replication in the text of the *Didache* (*Did.* 8.2). Whether the Didachist has drawn this form from some version of the Gospel of Matthew or simply knows it from the common materials of the early Christian experience, this citation is clear evidence of the typical usage of prayer in ancient church settings.

Elsewhere in the New Testament readers are enjoined to pray without ceasing both for the common life of the church and for those who exist outside the confines of the Christian faith (Matt 5:44; 2 Cor 9:14; 1 Thess 5:17). Paul acknowledges in every letter that he is praying either for his readers or for those about whom he offers quite specific advice (2 Cor 13:7; Col 1:9; 2 Thess 1:11). The author of Hebrews requests that those to whom the text is addressed "pray for us" (Heb 13:18), a plea that is typical of early Christian authors (Col 4:3; 2 Thess 3:1). The author of Acts observes that the early church was constantly in prayer within different situations, most noticeably when in times of distress or discernment (Acts 1:24; 6:6; 7:59; 9:40).

A survey of the texts of the fathers provides a similar concern for prayer, though to a much less obvious degree than within the New Testament literature. The author of *2 Clement* observes that, although fasting is better than prayer, prayer from a good conscience delivers a person from death (*2 Clem.* 16.4). This is a particularly interesting text within early Christian literature because it offers a conscious reflection on the value of prayer and its role within the Christian moral life.[35]

The bishop Ignatius offers sound observations about prayer throughout his letters. As he notes, he is dependent upon the prayers of the Ephesians as he anticipates his fight against the wild beasts, though his notation that this be accomplished "successfully" is not altogether clear here (Ign. *Eph.* 1.2). Indeed, as he observes later in the same text, the prayer of only one or two believers may bring harmony to an entire

---

[35] One might compare this same idea with Matt 6:1–18, in which the context of a Jewish ethical matrix on alms, prayer, and fasting provides the framework for the inclusion of the Lord's Prayer; see Hans Dieter Betz, "A Jewish-Christian Cultic *Didache* in Matt. 6:1–18: Reflections and Questions on the Problem of the Historical Jesus," in *Essays on the Sermon on the Mount* (trans. L. L. Welborn; Philadelphia: Fortress, 1985), 55–69.

church community (Ign. *Eph.* 5.2). Undoubtedly, this may be to some extent a conscious reflection of the Matthean text in which we read "where two or three are gathered in my name, I am there among them" (Matt 18:20). Paul expresses a similar idea as he writes to the Corinthians in 1 Cor 5:3–4, which suggests that this concept of "Christian presence" was widely understood among the developing churches of the late first and early second centuries. Elsewhere, like the author of Hebrews in the New Testament, Ignatius asks that the Romans remember him in their prayers (Ign. *Rom.* 9.1), and that the Trallians remember the church of Smyrna in their prayers (Ign. *Trall.* 13.1).

As to other texts among the fathers, Polycarp, like his close friend Ignatius, is shown to be one who prays both for the church and for the persecutors of the church (*Mart. Pol.* 7.2–8.1). Indeed, the person who penned the martyrdom of this famous bishop observes that Polycarp prayed for two straight hours prior to his arrest. Undoubtedly, this scene has been offered as a reflection of Jesus' own prayer for the church as found in the parallel text of John 17.

Finally, prayer is a concern in several interesting passages of the *Shepherd* as well. In the parable of the virgin spirits whom Hermas encounters toward the end of his experiences, he is enjoined by the virgins to lie in the midst of them and to pray (*Herm.* 88), which he acknowledges to the reader that in fact he did. One can hardly object that the presence of prayer in such a stimulating context reveals a special devotion to the concept for those who would be faithful to Christ, at least as seen by the author of the *Shepherd*.

Loosely associated with the idea of prayer in early Christian literature is the presence of hymns throughout our literature. In the New Testament one is immediately drawn to texts such as the Gospel of John and the letters of Paul. The well-known prologue on "the Word" of John 1:1–18 clearly reflects an early hymn that was widely known among the second-century churches, either in a form commonly used by the Johannine community or by competing strains of "Christian" followers. The roots of this hymn are not entirely clear, to be certain, but its elements reflect a theology that associates the role and function of the Messiah both with the creative principles of God as expressed in the character of the person of Wisdom and with the salvific beliefs of God as found in the actions of a wonderworker who lived and acted among God's people. The parameters of such a concept may be broadly defined according to first-century views of God's relationship with the world, especially since the definition of exactly who Jesus was as the Christ continued to be debated by the church through a series of ecclesiastical councils that extended through the fifth century.

It is perhaps noteworthy that other hymns in the New Testament reflect a similar concern for the definition of exactly who Jesus is as the Christ and how he performed his role among those to whom he ministered. For example, the now well-known hymn of Phil 2 by Paul illustrates similar tendencies (see Phil 2:5–11). The basic concern of the hymn is directed toward the nature of who Christ Jesus is, how he chose to divorce himself from divine privileges in order to act in a human capacity, with the result that he was brought to crucifixion, found worthy of exaltation by God, and worthy of praise by all those who would follow him. As is widely recognized today, this hymn most likely has been adopted and adapted by Paul to fit the particular context of his letter to Philippi. For our present purposes, it is intriguing that the early nature of the hymn so closely identifies a primary concern of the earliest churches, much like the hymn of John 1:1–18. That concern was the identification of the nature and function of Jesus as the Messiah.[36]

The circumstances of the use of hymns in the apostolic fathers might be paralleled with that in the New Testament, except that there is a clear paucity of hymnic sections throughout these works. The single exception here may be found toward the beginning of *2 Clement*, at *2 Clem.* 1.4–8. These five verses offer what is in essence a synopsis of the doctrinal argument that the author has chosen to pursue in the remainder of *2 Clement*. The theological foundation of the hymn is focused upon the activity of Christ as it relates to the situation of the early church. As the author of the text observes, even as humanity was blinded by ignorance and false religions, Christ had pity and called forth in an effort of salvation. He offered light to those who were perishing, "as a father he called us sons" (*2 Clem.* 1.4). Though there is some concern in this hymnic fragment for the nature of who Christ is,

---

[36] One might add Heb 1:5–14 to the New Testament collection of hymns, though the distinction is not as clear. These verses offer an assemblage of passages from the royal psalms of Jewish Scripture, which, naturally, were themselves hymns in their original form. Presumably, the presentation of these fragmentary psalms is intended to serve the form of a hymn for early Christian worship as well. In either case, the concern to identify the role of Christ (here as compared to the angels) stands as the dominant concern of the author.

the focus is less upon a definition of the role of Christ than on an explanation of how Christ functions on behalf of the believing community.

If these verses can indeed be accepted as a form of early Christian hymn, then there has been a basic shift in perception about the function of hymns by the second-century church, as is illustrated by this text. Hymns are no longer designed primarily to offer praise for the reality of the nature of Christ, but rather to offer recognition for the reality of how Christ functions in the world for those who would seek to be his followers.

CONCLUSION

This brief review of materials shared between New Testament literature and the works of the apostolic fathers reveals several factors worthy of note for anyone doing research in the field. In the first instance, the basic forms of the New Testament tradition—letters and homilies, apocalyptic texts and martyrdoms—are represented for the most part in the fathers as well. The numerous letters of Scripture find convenient parallel in the fathers, and apocalyptic materials among the apostolic writings have parallels among the postapostolic texts. It certainly is true that there is not necessarily a one-to-one balance in this regard, of course. There is only one martyrdom in the New Testament, that of Stephen in Acts (unless one wishes to call the crucifixion of Jesus a martyrdom as well), and this is but a small portion of a much larger work. In the apostolic fathers there is only one martyrdom as well, that of Polycarp. However, the account of the bishop's death encompasses the pages of an entire work and clearly is the locus of a major tradition that develops into a specific genre throughout later Christian literature.[37] Further, though technically not characterized by the genre of martyrdom, the letters of Ignatius speak constantly to the anticipation of death and thus have the particular flavor of martyrdom about them.

What holds true with respect to genre holds true with respect to specific categories of material as well. So, the prolific use of sayings throughout the New Testament finds a similar usage throughout the fathers. This is only natural, of course, since such is a primary way by

---

[37] Compare the early-third-century *Martyrdom of Saints Perpetua and Felicitas* and, slightly later, *Acts of Cyprian* as apt examples.

which wisdom in any faith is disseminated. The act of praying and the desire for prayers appear throughout all of the material. Parables are to be found in both collections of texts as well, but they are limited to very specific writings at each stage. Other categories find a different level of acceptance. In the New Testament there is a scattered usage of traditional, early Christian hymns, while the fathers are less disposed to such materials. In addition, the way in which hymns are used in *2 Clement* suggests that their focus—the need to identify the role and function of who Christ is—has undergone a slight change.

As one might expect, most categories of texts are prevalent both in the New Testament and in the fathers. This makes sense in light of the fact that the apostolic fathers, as noted previously, is only a secondary collection of materials that have been thrust together by modern scholars, primarily on the premise that what appears here is similar to what is found in Scripture, and secondarily on the idea that these writings, like those in the New Testament, were widely employed throughout the second-century church. At the same time, this brief survey indicates that most of the materials used in both collections have been employed for similar purposes, if not in similar ways. Sayings remain consistent throughout, as does the use of the letter form. So too, most of the authors of the apostolic fathers no longer find a need for hymns or for the parables of Jesus. Nor do they find a use for miracles as a way to authenticate the authority of specific early Christian figures.

The use of particular genres and materials in our literature indicates the individual concerns of church communities and their leaders. The consistency of certain forms reveals the typical progression of definite categories as the developing church implemented them. At the same time, some images lost their value as dynamic views of what it meant to be Christian in a gradually changing atmosphere of faith.

FOR FURTHER READING

Though much of the truly interesting research on early Christian literary forms is widely scattered among studies focused upon individual texts, there is some broad help to be found in the following:

- Aune, David E., ed. *Greco-Roman Literature and the New Testament: Selected Forms and Genres.* Society of Biblical Literature Sources for Biblical Study 21. Atlanta: Scholars Press, 1988.

- Longenecker, Richard N. *New Wine into Fresh Wineskins: Contextualizing the Early Christian Confessions.* Peabody, Mass.: Hendrickson, 1999.

- McDonald, James I. H. *Kerygma and Didache: The Articulation and Structure of the Earliest Christian Message.* Society for New Testament Studies Monograph Series 37. Cambridge: Cambridge University Press, 1980.

- Strecker, Georg. *History of New Testament Literature.* Translated by C. Katter, with H.-J. Mollenhauer. Harrisburg, Pa.: Trinity Press International, 1997.

- Wilder, Amos N. *Early Christian Rhetoric: The Language of the Gospel.* Cambridge, Mass.: Harvard University Press, 1971.

A large variety of introductions to ancient Christian letter style are also available, including:

- Stirewalt, M. Luther, Jr. *Studies in Ancient Greek Epistolography.* Society of Biblical Literature Sources for Biblical Study 27. Atlanta: Scholars Press, 1993.

- Stowers, Stanley K. *Letter Writing in Greco-Roman Antiquity.* Library of Early Christianity 5. Philadelphia: Westminster, 1986.

- White, John L. *Light from Ancient Letters.* Foundations and Facets. Philadelphia: Fortress, 1986.

Chapter 3

Codes of Conduct and Christian Thinking

It seems fair to say that the earliest Christian communities, whatever their numbers and regional locations, were composed primarily of Christian Jews whose views of Judaism were challenged by the call to faith that was shared by the early Christian evangelists. This reality seems to be suggested by our earliest witnesses to the spread of the Christian faith, as is illustrated by the letters of Paul. It is also evident in the depiction of the spread of the Christian mission that is portrayed, admittedly somewhat anachronistically, by the author of the New Testament book of Acts. The specific nature of those persons of faith who first responded to the nascent Christian message certainly has received extended debate among scholars. Let it suffice for us simply to say here that Judaism was most likely the first mission field of the earliest Christians and served as the ground soil for the ultimate rise of church communities.

From this initial foundation two successive factors must be taken into consideration. In the first instance, whatever the composition of the earliest groups of Christian believers, their numbers quickly became infiltrated with non-Jewish believers. These people, whether the God-fearers of those early synagogues that were scattered throughout the Diaspora or otherwise, brought with them the customs and traditions of divergent Mediterranean faiths. In some cases, the attraction to Judaism, and hence to primitive Christianity, undoubtedly was driven by a lack of satisfaction with these more traditional belief systems. In other instances, the shift toward Judeo-Christian ideas may have been less of a quest for satisfaction and simply an attempt to establish roots within a new cultural setting. In other words, a change of faiths was not always religiously motivated.

Second, what is commonly called first-century Judaism, that is, the religious milieu within which the earliest roots of Christianity took hold, was hardly a cloth woven from a single fabric. Indeed, mixed within this "Judaism" of the period was a variety of theological and ethical considerations, as has long been recognized by modern scholars. To some large degree this variety was determined by geographical situations or by political circumstances. In other cases, language and local custom often came into consideration for local synagogues. Additional factors such as wealth, stability, access to regional authorities, the ebb and flow of intolerance among the local populace, connections with distant Jewish communities, and family concerns all served to determine the nature of scattered synagogues and the vision of what it meant to be Jewish among both the leaders and congregants of those centers of worship.

For our current discussion, we must ask two questions concerning which the nature of the late-first- and early-second-century churches played a decisive role: Among the scattered Christian communities of the period, which themselves were established and nurtured according to numerous theological and ethnic considerations, what was the nature and function of ethics? And, is there a pattern of ethics within the literature of the New Testament that is either continued among the apostolic fathers or dismissed within that corpus of texts? It is my conjecture that certain ethical patterns are indeed to be found among the scattered writings of Scripture that reflect the view of the authors of those texts, as well as the communities to which they were addressed. Further, I believe that the patterns that exist there are continued in part among the writings of the fathers, but are in many cases shifted in those texts as well.

SCHOOLS OF THOUGHT AMONG FIRST-CENTURY CHRISTIANS

The earliest evidence of a single ethical perspective to be found within the New Testament may be distinguished within the writings of the apostle Paul. Studies of the ethics of Paul may be found in various collections of secondary literature. My concern here is not so much to distinguish the nature of Paul's own ethical positions, but rather to consider how they functioned within his view of the developing Christian church.

Apocalyptic Themes

Paul's earliest writing, 1 Thessalonians (and perhaps 2 Thessalonians, if that letter may indeed be attributed to Paul), reveals a trend that is immediately evident to any reader of Scripture: a concern for apocalyptic.[1] As was mentioned previously in chapter 2, apocalyptic as a genre was widely scattered within both Christian and non-Christian literature of the first and second centuries. On the one hand, such materials were designed to challenge the faithful toward a consideration of future events and the need to be prepared for difficult times that lay ahead. In this respect, one naturally perceives within many works the obvious call to "stay alert" and to "be aware." On the other hand, apocalyptic texts were written less with a concern for the future and more with a view toward the present. Here one finds that the author's primary concern is with the ethical lifestyle of the audience instead of what may actually lie ahead in days to come.

It is perhaps impossible to know the intention originally associated with those materials that Paul has presented in 1 Thess 4:13–5:11. The now familiar imagery of early Christian apocalyptic is rife within this short selection of verses: the coming of the Lord, the sound of God's trumpet, the rising of the dead, the arrival as a thief in the night, and the call to be children of light. I do not doubt that the words here are those of the apostle, but there seems little question that the imagery reflects late Jewish apocalyptic material and may be drawn from widely known Christian sources.[2] If indeed his language stems from a

---

[1] For helpful discussions on the relationship of apocalyptic language and eschatological thinking in Paul with respect to Pauline ethics see Robin Scroggs, *Paul for a New Day* (Philadelphia: Fortress, 1977), 59–74; Victor Paul Furnish, *Theology and Ethics in Paul* (Nashville: Abingdon, 1968).

[2] Parallel language appears in Mark 13 and its synoptic parallels. As Jan Lambrecht notes, "Abundant use of apocalyptic motifs is made in both sections [4:1–5:22] in contrast to what precedes and follows and both make use of creedal material" ("A Structural Analysis of 1 Thessalonians 4–5," in *The Thessalonians Debate: Methodological Discord or Methodological Synthesis* [ed. K. P. Donfried and J. Beutler; Grand Rapids: Eerdmans, 2000], 165); see also Christiaan Beker, *Paul the Apostle: The Triumph of God in Life and Thought* (Philadelphia: Fortress,

combination of these categories, it is impossible to determine any particular "original intention."

On Paul's own part, however, the intention is clearly stated: "Encourage one another and build up each other, as indeed you are doing" (1 Thess 5:11). Though a reading of this one verse alone suggests simply the encouragement of fellow Christians in the midst of ordeal and concerns about those who have died, as suggested already by 1 Thess 4:13, the surrounding context of the letter implies something more. Indeed, the essence of 1 Thessalonians is a call for an adherence to an ethical lifestyle. The apostle reminds his readers that he neither came to steal from the Thessalonian church nor to sponge off of it (1 Thess 2:5–12), but rather to serve as a model for faith. So too, he chides his audience to live publicly moral lives (1 Thess 4:1–12), controlling passions, living quietly, and paying attention to one's own affairs. Finally, he concludes with further words about the need to remain at peace, to be patient with the weak, to seek to do good deeds, and to pray constantly (1 Thess 5:12–24). It is in this manner that the spirit of God is able to enter into the life of the community and the believer's body and soul may "be kept sound and blameless at the coming of our Lord Jesus Christ" (1 Thess 5:23).[3]

It is curious that Paul, for the most part, abandoned basic apocalyptic imagery in his remaining letters. This is not to say that no similar terms and phrases are to be found in his subsequent writings, but simply that he chose not to focus upon apocalyptic materials as a primary genre. Of course, Paul's concern for the ethical lifestyle among believers in Christ Jesus never waned. Quite the contrary, the Pauline

---

1980), 135–81; John J. Collins, *The Apocalyptic Imagination: An Introduction to the Jewish Matrix of Christianity* (New York: Crossroad, 1984), 205–15; Ulrich B. Müller, "Apocalyptic Currents," in *Christian Beginnings: Word and Community from Jesus to Post-Apostolic Times* (ed. J. Becker; trans. A. S. Kidder and R. Krauss; Louisville: Westminster/John Knox, 1993), 281–329.

[3] Second Thessalonians, which is closely modeled on the concerns of 1 Thessalonians, holds a similar connection between the use of apocalyptic and the call for modest and appropriate behavior. If this writing does indeed come from Paul, it offers little that is worthy of additional comment, with a single exception. The text of 2 Thessalonians clearly is devoted more toward an apocalyptic focus than toward ethical implications, which is a reverse of 1 Thessalonians. If the letter actually comes from another hand, then this change in focus may represent either the particular concerns of the author, couched within a Pauline school of consciousness, or evidence of the changing function of apocalyptic texts within the developing church.

emphasis upon appropriate living is well known. For one reason or another, Paul chose to make his arguments for ethics according to the logic of rabbinic persuasion in subsequent letters or simply made his calls to an ethical lifestyle based upon the threat of a final judgment by God.[4] This may have been because he did not encounter the results that he had wished for from an apocalyptic approach. Or, as others have suggested, he may have found the call to be watchful for the immediate coming of the Son of Man to have lost its immediacy for Christian faith. In either case, Paul continued to argue for a correct Christian lifestyle for his readers, clearly directed toward Jewish norms but away from the rigorist interpretations of strict Torah observance.

The similar concern for apocalyptic is perhaps best addressed elsewhere, in the Gospel of Mark, a text whose famous sayings in chapter 13 were adopted by the authors of the Gospels of Matthew and Luke and expanded in those texts with additional materials. The sayings of Mark 13 are clearly apocalyptic, but they only belie the immediacy with which the author of the gospel text perceived the entire mission of the historical Jesus in the opening chapters of the work. Whether we can assign the sayings and warnings of Mark 13 with the actual teachings of Jesus has received considerable debate. Indeed, the issue has provoked a conversation that traditionally has divided scholars according to those who find within the teachings of Jesus an essentially existential concern for the growing kingdom of God within the world and those who believe that Jesus made a call for faithful attention to the coming Day of the Lord as his primary concern.

Regardless of how one interprets the mission and message of Jesus with respect to apocalyptic, it is clear that the authors of the Synoptic Gospels understood the message of future warnings to be a central premise. This is particularly evident within a text such as the Gospel of Matthew, where an editorial consciousness has attached imagery about the judging of all humanity at the end of times throughout the gospel text. At the same time, however, it is noteworthy that each of the synoptic authors has collected the bulk of warnings about the future into some final speech from Jesus prior to his passion experience. Such a literary position reminds one of the last words of a condemned person—that is, those words that bear the most significance within a person's life and deserve the right to be heard by those who seek

---

[4] See, for example, Rom 2:1–16.

wisdom. Though Matthew and Luke may simply be following the cue of Mark in this regard, one must be impressed that these words appear in such a crucial literary position in all three texts. This positioning is all the more impressive when compared with the Gospel of John. The Johannine author is not nearly as interested in apocalyptic imagery, and in the final words of Jesus (John 14–17) the author has substituted an address of love and community concern to the readers of the gospel text.[5] This difference between the Synoptic Gospels and that of John undoubtedly indicates a basic approach to ethics within the two traditions that separates over the question of apocalyptic emphasis: the synoptic authors envision the apocalyptic genre as the motivator for authentic Christian actions and an ethical lifestyle; the author of John pictures the figure of the risen Christ as the central image through whom true believers must be inspired to live in accordance with gospel teachings.

Finally, a brief word on the book of Revelation is needed here. Many who have read this text over the centuries have been immediately attracted to its call for vigilance in the face of the unknown. For those who are persecuted, it offers reassurance of God's coming rescue. For those who are the persecutors, it offers the warning of God's coming judgment. And yet, the author explicitly states at the beginning of the work that the message is for seven specific church communities in Asia Minor (Rev 1–3). Unlike the approach taken by Paul and the authors of the Synoptic Gospels, the author of Revelation does not explicitly direct an apocalyptic message toward the conscious repentance of all the world, at least not as a primary motivational factor behind the writing of the work. Whether John of Patmos was more concerned for the destruction of the churches of Asia Minor or for their repentance is unclear and simply the matter of modern speculation. Indeed, as is stated in the text, "Let the evildoer still do evil, and the filthy still be filthy" (Rev 22:11). But surely the later church tradition that chose to place this work as the concluding text of the New Testament canon intended for it to serve as a call for general Christian repentance and the living of an ethical lifestyle.

---

[5] This is perhaps all the more perplexing for those who would link the authorship of the Gospel of John to that of the book of Revelation, since the apocalyptic concerns of the latter indicate a view that is more in line with synoptic tendencies than with Johannine ideas. This is not to deny that people "change their minds" throughout their lives according to life's circumstances. All the same, such would be a significant change indeed.

Again as suggested previously in chapter 2, the role of Revelation as a call to action (one way or another) perhaps served as a model for the materials of *Did.* 16. In this writing from the apostolic fathers, a text that otherwise indicates little trace of apocalyptic considerations, the materials of chapter 16 reflect all three of the New Testament traditions stated above. The intensity and canonical positioning of Revelation is clearly reflected in the design of *Did.* 16. The imagery of 1 Thessalonians and Mark 13 is likewise apparent in this same chapter. What is most intriguing about this synthesis of New Testament apocalyptic perspectives by the Didachist is that the urgency of apocalyptic as a meaningful call to the immediate return of the Lord upon the clouds seems sharply diminished. All of the correct terms and warnings are in place, but the remainder of the text suggests no particular reason to worry about such warnings, except in some formal sense. Instead, the final warnings of the *Didache* stand simply as an appropriate closing statement about the importance of what has preceded these materials: a call to follow the path of life (*Did.* 1–6), a series of instructions on the appropriate observance of liturgical matters (*Did.* 7.1–10.6), and a reminder about the best way to handle wandering authorities and to respect local leaders (*Did.* 7.7–15.4). The average reader of the *Didache* is hardly prepared for the apocalyptic conclusion that appears in chapter 16. Its presence seems more a matter of form than of urgency.

In the *Shepherd of Hermas* a similar transition seems evident. The apocalyptic beast encountered by Hermas in chapters 22–23 rises (and falls) mostly as a curious moment in the experiences of our hero. Certainly there is a brief acknowledgment of the value of apocalyptic materials as motivators for ethical living here, but it is hardly more than that. It is worthy of note that our author never returns to this image in any other way in this, the longest, writing of the apostolic fathers.

We must ask, then, what conclusions we may draw from this analysis of the apocalyptic genre as an aid to understanding early Christian ethics. In the first instance, the authors of the New Testament clearly were dependent upon the motivation of apocalyptic materials as known and used within the Jewish Scriptures. From Paul to the synoptic authors to the book of Revelation, such materials were known and used as an aid toward the adjustment of early Christian attitudes about appropriate living. The effect of such calls remains a mystery for the modern researcher, of course. However, it is perhaps worthy of note that these same materials often serve as tremendous motivations for the twenty-first-century reader of these texts.

Second, though apocalyptic materials were widely known and used by first-century Christians, their influence upon the apostolic fathers seems minimal at best. The text of the *Didache* appears at first glance to be a legitimate reflection of the way that New Testament authors made use of apocalyptic themes as a motivational tool. This does not prove to be true, however, upon a closer consideration of the way that *Did.* 16 functions for the remainder of the text. So too, the author of the *Shepherd* seems little bothered by apocalyptic imagery, except as a momentary image for reflection. For the most part, apocalyptic materials are not otherwise employed in the apostolic fathers as a source of motivation for correct ethics.

Virtue and Vice Lists

Two common tools that were often employed by New Testament authors in the pursuit of ethics were so-called virtue-vice lists and household codes. Though these genres were offered to their readers in order to achieve similar effects throughout early Christian literature, the means by which they were used and the frequency of that usage perhaps demand that they be discussed separately.

Virtue and vice lists appear randomly throughout the New Testament. They are drawn both from Jewish sources and from Hellenistic literature. It is not possible to argue that any particular author was exclusively dependent upon one tradition or another for the employment of such lists. Instead, the modern student must come to recognize that such materials simply were "in the air."[6] Indeed, virtue and vice lists are found in a variety of early Christian scriptural sources. Paul incorporates a number of such lists throughout his writings. One finds a clear example in Gal 5:19–21, where virtues are associated with "the works of the spirit," and vices are labeled as "the works of the flesh." Elsewhere, Paul is particularly concerned to list the vices of fleshly living, as is seen in Rom 1:29–30, 1 Cor 5:10–11, 1 Cor 6:9–10, and 2 Cor 12:20. Often,

---

[6] For an interesting discussion of the background behind both virtue and vice lists and the household codes see the general review of early Christian literature in James I. H. McDonald, *Kerygma and Didache: The Articulation and Structure of the Earliest Christian Message* (SNTSMS 37; Cambridge: Cambridge University Press, 1980).

similar materials are used to characterize the life of the faithful follower of Christ Jesus.[7] The apostle makes additional use of virtue and vice lists as he issues various rhetorical appeals to his readers, as may be found in Rom 8:35–39 and 2 Cor 11:22–29.

Much like the writings of Paul, writers from within the Pauline school make use of similar lists. The author of Colossians encourages the church in Colossae to die to various vices (fornication, impurity, passion, etc.) and to be clothed in numerous virtues (compassion, kindness, meekness, patience), but most especially in love (Col 3:5–17). So too, the author of the letter to the Ephesians instructs all Christians to avoid fornication and impurity of any kind, but also greed and useless talk (Eph 5:3–5), since such persons have no inheritance in the kingdom of Christ and of God. Later in this same trajectory, the author of 1 Timothy lists the by-products that result from listening to false teaching (envy, dissension, slander, etc.) and urges instead pursuit of the virtues of righteousness, godliness, faith, love, and so forth (1 Tim 6:3–12). A similar warning is repeated in the text of 2 Timothy (2 Tim 3:1–9).

It is perhaps not surprising, therefore, particularly in the light of a desire among many second-century Christians to model their faith upon the teaching and ministry of the apostle Paul, that virtue and vice lists are found within both the Ignatian correspondence and the letter of Polycarp. A subtle and innovative use of such lists is offered by Ignatius in Ign. *Eph.* 10.1–3, for example, where the Ephesians are counseled to instruct others through their own deeds: respond to anger with gentleness, to boasts with humility, to slander with prayers, to errors with faith, to cruelty with gentleness. As he himself states in this same passage, Ignatius views the performance of such traits to serve as an imitation of the Lord.[8] Polycarp, in his letter to the Philippians, also offers a short list of virtues that he believes to represent the example "of the Lord": being immovable in faith, loving fellowship, cherishing others, being united in truth, yielding to others in gentleness, despising no one (Pol. *Phil.* 10.1).[9] It is not particularly surprising that he, like Ignatius,

---

[7] See 1 Cor 4:11–13; 2 Cor 6:4–10.

[8] William R. Schoedel notes that being an imitator of the Lord, "becoming disciples" (Ign. *Eph.* 1.2), and "attaining God" are typical Ignatian themes that the bishop associates with martyrdom (*Ignatius of Antioch: A Commentary on the Letters of Ignatius of Antioch* [ed. H. Koester; Hermeneia; Philadelphia: Fortress, 1985], 70).

[9] It is possible that this single verse is composed of allusions to 1 Cor 15:58 or Col 1:23, 1 Pet 2:17 or 3:8, Rom 12:10, and 2 Cor 10:1; so Kenneth Berding,

associates such traits with the Lord's example. There is much in Polycarp's letter that indicates a close agreement with the views and style of Ignatius. Presumably, they were well acquainted, and one borrowed from the other in the many ideas that they seem to have shared.

Of course, this use of lists is by no means restricted to Pauline materials or to those who reflected the consciousness of the Pauline school. The so-called Catholic Epistles of the New Testament make occasional use of the lists as well. The author of the book of James offers a brief reflection on two types of wisdom: that which comes down from above and that which does not. The first is characterized by traits such as purity, peace, gentleness, and mercy; the second produces envy, selfishness, disorder, and unspiritual activity (Jas 3:15–18). In another interesting image, the author of 1 Peter warns the faithful Christian to remove all "malice, guile, insincerity, envy, and slander" (1 Pet 2:1). Those who can achieve this end will become as "living stones" in a spiritual house, built for the Lord, as the author of the text insists.

These two images, particularly as they are associated with virtue and vice lists, have interesting parallels in the apostolic fathers. In the *Shepherd of Hermas,* parables and teachings about the church likewise tap into the vision of Christians who serve as stones that are used to build a tower that is meant to be seen as a metaphor for the body of Christ. The author of the *Shepherd* offers several instances where the reader is instructed to pay special attention to how the church has been constructed with carefully weighed and shaped stones. Within this construction, numerous types of stones have been used. Some of these are round and worn; some are newer and squared; some are heavy, and others are light. But even in this variety, only the best have been employed.[10]

Apart from this lively image of the church as a construction of "Christian stones," the author of the *Shepherd* made a second, even more important, advance upon the use of virtue and vice lists. I refer here to the anthropomorphic figures of virtue that first appear in chapter 16. In this passage, the virtues (faith, self-control, sincerity, knowl-

---

Polycarp and Paul: An Analysis of Their Literary and Theological Relationship in Light of Polycarp's Use of Biblical and Extra-Biblical Literature (VCSup 62; Leiden: Brill, 2002), 101–3.

[10] See especially chapters 10–17 and 78–110 of the *Shepherd.* At the same time, I do not think it necessarily significant that the author of *2 Clem.* 14, while talking about the "spiritual" nature of the church, does not choose to employ virtue and vice lists in that particular discussion.

edge, innocence, reverence, love) are depicted as young women who assist in the construction of the tower that is the church. As the author of the *Shepherd* says, "Whoever serves these and has the strength to master their works will have a dwelling in the tower with the saints of God" (*Herm.* 16.8). These women appear variously in later texts, but eventually they are addressed as specific images once again in chapter 92, where they are further identified as virgins and their numbers are enlarged by the additional virtues of cheerfulness, truth, understanding, and harmony. Beside these virgins have now appeared women in black clothing who represent the reality of vices in the struggle of all Christians: unbelief, self-indulgence, disobedience, grief, and so forth. Each of these figures has a place in daily living. The embodiment of virtues and vices by the author of the *Shepherd* undoubtedly went far in the later anthropomorphic use of such images in the morality plays of the Middle Ages and Renaissance Christianity.

The *Didache* offers an image of virtue and vice lists that reflects an awareness both of the role of Wisdom in the creation of the Christian conscience and of the place of the ethical implications of any attempt to apply moral categories to practical living. The text of *Did.* 2–5 offers clear virtue and vice lists that have incorporated within them an awareness of the Decalogue of the Jewish Scriptures. The reader is warned not to murder, commit adultery, steal, and so forth. Associated with these evils, however, is practical advice designed to protect the reader from being led to these sins: do not be angry, for anger leads to murder; do not be lustful, for lust leads to fornication; and so on (*Did.* 3.1–6). Instead, the observant Christian should be humble, patient, merciful, innocent, quiet, and good, since these are the correct moral choices of ethical Christians (*Did.* 3.7–10). The framework for such instructions is the application of wisdom language that appears in the book of Proverbs through the use of the address "My child."[11] The Didachist has provided a most intriguing combination of Torah language and wisdom idiom to produce a text that is unique in early Christian literature, a writing that clearly was designed to instill an ethical consciousness in the lives of new Christian believers.[12]

---

[11] See, for example, Prov 1:8, 10, 15; 2:1; 3:1, 11, 21; 4:1, 10, 20; 5:1; 6:1, 20; 7:1.

[12] These materials have an obvious parallel in *Barn.* 18–20, of course, and will be discussed below in relation to the "two ways" image that appears throughout late Jewish and early Christian literature.

Finally, we should take notice of the materials of Mark 7:21–22, which gives a short list of vices that Jesus purportedly believed to originate with people and, hence, to defile them.[13] Lists of virtues and vices in the Gospels are rare, to be certain. It is most likely that the usefulness of such lists as a means by which to inspire the ethical lifestyle of early followers may not have been of specific concern to the historical Jesus. At the same time, the authors of the Gospels may not have seen them as a genre of materials that served as well as did apocalyptic warnings. We must never lose sight of the fact that ethical codes such as virtue and vice lists never stood alone in Christian literature, but rather were offered as support and validation for the soundness of the church's teachings. In the case of the Gospels, the authors of these texts were more interested in the authority of Jesus as the ultimate rationale behind the actions of those who encountered the Messiah than in the specific use of traditional, ethical codes as the justification for any particular Christian lifestyle.

It is this very combination of the teachings of Jesus together with virtue and vice codes that we find assembled within a single writing of the apostolic fathers. The text of *1 Clement* is scattered with virtue and vice lists that appear in various forms. At *1 Clem.* 8.4, for example, the characteristics of the suitable Christian are offered as a list of virtues that relate to social justice for those who have been wronged, the orphan, and the widow. In *1 Clem.* 30.1, those who are "the portion of the Holy One" are enjoined to forsake the practices of slander, impure embraces, drunken lust, adultery, and pride. Later, in *1 Clem.* 30.8, short comparative lists are offered: boldness, arrogance, and audacity are for those who are cursed by God; graciousness, humility, and gentleness are for those who are blessed by God.[14] Furthermore, those who are "of the mind of God" are charged to cast off unrighteousness, lawlessness, covetousness, strife, malice, deceit, gossip, slander, hatred of God, pride, arrogance, vanity, and inhospitality (*1 Clem.* 35.5). Though the Romans could hardly have known spe-

---

[13] Admittedly, this is the single example in the Synoptic Gospels and may be the work of a later hand. This is not to say that Jesus was not a user of such lists, of course, particularly in light of the fact that they paralleled common rabbinic usage of the period.

[14] As is argued by Lindemann, the author of *1 Clement* clearly has followed a Pauline rhetorical scheme here in offering an "indicative/imperative" approach to ethics in this chapter; see Andreas Lindemann, *Die Clemensbriefe* (HNT 17/1; Tübingen: Mohr, 1992), 96–97.

cific episodes of each of these vices within the church at Corinth, the clear employment of this vice list is surely intended to call the Corinthians to a general reexamination of their ethics and lifestyle. The foundation of this examination would be intended to serve as a means by which to question the election and maintenance of local church leaders, of course. So then, the acceptable virtues of a true Christian church—faith, repentance, genuine love, self-control, sobriety, and patience (*1 Clem.* 62.2)—could be anticipated as the fruit of the Corinthian situation.

Household Codes

We turn now briefly to the situation of the so-called household codes.[15] Unlike the virtue and vice lists, these codes appear only in very specific contexts within the New Testament and the apostolic fathers. Such codes clearly are dependent upon a hierarchy of authority within the Mediterranean household, a hierarchy that quickly was utilized by the earliest Christian communities in order to provide some ethical structure for the late-first-century church. In their earliest forms the household codes were offered as a means by which Christians could regulate the social relationships within a religious organization that, though theoretically composed of believers in Christ who had no social or political or economic distinction, served as a melting pot of divergent backgrounds and classes. Drawn from models of both Greek and Roman antiquity, as well as from the popular practices of Hellenistic Judaism, the codes appeared first within Christian literature among the works of deuteropauline authors.[16] It seems relatively clear that these codes, whatever the many reasons for their use, generally functioned in at least two basic ways. First, the codes provided a system of ethics that was broadly familiar to Hellenistic converts. Thus, as non-Jewish Christians joined the house churches of the first century, the codes provided a system of institutional management that could be subsumed under the general rubric of the "household of God." Second, the codes became a means by which the authors of early Christian literature could appeal for harmony according to systems that had long been established within society and were generally respected as acceptable social norms.

---

[15] For a slightly more extended presentation of the following material see Clayton N. Jefford, "Household Codes and Conflict in the Early Church," *StPatr* 31 (1997): 121–27.

[16] See Col 3:18–4:1; Eph 5:21–6:9.

The authors of Colossians and Ephesians show that they can harness the power of such codes and apply them freely in different contexts. For the author of Colossians, the codes are offered as an "earthly" structure of ethics that stands in open confrontation with a divergent "philosophy" that confronts the church at Colossae. The elements of "principalities and powers" (Col 2:5), "elemental spirits" (Col 2:8, 20), and "festivals, new moons, (and) Sabbaths" (Col 2:16–19) suggest a competing system, perhaps gnostic in form, against which Colossians was written. The application of household codes by the author clearly offers a more widely acceptable social norm—the system of the *paterfamilias,* in which the father figure held ultimate authority within the community—that could serve to ground the fledgling Colossian church in a world of both social and individual ethics.

Though not confronted with the same sort of philosophical challenge that the author of Colossians faced, the author of Ephesians likewise wrote in conflict with some sort of "false teaching" that was circulating among the Ephesian Christians. For the author of Ephesians, the household codes serve to support a religious institution under the rubric of "body of Christ" that disavowed any validity to pagan customs or false lifestyles (Eph 5:21–6:9).[17]

As with the virtue and vice lists, later deuteropauline authors were quick to incorporate household codes as a means by which to determine appropriate Christian ethics. The tenor of the codes takes a significant turn in this situation, however. In texts such as 1 Timothy (1 Tim 3:1–13; 5:1–6:2) and Titus (Titus 2:1–10), the codes are associated with two noteworthy concerns for the developing hierarchy of the church. On the one hand, the structure of the codes is utilized as a justification for the structure of the hierarchy of the church according to the order of bishop, presbyter, and deacon. Each of these ecclesiastical offices was viewed within the authority of the head of the Christian household, a society whose members were expected to be respectful of its "elders." On the other hand, the question of submission is clearly considered in

---

[17] Though clearly not of the Pauline school, the household code that appears in 1 Pet 2:11–3:12 may have been applied here in a way that is roughly parallel to that of Ephesians; see Jefford, "Household Codes and Conflict," 123. All three of these texts—Colossians, Ephesians, 1 Peter—may be interconnected within a "gnostic-patristic" trajectory, according to Elisabeth Schüssler Fiorenza, *In Memory of Her: A Feminist Theological Reconstruction of Christian Origins* (New York: Crossroad, 1984), 251–84.

this use of the codes. Wives are to be submissive to their husbands, younger Christians (either in years or faith) to their elders, and slaves to their masters. Between these two considerations—hierarchy and re-spect—the household codes seem to have served the authors of the Pastoral Epistles quite well late in the first century.

It is perhaps in this same tenor that the household codes are used by the author of *1 Clement*, as well as by the bishops Ignatius and Polycarp. Much like the Pastoral Epistles, *1 Clement* employs the codes as a means by which to resolve conflicts within the community. The quarrel is not that of the author's own community at Rome, of course, but that of the intended recipient of the letter, the church at Corinth. So, in *1 Clem* 1.3 and 21.6–9 we find our author's use of the codes, which are offered as a standard by which the Corinthians are expected to regulate their activities. Indeed, having departed from such codes was clearly seen by the Romans as an important reason why the Corin-thian situation had fallen apart. It is unclear whether the Corinthians themselves actually supported household codes as a standard for ethics and hierarchy, but the Romans certainly did. For Rome, the model of *paterfamilias* was an acceptable authority for church structure and a sure avenue by which to be aligned with God's desire for harmony and the resolution of conflicts.

Ignatius and Polycarp appear to have used the codes in a similar fashion. In his letter to Polycarp (Ign. *Pol.* 4.1–6.1) Ignatius outlines a specific standard by which widows, slaves, and wives are to be treated within the church community. Much like the New Testament letters to Colossae and Ephesus, Ignatius envisions the household codes as a means by which to resist "those who teach an unusual doctrine" (Ign. *Pol.* 3.1–2). To some extent, Polycarp likewise respects the codes as a model around which to structure the correct teachings of his own church community at Smyrna. In his letter to the Philippians (Pol. *Phil.* 4.2–6.3) Polycarp gives instructions for wives, widows, young men, deacons, and presbyters within the light of the threat of "false teach-ings" of Docetism. The extent to which he already was in agreement with Ignatius on these issues is unclear. What is clear, however, is that he took the opportunity of Ignatius's letter to model his words on those of the bishop of Antioch.

Finally, household codes appear briefly in the texts of the *Didache* (*Did.* 4.9–11) and *Barnabas* (*Barn.* 19.5, 7). The primary concern of each reference is the instruction of youth and the appropriate relationship between masters and slaves. For the sake of argument, I assume here that the authors of these two writings have drawn upon a similar source for these insights.[18] Each code is integrally related to the remainder of the "two ways" teaching that provides the context for the code. That context is intimately related to the question of ethics and is dominated by a clear warning against the threat of a false lifestyle.

In each use of the household codes we find a concern for Christian ethics as it was intended both for average Christians in their interpersonal relationships and for the leaders of the community in their interactions among themselves. The model of the contemporary household structure served the early church well. It is all the more interesting, therefore, that the codes quickly disappeared from Christian literature after the middle of the second century. One must assume that this disappearance is associated with some recognition among the second-century Christian apologists and heresiologists after them that the household codes were no longer necessary or useful as a standard by which to establish an ethical Christian lifestyle.

It is my belief that the disappearance of the codes is associated with the rise and establishment of ecclesiastical hierarchies. Once the power of the bishop and other church administrators had been firmly emplaced and was widely acknowledged both within and among church communities, any appeal to social codes became irrelevant. Further, a return to such standardized codes may have been envisioned as a threat to idiosyncratic positions that were held by individual bishops within the churches. Thus, the codes became not only superfluous, but also a threat to hierarchy. Consequently, it seems only natural that they would have disappeared from the literature.

Two Ways

Much has been written on the theme of the "two ways" tradition within early Christian literature.[19] The roots of this theme, as with

---

[18] This assumption begs the literary question of whether the author of the *Didache* composed the "two ways" (*Did.* 1–5) based upon *Barn.* 18–20, whether the author of *Barnabas* made use of *Did.* 1–5, or whether each was dependent upon some common source. This last option has been the preferred choice of scholarly opinion during the last half century.

[19] For informative examples see M. Jack Suggs, "The Christian Two Ways Tradition: Its Antiquity, Form, and Function," in *Studies in New Testament and Early Christian Literature: Essays in Honor of Allen P. Wikgren* (ed. D. E. Aune;

those of the virtue and vice lists and the household codes, are firmly established in both Hellenistic and Jewish traditions. Jewish Scripture advocates a two ways approach to life both within the Torah and among the prophets.[20] The premise itself eventually was incorporated into the later literature of the second-century temple period and the writings of Qumran.

New Testament literature supports the two ways idea, but only in two texts. The first of these passages is in Paul's letter to the Galatians. The apostle includes a basic two ways motif at Gal 5:17–24, where he contrasts the works of the Spirit of God with the works of the flesh. Included here is a list of works from both ways: a basic list of virtues associated with the Spirit of God, and another of vices associated with the flesh. Works of the Spirit include love, joy, peace, patience, kindness, generosity, faithfulness, gentleness, and self-control (Gal 5:22–23); works of the flesh include fornication, impurity, licentiousness, idolatry, sorcery, enmity, strife, jealousy, anger, quarreling, dissension, factions, envy, drunkenness, and carousing (Gal 5:19–21). Clearly, the works of the flesh require a much busier lifestyle than do the works of the Spirit, at least as Paul perceives the situation.

The second appearance of the two ways motif in the New Testament is at Matt 7:13–14.[21] These verses have a rough parallel in Luke 13:23–24, but the Lukan version does not reflect what might be considered as a true two ways theme. As the text of Luke reads, "Strive to enter through the narrow door; for many, I tell you, will try to enter and will not be able." The choice for the potential follower of Jesus, then, is one of the basic choices of living—either enter the door or do not! This does not compare exactly with the Matthean passage, in which the reader is encouraged to enter through the narrow gate; "for the gate is wide and the road is easy that leads to destruction . . . for the gate is narrow and the road is hard that leads to life . . ." Here, of course, is a true

NovTSup 33; Leiden: Brill, 1972), 60–74; Jan Bergman, "Zum Zweiwegemotiv: Religionsgeschichtliche und exegetische Bemerkungen," *SEÅ* 41–42 (1977): 27–56; and most recently, Huub van de Sandt and David Flusser, *The Didache: Its Jewish Sources and Its Place in Early Judaism and Christianity* (CRINT 3/5; Assen: Royal Van Gorcum; Minneapolis: Fortress, 2002).

[20] See, for example, Deut 30:15; Jer 21:8.

[21] For a more expansive discussion of the two ways theme in Matthew, Luke, and the *Didache* see Clayton N. Jefford, *The Sayings of Jesus in the Teaching of the Twelve Apostles* (VCSup 11; Leiden: Brill, 1989), 22–29, 146–59.

choice—that is, the choice between two ways. The image found in Matthew is that of two gates, one of which leads to destruction and one to life.

Because Matthew alone among the Gospels preserves what may be considered as a true two ways motif, it is not surprising that the theme appears once again in the text of the *Didache,* a writing that shares much in common with Matthean sources, if not the Gospel of Matthew itself. Both the *Didache* (chapters 1–5) and *Barnabas* (chapters 18–20) preserve the idea of the two ways, and, as is suggested by the close structuring of the two ways materials that appear in these writings, presumably they are dependent upon a common source.

As has been suggested above, the version of the two ways that appears in the *Didache* has been cleverly edited to include not only the two ways motif, but also a carefully crafted presentation of both a virtue and vice list and a brief household code. To combine all three of these elements into a single text, the Didachist must have devoted considerable thought to the project. Moreover, the virtue and vice lists reflect the careful consideration of the Decalogue as a source upon which to develop basic tenets for Christian ethics and lifestyle. It is undoubtedly fair to describe the model of "life and death" in this text as somewhat codified. Linked with virtues and vices, codes and Jewish Torah, the two ways theme has been formally adapted by the author into a catechetical format that exemplifies the Christian way of life and its alternative choice.[22] Clearly, the two ways model has been offered to a specific church community as a guide to ethics for new converts and lifelong members alike.

The two ways motif that appears in *Barnabas,* though similar in its presentation of elements, is not as closely worked as that which we find in the *Didache.* In *Barnabas* the ways of life and death are associated with the angels of light and darkness (*Barn.* 18.1–2). This vivid imagery is not paralleled in the *Didache,* though traces of the view may be found in the perspective of Qumran and probably was widely respected among first-century Jews and Christians alike. This suggests that the two ways motif in *Barnabas* may have been seen with a slightly different light than what is found in the *Didache.* An apocalyptic focus is strongly suggested here. Furthermore, the motif is found not at the beginning of the text of *Barnabas,* but at the end. To some extent, this late appear-

---

[22] So McDonald, *Kerygma and Didache,* 96–97.

ance of the theme may be attributed to the likelihood that chapters 18–20 are a secondary addition to the original version of the writing. This makes sense to the extent that the two ways motif is not otherwise apparent in the text. At the same time, the choice to conclude *Barnabas* with the two ways theme, both with its inherent angelology and its position as the final statement of the work, suggests that the author may have intended the teaching of the two ways to serve as something of a reinforcement to general teachings of the work rather than as a directive for specific Christian living. In either case, of course, the question of ethics lies just beneath the surface of the issue and most likely was not far from the mind of the author.

A final example of the two ways motif may be found in the *Mandates* of the *Shepherd of Hermas* (see *Herm.* 35–36, especially 36.10). The traditional lists of virtues and vices that are found with the two ways motif in the *Didache* appear here as well, though the imagery of the ways is more closely linked with the angelology of *Barnabas*. Whereas *Barn.* 18 speaks of an angel of light and an angel of darkness as the rulers of the ways, the author of the *Shepherd* speaks of the angel of righteousness and the angel of wickedness. This association of semidivine figures with a concern for ethics appears to have been common in the Mediterranean world of the first and second centuries, as is indicated in the two ways parallels of Qumran. Undoubtedly, some connection among these texts is suggested by such imagery, though no specific conclusions are evident.[23]

Two Themes within Early Christian Literature

Discipleship

The lifestyle of the earliest churches was shaped around more than the merely formal elements of ethical teaching that have been expressed above. Throughout the New Testament the evidence of early Christian attempts to live a new life in Christ are witnessed throughout the various perspectives of the authors. In many respects, the views that these authors offer are similar in scope. In many other ways, they diverge according to the particularities of community background and outside influences. The following review is an attempt to identify two ethical themes from within the Gospels that find no specific correspondence

---

[23] See the discussion in Carolyn Osiek, *Shepherd of Hermas: A Commentary* (ed. H. Koester; Hermeneia; Minneapolis: Fortress, 1999), 122–25.

elsewhere within the New Testament and only limited development within the apostolic fathers.

We examine the Gospel texts here, not because these writings necessarily reflect the earliest approach to ethics in Christian antiquity, but because they preserve our oldest known attempt to associate an ethical understanding of the Christian faith with the figure of Jesus of Nazareth. Indeed, it seems much more likely that the understanding of ethics that Paul portrayed, at least in his earliest writings, is much more primitive in scope than is that of the Gospels. Furthermore, the Pauline understanding of ethics seems to be that which is most widely shared among early Christian authors. All the same, it seems prudent to look at two gospel themes that had only limited appeal among later authors.

The Gospel of Mark, which I take to be the earliest of our gospel texts, clearly is oriented around the importance of the passion narrative. It does not seem that the author of our work is particularly concerned to talk about the importance of the death of Jesus as a component of salvation, or even how this may have served as a necessary ingredient of theology.[24] Instead, the author seeks to explain the circumstances that led to the crucifixion and to define the implications of Jesus' death for Christian living. Our concern, of course, is with those implications. Most commentaries typically identify these under the joint theme of "discipleship," the significance of which is emphasized in the central chapters of the text (roughly the materials of Mark 8–10). Here the reader is told three times that the Son of Man was destined to die (Mark 8:31–33; 9:30–32; 10:32–34), that Jesus is not like one of the prophets, but is an embodiment of the expected Messiah (Mark 8:27–29), and that Elijah has indeed returned in the figure of John the Baptizer as the forerunner of God's expected savior (Mark 6:14–16; 11:32). Associated with these comments about the reality of Jesus as the expected Messiah, however, are certain scenes in which the attitude of being a Christian is vaguely identified. As is typical with the Markan approach, many of these episodes are offered to the apparent detriment of the disciples. They are unable to heal a boy who is possessed by an unclean spirit because they are inadequate in prayer (Mark 9:14–29). They are reprimanded because they fight over who should be considered the

---

[24] Though some hint of this undoubtedly is shared in Mark 10:45: "For the Son of Man came not to be served but to serve, and to give his life a ransom for many."

greatest among them, while someone outside the group is commended simply for having acted in the "name of Christ" (Mark 9:33–41). They are informed that those who receive the kingdom of God as children will enter it, while those who refuse to abandon their earthly possessions will find it difficult to enter (Mark 10:13–31). Finally, those who seek places of honor with Jesus in the life to come are instructed that service, not requests for glory, leads to honor (Mark 10:35–45).

Through this series of brusque rebuttals, the reader gradually gains a feeling for the Markan view of Christian ethics. The imperative of ethics is associated with the demands of discipleship. Discipleship results from a believer's recognition that the cross carries ultimate validity for Christian faith. It insists upon prayer and humility; it demands innocence and a dependence upon spiritual realities instead of earthly treasures; it seeks to serve with only the promised rewards of faith ahead. In a sense, these factors lie at a deeper level of ethics than do the lists of virtues and vices and household codes that appear elsewhere in the New Testament literature. What is demanded here is a more intimate and involved level of ethics than merely the adherence to a set of standards as stated by the authority of an individual text or of a religious leader. As many have observed, this attention to discipleship (and hence, ethics) clearly comes through in the Gospel of Mark in a historical moment of crisis and persecution, most likely from some source outside of the Markan community. Combined with an attention to apocalyptic, as noted above, this is a powerful statement of ethics that our author has attributed to the teachings of Jesus.

The rest of the New Testament, though undoubtedly not in disagreement with the Markan view of discipleship, makes no specific use of this theme. Curiously, neither do the writings of the apostolic fathers, except perhaps for Polycarp, as we will see below. I say "curiously" in light of the ancient tradition from Eusebius that places the writing of this gospel text in Rome.[25] We might expect that, if such a proposition can be accepted as in some sense historical, one might find this most basic of Markan themes to have survived somewhere within the literature of that region, namely, *1 Clement* and the *Shepherd of Hermas*.[26]

[25] Eusebius, *Hist. eccl.* 3.39.15.
[26] Though in chapter 1 above I placed *2 Clement* within a Corinthian setting, some would include it here as well. The point ultimately is rendered moot, however, since the absence of the Markan discipleship theme in the text does not provide any solid ground on which to debate the issue of provenance.

At first glance, the circumstances of *1 Clement* do not necessarily lend themselves to the use of the Markan discipleship theme. The church at Rome has been requested to make some comment upon the removal of, or at least challenge to, the well-respected presbyters of the Corinthian church community. The result in Corinth has been general turmoil and divided loyalties within the congregation. The Romans open their response with general applause for the Corinthian church and, interestingly enough, an acknowledgment of the way that the community has conducted itself according to the vague parameters of an orderly household. In other words, the Corinthians are reminded that they have "lived in accordance with the laws of God," having submitted to leaders, given honor to elders, given instruction to the young, and having charged women to perform their duties with a blameless conscience and in dignity and discretion (*1 Clem.* 1.3). Further, the Corinthian church is compared against the standard of a loose list of virtues—humility, peacefulness, confidence, sincerity, awe—against which it has measured well, so that the "commandments and ordinances of the Lord" are written on the hearts of its members (*1 Clem.* 2:1–8).[27]

From this point forward, the author of *1 Clement* begins to offer examples from Scripture of how disobedience with respect to the law of God has led to disorder. The sequence of episodes includes the recognition of Cain and Abel, Esau and Jacob, Noah, Lot, and several others. Soon thereafter, the tenor of the argument shifts, and the basic elements of a valid Christian lifestyle are set forth (chapters 4–39). This discussion, which serves as the major body of the letter, is basically a statement of the ethical position of the Roman church from the first century. Because of the consequences of jealousy, as outlined by the primary scriptural figures previously offered, dire consequences inevitably result. The faithful person is ultimately enjoined to undertake repentance (chapters 4–8), practice obedience and faith, exist together with piety and hospitality (chapters 9–12), live in humility and peace (chapters 13–20), and engage in a virtuous lifestyle (chapters 21–23).

The author does not call for "discipleship" specifically by name, but the features of that existence are clearly related to the perspective of the Gospel of Mark. This theme is casually linked with the promise of the "coming resurrection," illustrated by the parable of the Sower, as a

---

[27] With the conclusion drawn from Prov 7:3.

call to right actions within the Corinthian church (*1 Clem.* 24.1–5). In the final analysis, however, the question of crucifixion as a motivation for Christian ethics is never invoked. Nor, despite the characteristics of Christian ethics that appear throughout the letter, does this motif seem to lie behind the arguments of the author.

As with *1 Clement,* the *Shepherd of Hermas* likewise makes no specific appeal to the "cross/discipleship" motif that lies behind the Markan argument. This is particularly noteworthy, since if there is a text among the fathers where one might expect to find such language, it might be that of the *Shepherd.* The narrative line of the *Shepherd* features both a potential disciple—that is, Hermas—and the witness of the presence of God in the figures of the woman (depicted at various ages) and the shepherd. This last figure often appears to function as the embodiment either of the Christ or of the Holy Spirit. If the Markan theme of "cross/discipleship" lies behind the mind of the author of the *Shepherd,* it could easily have been applied to its best advantage here.

Perhaps the only clear texts among the fathers where the "cross/ discipleship" motif are baldly expressed are Polycarp's *Letter to the Philippians* and the *Martyrdom of Polycarp.* These works indicate the divergent path of interpretation that developed within the early church in response to the death of Jesus.

Let us begin with the *Martyrdom of Polycarp.* The explicit imagery of the death of the bishop Polycarp is starkly portrayed against the various elements of the death of Jesus that appear throughout the several passion narrative episodes of the New Testament gospels. Scholars safely stand in agreement on this observation. The problem of Polycarp's death with regard to our discussion of ethics, however, is that the employment of the "cross/discipleship" theme in the *Martyrdom* was not applied to a general call to ethics among the early Christians. This is to say, the author of the *Martyrdom* does not conclude with a statement such as "Having now seen how the great Polycarp *died* for his faith, let us all *live* a life of virtue and moral fortitude for the faith of Christ!" The best that can be found is a closing farewell from the author to the church at Philomelium, the original audience of the letter: "We bid you farewell, brothers, as you walk by the word of Jesus Christ which is in accord with the gospel" (*Mart. Pol.* 22.1). Instead, the death of Polycarp was soon put into a form by which Christians were, if perhaps implicitly, exhorted to follow the example of the bishop in their own witness to the Christian faith. At least, this is the sense in which later Christian martyrs interpreted the witness of Polycarp's death. Indeed, the call to martyrdom became a commonly recognized concern for later bishops who found a number of the Christian faithful who were anxious to die for their faith in Christ and hence receive some sort of salvation. The resulting cult of the martyrs was hardly designed as an impetus toward Christian ethics, but instead was a call to the witness of faith through a noble death.[28]

A slightly different approach appears in Polycarp's letter, and it is a movement that seems much more comfortable with the perspective of the Gospel of Mark. Polycarp's address to the Philippians is couched in a discussion of righteousness and is directed toward the sound activities of church authorities—that is, presbyters and deacons. As a conclusion to his instructions (see Pol. *Phil.* 8.1–2), the bishop encourages the Philippian Christians to hold to their hope in Christ, "who bore our sins in his own body upon the tree" and thus endured death in order that his followers might experience life. He then challenges them to become "imitators of his patient endurance" and to "suffer for the sake of his name." After this, they are urged to obey the teachings of righteousness and to follow the "example of the Lord" with love, mutual appreciation, truthfulness, charity, humility, and so forth (Pol. *Phil.* 9–10). In this sequence Polycarp clearly reflects an understanding of "cross/discipleship" that was previously advocated by the author of Mark, though the theme has few clear parallels elsewhere.

It may be safe simply to conclude that this important Markan theme of ethics engendered through Jesus' suffering on the cross did not find a school of thought that can be widely traced either within the New Testament or among the apostolic fathers outside of the specific image of martyrdom found with the death of the bishop Polycarp. The single exception to this "martyrdom trend" may be discovered in the letter of Polycarp himself. We should observe that, though the theme served as a ready tool for the endorsement of a form of Christian ethics that was widely approved throughout the early church, the specific form of "cross/discipleship" as a moral principle was not widely utilized outside of the martyrological tradition.

---

[28] For both a Jewish and a Hellenistic background to this tradition, with textual examples through the third century, see Jan Willem van Henten and Friedrich Avemarie, *Martyrdom and Noble Death: Selected Texts from Graeco-Roman, Jewish and Christian Antiquity* (London: Routledge, 2002).

Righteousness

Let us turn briefly now to the Gospel of Matthew. The author of this gospel undoubtedly recognized the view of ethics that was endorsed by the Gospel of Mark, but made a clear addition to the concept that seems much more acceptable to the subsequent theology of the apostolic fathers. As is widely recognized, the author of Matthew has consciously inserted various "sayings of Jesus" at those places in the Markan story where we are told that Jesus taught the crowds, though no specific teachings are provided for the reader. Inserted among these teachings are various materials that give some suggestion of ethics as seen from the perspective of Matthew's Gospel.

Perhaps the most commonly accessed portion of Matthew's Gospel in any discussion of ethics is the so-called Sermon on the Mount (chapters 5–7). This text has been variously called a second Pentateuch, a new Christian law, and a model for Christian ethics. The author leads us to this conclusion, as well as to similar interpretations, through a consistent usage of Mosaic themes. This focus is often upon promise/fulfillment texts from Jewish Scriptures and parallels between the life of Jesus and events in the days of Moses.

Wedged between these texts is a theme that is treated by the author of Matthew in a singular manner: the motif of righteousness. Curiously, the term "righteousness" is not a word that appears commonly among the New Testament gospels. The Gospel of Mark does not use the word at all, while Luke offers only one instance, in the context of Zechariah's prophecy (Luke 1:75). The Gospel of John employs the term twice, both times within the context of Jesus' comments about the work of the coming Spirit of God, or the "Advocate" (John 16:8, 10). None of these authors makes any specific comment upon "righteousness," either as a concept or as it applies to the life of a Christian.

The Gospel of Matthew, therefore, seems all the more important in this regard, since this gospel uses the term six times. Furthermore, the term is used with a very specific meaning in mind. One sees in Matt 3:14–15, for example, that Jesus responds to the Baptizer's query of "I need to be baptized by you, and do you come to me?" with the response of "Let it be so now; for it is proper for us in this way to fulfill all righteousness." The meaning of this answer is not altogether clear, to say the least. And yet, the chief priests and elders of the people (and hence the reader) are told later that "John came to you in the way of righteousness and you did not believe him" (Matt 21:32).

The meaning of righteousness is explained for us by its other four usages in Matthew, all of which appear in the Sermon on the Mount. In the first of these references (Matt 5:6) we are informed that "those who hunger and thirst for righteousness . . . will be filled." This is not explicitly informative for Christian ethics, except perhaps to emphasize that the desire for justice will be met for those who seek it. A little more helpful is the last of our references (Matt 6:33), where the reader is charged to "strive first for the kingdom of God and his righteousness," thus to suggest that there is some intimate connection between these two concepts, righteousness and God's kingdom.[29] The key to the idea of righteousness for the Gospel of Matthew, so it would seem, remains in the remaining references that appear in the materials of Matt 5:17–20. The first two of these verses (Matt 5:17–18) have a clear parallel in Luke 16:17. The focus is upon the necessity of the Scriptures (here, "the law and the prophets"), which Jesus is shown to explain will not pass away until all that they say has been accomplished. The following materials (Matt 5:19–20) are specifically Matthean and reveal the author's unique understanding of righteousness. The reader is informed that those who break the law and the prophets or who teach others to ignore them will be called "least in the kingdom of the heavens." Indeed, no one enters the kingdom whose righteousness does not exceed that of the scribes and Pharisees. According to the first-century Jewish understanding of piety and righteousness that was associated with the scribes and Pharisees, this may well be seen as a significant challenge indeed. Traditionally, scholars have come to associate this charge with the concept of personal motivation and not with a measurement of results. This is to say that it is not necessarily the product of a person's actions that are under examination, but instead the nature of the mindset of faith that motivates a person to undertake those actions.

This leaves the author of Matthew with an understanding of righteousness and the kingdom of God that is most compelling. From the outset, it is only through the exercise of righteousness by the motivation of faithful intention that anyone may enter the kingdom of God. This, of course, may be achieved by anyone whose heart is in the right place, so to

---

[29] I take the rather rare Matthean usage of the phrase "kingdom of God" (rather than the typical "kingdom of the heavens") to be a sign of some special significance to be attached to this passage by our author.

speak. Once within this kingdom, however, a person's status and role is determined by his or her faithfulness to "the law and the prophets." This becomes the standard by which a person's attainment of righteousness is thus measured. Finally, the goal of this exercise is to be perfect as God is perfect (Matt 5:48). This perfection is not so much a value that should be defined by Greek values, such as the quest for some Platonic existence that may always remain more as an ideal than as a practical reality. Instead, it is a typically Jewish understanding that is related to relationships. Thus, the reader is charged to relate with God in a complete relationship, and thus to relate to others in a similar manner.[30]

As any informed student of the New Testament will immediately note, the apostle Paul makes constant and repeated use of the term "righteousness" as well.[31] This holds true both for the apostle and for those who subsequently wrote under his name, the so-called deutero-pauline school.[32] Paul's understanding of righteousness seems to differ somewhat from that of the Gospel of Matthew, however. For Paul, righteousness is obtained specifically as a gift of God (Rom 5:17). Indeed, the righteousness that any Christian receives is the "righteousness of God," given in response to personal faith, as with Abraham (see Rom 4:1–25; 9:30; Gal 3:6; Phil 3:9). As Paul notes, Israel long pursued the attainment of righteousness through the rigorist fulfillment of the law (Rom 2:12–16; 10:1–4). In this pursuit, however, there was no satisfaction. The ultimate attainment of righteousness comes only through that faith which God recognizes as worthy (Rom 1:16–17).

Those who subsequently wrote under the name of Paul within our New Testament literature, as well as the remaining authors who used the term "righteousness," tended to think of the concept more in line with the traditional understanding of justice. Righteousness in this context may be closely linked with the adjective "righteous" and the characterization of the "righteous person," ideas that appear prominently throughout the New Testament, including the Gospels. The synonym

[30] It is intriguing to note that Clement of Alexandria, making use of Matthew's language, later interprets this same theme of righteousness with respect to the gnostic perfection (καθαρισμός) of the purified soul; see Clement, *Strom.* 4.113.6–114.1; 6.7.60.

[31] See, for example, Rom 1:17; 3:21–22, 25; 4:3, 5–6, 9, 11 (bis), 13, 22; 5:17, 21; 6:13, 16, 18–20; 8:10; 9:30–31; 10:3 (bis), 5–6; 14:17; and fifteen other times outside of his letter to the Romans!

[32] So Eph 4:24; 6:14; 1 Tim 6:11; 2 Tim 2:22; 3:16; 4:8; Titus 3:5.

"justice" may easily replace "righteousness" in each of these examples: "for your anger does not produce God's righteousness" (Jas 1:20); "in righteousness he judges and makes war" (Rev 19:11); "[God] saved Noah, a herald of righteousness" (2 Pet 2:5); "put on the breastplate of righteousness" (Eph 6:14).

The question for consideration, of course, is whether any of the authors of the apostolic fathers recognize an understanding of righteousness similar to that which appears in the Gospel of Matthew, or whether these texts are likewise dependent upon the traditional use of righteousness interspersed throughout the New Testament. For Matthew, righteousness is not seen as a goal to be attained through God as a specific reward for faith (as it is, to some extent, with Paul), nor is it seen as the product of faithful adherence to the teachings of Scripture or the fruits of justice that come from a devoted Christian existence (as it is, to some extent, with the rest of the New Testament literature). Instead, righteousness for Matthew is the product of a pure motivation, out of which comes the ability to act in accordance with the Jewish Scriptures and to fulfill all that God has commanded there, thus to be perfect in a divine sense.

As with the New Testament, the concept of righteousness appears in numerous cases throughout the apostolic fathers. *First Clement* contains several examples. In *1 Clem.* 3.4 the Corinthians are told that because of the revolt within the church there, "righteousness and peace stand at a distance."[33] Shortly thereafter, Paul is offered as a model of one who "taught righteousness to the whole world" (*1 Clem.* 5.7). In *1 Clem.* 33.8 the Corinthians are charged to "do the work of righteousness," while righteousness is designated to be a gift of God in *1 Clem.* 35.2. Further, the Corinthians are reminded of the observation of Scripture that "I will appoint their bishops in righteousness and their deacons in faith."[34] Elsewhere, the author of *1 Clement* quotes variously from the writings of Paul or from scriptural passages that Paul used,[35] thus to suggest that the understanding of righteousness that is endorsed here is primarily Pauline in form.

---

[33] Based upon Isa 59:14.
[34] Drawn from Isa 60:17, which is a Greek mistranslation of the Hebrew text.
[35] See *1 Clem.* 10.6 and 31.2 (based on Gen 15:5–6, paralleled throughout Rom 4:1–25); 13.1 (based on Jer 9:23–24, paralleled in 1 Cor 1:31; 2 Cor 10:17); 18.15 (based on Ps 51:1–17).

The *Shepherd of Hermas* likewise makes numerous references to righteousness as a component of the Christian construct of faith. In *Herm.* 9.6 the church as an elderly woman asks Hermas to pray to God for righteousness, so that he might "take some part of it to your family." This view clearly suggests that the author envisions righteousness to stand as a commodity given by God as a reward. This is reinforced elsewhere in the text when the reader is instructed to cast off evil and "put on every virtue of righteousness" (*Herm.* 26.2), to avoid anger that leads one away from righteousness (*Herm.* 34.1), to use "words of righteousness" (*Herm.* 38.9), and to avoid any ignorance of righteousness (*Herm.* 40.5). This holds true as well when Hermas is asked to speak to church officials in order that they may pay attention to the "ways of righteousness," since there are many who live for only a short time in righteousness (*Herm.* 6.6 and 14.4, respectively). Finally, Hermas is shown the imagery of those Christians who once practiced lawlessness but now have repented and "practice every virtue and righteousness," as well as those who once were righteous but eventually "fell asleep in righteousness" (*Herm.* 76.3 and 93.7, respectively). Our term appears in numerous other instances throughout the work, but for the most part its meaning is typical of common Christian usage that equates righteousness with justice as reflected throughout most of the New Testament.

Elsewhere in the fathers the term "righteousness" appears variously in a number of texts. The bishop Ignatius seems to shun any use of the concept, perhaps because of the potential association with Jewish themes that he wished to avoid. Indeed, we find only one instance of the term "righteousness" in the Ignatian correspondence. This appears specifically within a creedal formulation offered to the church at Smyrna, a passage in which Ignatius notes that Jesus was "baptized by John in order that all righteousness might be fulfilled" (Ign. *Smyrn.* 1.1).[36]

Unlike Ignatius, the bishop Polycarp does not seem nearly as reluctant to use the term. In his letter to the church at Philippi he invokes righteousness as a constant theme. Indeed, he insists that his comments on the theme are a response to the queries of that very church (so Pol. *Phil.* 3.3). What follows is an understanding of righteousness that closely parallels that of Paul. As he observes in a discussion of the witness of Paul, one must be formed in faith, followed by hope and a love

---

[36] Based on Matt 3:15.

for God, Christ, and neighbor, for to be thus occupied is to fulfill "the commandment of righteousness."[37] He warns the Philippians to arm themselves with "the weapons of righteousness" (Pol. *Phil.* 4.1), and he insists that deacons must be "blameless in the presence of [God's] righteousness" (Pol. *Phil.* 5.2). He offers the hope of Christ as a guarantee of righteousness, encourages the Philippians to obey the "teaching of righteousness" (a phrase that remains undefined), and offers the example of Paul and the apostles, who worked not in vain, but in faith and righteousness (see Pol. *Phil.* 8.1; 9.1–2). There is no question here that the bishop understands righteousness to serve as the foundation upon which Christian ethics must be constructed. At the same time, however, no subsequent appeal to Jewish Scriptures is offered as a guideline for the framing of any particular system of ethics.

Perhaps the one text among the fathers that reveals some awareness of a system of ethics (aided by a respect for Jewish Scripture) based upon the idea of righteousness is the letter of *Barnabas.* In *Barn.* 1.6 the three tenets of the author's argument are set forth with a heavy emphasis upon the role of righteousness: "There are three basic doctrines of the Lord: the hope of life, which is the beginning and end of our faith; and righteousness, which is the beginning and end of judgment; and love shown in gladness and rejoicing, the testimony of righteous works." The insistence upon one doctrine (the "hope of life" is our directive for faith) gives sufficient meaning to a parallel observation ("righteousness" is the directive for judgment) for us to understand immediately that *Barnabas* considers righteousness to be the product of personal decision. Already in *Barn.* 1.4 the author has made reference to the "way of righteousness" in a sense that roughly parallels the "way of light" (= "way of life" in the *Didache*) that appears later in chapters 18–20. This is reinforced in *Barn.* 5.4 when the author states that a person "deserves to perish if, having knowledge of the way of righteousness, he ensnares himself in the way of darkness."

Two specific texts in *Barnabas* seem to suggest a consideration of righteousness that closely reflects that of the Gospel of Matthew. Both of these fall within the context of specific questions: What was the covenant that God established in the tradition of Judaism? To whom does that

---

[37] This is the argument of Pol. *Phil.* 3.1–3. Berding (*Polycarp and Paul,* 63–66) points to possible allusions here to Gal 4:26, Rom 4:16, 1 Cor 13:13, Rom 13:8–10 and/or Gal 5:14.

covenant rightfully belong? In *Barn.* 13.7 our author addresses these issues with a question from the ancient tradition: "What, then, does [God]
say to Abraham, when he alone believed and was established in righteousness? 'Behold, I have established you, Abraham, as the father of the
nations who believe in God without being circumcised.'" The conclusion
seems obvious then, as derived from Genesis: Abraham became the
father of those who believed among the nations.[38] And because Abraham
himself received righteousness, he likewise was given the covenant of
God through Moses, though later it was rejected by the Jews because of
their sins. Indeed, at Mount Sinai the Jews made graven images for themselves and thus abandoned the covenant that had been promised to
Abraham and was only recently received by Moses.

A quotation of Isa 42:6–7 in *Barn* 14.7 sheds additional light
upon our author's use of the term through the argument that Jesus
himself inherited the covenant of God (first received by Moses) in
order to redeem humanity and prepare a holy people, as instructed by
the prophet Isaiah: "I, the Lord your God, have called you in righteousness, and I will grasp your hand and strengthen you." In other
words, Jesus was already summoned to fill the role of savior for all humanity within a state of righteousness. Indeed, as understood by the
author of *Barnabas,* the subsequent ministry and activities of Jesus
were a fulfillment of the words of the prophet Isaiah: he was a light to
the nations (Isa 49:6–7) who healed the brokenhearted, freed prison-
ers, gave sight to the blind, comforted those who mourn, and proclaimed the Lord's year of favor and judgment (Isa 61:1–2). After a
brief comment upon the role of the Sabbath and the temple, the author of *Barnabas* concludes with the "two ways" materials that chide
the reader to follow in this same activity, though specifically in
the guise of an ethical lifestyle (*Barn.* 18–20).[39] Here, then, is an
understanding of righteousness and ethics that looks very much like

---

[38] See Gen 15:6; 17:5. Paul uses these same texts in Rom 4:11, 17, though
with an emphasis upon the fact that righteousness was given to Abraham
through his faith. Hence, Abraham's witness serves as a model for the salvation
of even non-Jews.

[39] Whether this view of righteousness can be associated with the original
scripting of *Barnabas* depends in part upon whether one can accept the concluding "two ways" materials as original to the text, of course. If not, then the
focus upon the activity of Jesus "in righteousness," thus demanding an ade-
quate Christian response through the ethics of *Barn.* 18–20, may be primarily
the view of a rewriting of the text or the work of a later editor.

that of Matthew, yet finds little parallel among the remaining writings of Scripture and the apostolic fathers.

CONCLUSION

A typical ingredient of cultural and religious movements is the unifying element of ethical norms. No collection of like-minded individuals can function effectively as a unit unless there is some common agreement among its participants about guidelines for living. Such guidelines come to form the standard by which members can measure their faithfulness to the ideals of the community. Also, they serve as a gauge by which people can measure suitable responses to the actions of insiders and outsiders alike.

With respect to the situation of the New Testament and the apostolic fathers, the quest for ethical norms was of paramount importance. Each author wrote within a world of conflicting standards.

On the one hand, Jewish ideals and biblical ethics demanded a voice in the nascent church. Judaism was the bedrock of Christianity's origins, providing the soil from which the church's theology and morals sprang into a living reality among its followers. This may be seen quite clearly in the teachings of Paul, mainly as he confronted the lifestyle of the Corinthians. And yet, in a paradoxical sense, we see it even more distinctly in the convictions of those Christians against whom Paul struggled as he sought to free non-Jewish believers from the ties of synagogue life, specifically in the case of Galatians. Similar concerns are found in the Gospels, particularly in those instances where Jesus seems to support traditional religious values over against the scribes and Pharisees, who arguably sought to bolster an institutional ethic that was more in support of the claims of Torah than of the plight of common humanity. How much of this material is an accurate reflection of the teachings of Jesus versus the instruction of the late-first-century church is difficult to say with certainty. In either case, it is clear that ethical standards, defined by the nature of the kingdom of God, often stood at the heart of the matter.

On the other hand, the early church quickly found itself flooded with believers who had no Jewish roots. Some of these were what might be called "God-fearers," while others simply found themselves attracted to what Christianity had to offer. For many of these Christians, the existence of Jewish norms and concerns became a stumbling block to growth. The author of *Barnabas* suggests this problem early in the second century, as does the bishop Ignatius. For such writers, the quest for ethical guidelines was precarious, since they were caught between the standards of a Jewish faith that they wished to abandon and a loose assortment of moral interpretations that were offered by belief systems such as Stoicism, Cynicism, Mithraism, and the mystery religions.

Thus, individual churches and theologians were forced to work within a constantly evolving framework of ethical considerations. On a broad level, they had to decide whether the essence of Christian faith should be directed toward some future promise, often defined by the categories of apocalyptic and a future eschatology, or instead, whether it was not better suited to a practical ethic that was fashioned to suit the daily lifestyle of believers. For Paul, the synoptic authors, and the *Didache,* apocalyptic language ultimately was reshaped into a practical ethic for living that could be applied to the interactions of daily Christian living.

In a much more narrow sense, early church authors quickly learned to incorporate the elements of traditional ethical teachings that were characteristic of both Judaism and pagan religions into their moral frameworks. Virtue-vice lists, household codes, and the "two ways" tradition came to serve as elements by which Christians could shape their common activities. Their presence is broadly evident in the deuteropauline literature, 1 Peter, the *Didache* and *Barnabas, 1 Clement,* and the epistles of Ignatius and Polycarp. And their influence upon subsequent church values may be traced down to the present day.

Also important to this discussion is the attention that early Christian literature gave to the ideas of discipleship and righteousness as guidelines for ethical living. With respect to discipleship, the model of the faithful disciple that is offered in the New Testament gospels may be readily traced also to the teachings of Paul, as well as to those authors of the apostolic fathers who sought to evangelize in his image: Polycarp and Ignatius. Their quest to become faithful followers, both of Jesus Christ and of the apostles who followed him, evolved into a driving motivation for Christians. With reference to the theme of righteousness, the image of purity of spirit, fidelity to devotion, and a complete relationship with God already found its roots in the teachings of the Gospel of Matthew. Such considerations eventually were played out in the theologies of *Barnabas* and the *Shepherd of Hermas.* And the quest to experience a harmony with God within the framework of the kingdom soon became a dominant impulse among many early Christians.

For the early church, then, the question of how to form a unified Christian community that could exist around a single, ethical norm became a principal concern. Those who framed the standards for that norm ultimately became the focal points of other theological and ecclesiastical controversies, subsequently leading to a preservation of their writings as the foundational texts of ancient Christian literature.

FOR FURTHER READING

The following studies are most helpful in understanding the early Christian view of ethics from a New Testament focus:

- Countryman, L. William. *Dirt, Greed and Sex: Sexual Ethics in the New Testament and Their Implications for Today.* Philadelphia: Fortress, 1988.

- Meeks, Wayne A. *The Moral World of the First Christians.* Library of Early Christianity 6. Philadelphia: Westminster, 1986.

- Schnackenburg, Rudolf. *The Moral Teaching of the New Testament.* Translated by J. Holland-Smith and W. J. O'Hara. New York: Seabury, 1965.

- Theissen, Gerd. *Social Reality and the Early Christians: Theology, Ethics, and the World of the New Testament.* Translated by M. Kohl. Minneapolis: Fortress, 1992.

From the view of early Christian development within the ancient context, consider the following:

- Grant, Robert M. *Early Christianity and Society: Seven Studies.* New York: Harper & Row, 1977.

- Meeks, Wayne A. *The Origins of Christian Morality: The First Two Centuries.* New Haven: Yale University Press, 1993.

- Osborn, Eric. *Ethical Patterns in Early Christian Thought.* Cambridge: Cambridge University Press, 1976.

- Osiek, Carolyn. *Rich and Poor in the Shepherd of Hermas: An Exegetical-Social Investigation.* Catholic Biblical Quarterly Monograph Series 15. Washington, D.C.: Catholic Biblical Association of America, 1983.

- Wengst, Klaus. *Pax Romana and the Peace of Jesus Christ.* Translated by J. Bowden. Philadelphia: Fortress, 1987.

Chapter 4

Imagery of the New Testament Faith

An interesting feature of the apostolic fathers may be detected in the numerous images that the authors of these texts have drawn either from New Testament literature or from the common sources that biblical authors likewise have adopted. The following survey offers a collection of those images and draws some general conclusions about the choice of materials. I approach the texts in the reverse order of certainty that I have assigned to them in chapter 1.[1]

THE *EPISTLE TO DIOGNETUS*

The author of this letter makes only a limited use of New Testament imagery. This is particularly intriguing in light of the possibility that the text falls late in the second century, a time when, presumably, Christian writings from the first century would have been widely known and used by the apologists of the church. The twelve chapters of the text often are broken into two sections, chapters 1–10 and 11–12, possibly representing the union of a primary tractate with a separate homily fragment. The first chapters (1–10) reflect virtually no knowledge of

---

[1] I do not offer a discussion of the Fragments of Papias here, since that material is a broad collection of snippets that have been drawn from diverse sources and are provided to us by later editors. Those passages that remain do not provide a clear understanding of New Testament images as viewed by Papias.

New Testament imagery, with three possible exceptions. Within the author's discussion about the useless worship practices of the Greeks and Jews (*Diogn.* 2.1–4.6), scholars have occasionally pointed to an incident that involved Paul and Barnabas in Lystra as we know of it from Acts 14:8–18. This is a slim possibility at best, especially since the text of Acts serves no other obvious purpose for *Diognetus.* So too, the call to "not be anxious about food and clothing" (*Diogn.* 9.6), which at first glance seems to be a clear reflection of Matt 6:25–31, must be considered a most dubious parallel in light of the fact that the author makes no use of the Synoptic Gospels elsewhere in the text.[2] The likelihood that this is an intentional recollection of the Gospel of Matthew again seems remote at best.

The situation is decidedly different in chapters 11–12. Here there is a dual emphasis upon the writings of Paul and the theology of the Gospel of John. In the middle of a discussion about the tree of the knowledge of good and evil from Genesis, the reader receives a quotation from 1 Cor 8:1 that is assigned specifically to "the apostle" (ὁ ἀπό στολος): "knowledge puffs up, but love builds up" (*Diogn.* 12.5). Two observations deserve comment here. In the first instance, like the references that were dismissed in chapters 2–4 and 9 above, we have here only one reference to a single text from a known author of Scripture. Second, the quotation is offered with a specific point of reference to the work of Paul, thus to indicate that our author is privy to the work of Paul, either in written or oral form. The latter point seems to give some weight of authenticity to the quotation so that it might be accepted as the intention of the author. Clearly, however, though our author knows the work of Paul (at least to some limited extent), the apostle's writings are not of such value as to serve as a primary source otherwise in the argument.

A different case appears with our author's use of the theology of the Gospel of John and 1 John in these two chapters, which focus upon the use of the term "Word" as a reference to Christ. For example, in *Diogn.* 11.2–3 we read,

> Indeed, does anyone who has been rightly taught and has come to love the Word not seek to learn exactly the things only made known by the Word

---

[2] As Michael Holmes notes, Harmer and Meecham dropped this phrase as a later redaction (*The Apostolic Fathers* [2d ed.; Grand Rapids: Baker, 1999], 549 n. 7).

to disciples? To them the Word appeared and revealed these things, speaking quite plainly. . . . This is why [the Father] sent the Word, namely, that he might appear to the world; though dishonored by the chosen people, he was preached by apostles and believed in by Gentiles.

These lines are followed by later references to the Word as a teacher who is understood through grace (*Diogn.* 11.7), who "rejoices as he teaches the saints," and "through whom the Father is glorified" (*Diogn.* 12.9). Though these are only brief references to what is known from the New Testament, the theology is clearly Johannine in form. Interestingly, it is a theology that seems closely identified with the latter chapters of *Diognetus* only, and thus may not reflect the thought of the author of the first materials that lie in chapters 1–10, provided that the work comes from two different hands. In either case, one finds here a deep concern for a specific understanding of early theology as expressed by a late-second-century author.[3] And though there are few actual references to the New Testament materials, the tone of the concluding chapters indicates that our author is quite familiar with the specific theology and view of Johannine Christianity, a perspective that continued firmly in late Egyptian Christianity.

THE *EPISTLE OF BARNABAS*

This tractate, now letter, is most interesting in its use of early Christian imagery, primarily because it holds little concern for New Testament writings. In this regard, *Barnabas* is singularly parallel to the first ten chapters of *Diognetus*. This is not to say that our author works apart from any dependence upon Scripture. Indeed, the text of *Barnabas* relies heavily upon Jewish texts and images in order to provide a decidedly anti-Jewish interpretation of their meaning. It is perhaps all the more surprising, therefore, that the writings of the New Testament find so little a role in this argument.

Only a few specific parallels to New Testament texts appear throughout *Barnabas,* if not in any particularly significant way. In *Barn.* 4.14 one

---

[3] It is unfortunate that Helmut Koester did not address the situation of *Diognetus* here, since he considered the text to be from the third century at the time of writing (*Synoptische Überlieferung bei den apostolischen Vätern* [TUGAL 65; Berlin: Akademie-Verlag, 1957]).

reads the words "many called, but few chosen," which is widely known from Matt 22:14. Of particular interest here is the inclusion of the introductory formula "it is written," a phrase that is broadly employed in antiquity and indicates that the words hold a special significance for the author's understanding of tradition. If the text of *Barnabas* can indeed be held to come from the late first or early second century, as I assume that it does, this is a most interesting use of an introductory formula for a passage that would not yet have been recognized as an authoritative tradition throughout the contemporary churches.

Further along, in *Barn.* 5.9, our author employs another comment from the Synoptic Gospels: "he did not come to call the righteous, but sinners" (Matt 9:13). This phrase is not specific to the Gospel of Matthew, of course, but certainly it reflects a theme that Matthew knows well.[4] Since Matthew was so widely recognized among the numerous churches of the early second century, and since the author of *Barnabas* makes no references to any other text from the Gospel of Mark, it seems suitable to attribute this particular text to the Matthean tradition.[5]

Another reference, appearing in *Barn.* 7.11, possibly reflects a knowledge of Acts 14:22, though this is uncertain. The author of *Barnabas* writes here, "Likewise, [Jesus] says, 'those who desire to see me and to gain my kingdom must receive me through affliction and suffering.'" In Acts 14:22, Paul and Barnabas encouraged the disciples of Lystra, Iconium, and Antioch with the words "It is through many persecutions that we must enter the kingdom of God." The idea clearly is the same, including the reference to "kingdom," though it is unclear whether this is the author's unique usage of a text from the book of Acts. If so, then we have a parallel to a singular reference of materials from Acts 14 that appears in *Diognetus* as well. This is interesting, to say the least. At the same time, it must not go without observation that one of those to whom this activity was attributed in Acts was the apostle Barnabas, after whom our current work is named.

It is particularly interesting that the concluding chapters 18–20, which include the "two ways" theme, do not contain any New Testa-

---

[4] Cf. Mark 2:17 and Luke 5:32 (with "sinners to repentance").

[5] See the discussion on *Barn.* 5.8–9 by Édouard Massaux, *The First Ecclesiastical Writers* (vol. 1 of *The Influence of the Gospel of Saint Matthew on Christian Literature before Saint Irenaeus;* trans. N. J. Belval and S. Hecht; ed. A. J. Bellinzoni; NGS 5/1; Macon, Ga.: Mercer University Press, 1990), 59–62.

ment parallels. This stands in decided contrast to the similar materials of *Did.* 1–6, in which references to materials from the Synoptic Gospels are clearly present. These New Testament references in the *Didache* have long been recognized as the work of an editorial hand, which suggests either the early nature of the materials in *Barn.* 18–20 or a lack of editorial manipulation with respect to those materials. For the moment, it is sufficient to conclude that these chapters, together with the paucity of New Testament citations elsewhere in *Barnabas,* perhaps speak to the early nature of the writing or the author's lack of knowledge of contemporary Christian literature. One might argue as easily, however, that the subject matter of the text did not inspire the author to utilize early Christian sources in the presentation of the themes in question.[6]

2 CLEMENT

As I have noted in chapter 1 above, I attribute the text of *2 Clement* to the setting of Corinth. On the one hand, the attribution of the text to Corinth might suggest a familiarity with the various New Testament materials that may have gravitated to such a large center of early Christian faith, including works by Paul, the sources that the author of Acts includes about the city in the account of Paul's missionary journeys in and around that region, and perhaps even the witness of the Gospel of Luke. On the other hand, whatever reflection of the New Testament may be found in *2 Clement* may simply be the witness of an author who was intimately familiar with the Corinthian situation, whether an author from the city of Rome or possibly from Alexandria. In either instance, there is perhaps no particular wonder that this text bears the specific marks of the first-century church as preserved in the New Testament.

---

[6] If indeed both *Barnabas* and *Diognetus* may be attributed to the environs of Alexandria, it is perhaps somewhat intriguing that neither of them makes particular use of other early Christian sources. In the former case, this might be forgiven in the light of the text's early nature. In the latter case, and particularly in the light of the wonderful library and catechetical school that developed in the city, it puts some strain on the hypothesis that all of *Diognetus* was written in Alexandria or, otherwise, was produced at such a late date in the second century.

From the opening words of *2 Clement,* our author provides a specific awareness of the work of Acts, recalling an episode at Caesarea Philippi in which Peter instructs Cornelius that God has commanded us to think of the risen Christ as "judge of the living and the dead" (so Acts 10:42). Of course, this same phrase appears elsewhere in the New Testament, specifically in 1 Pet 4:5, whose testimony is likewise associated with the name of Peter, either as an authentic witness to the preaching of the apostle or in sympathy with the situation of Acts. Both texts are decidedly late in the development of the New Testament literature, and neither serves as a particularly significant source for our author.

There is a second possible reference to 1 Peter, however, which appears in *2 Clem.* 16.4: "love covers a multitude of sins." The parallel in 1 Pet 4:8 presumably is based upon similar terminology that appears in Prov 10:12: "Hatred raises strife, but love covers all offenses." The Greek verbs are not the same in each case, with our two Christian texts employing ἀγαπάω, while the LXX uses φιλέω. This variation is not especially significant except to suggest that both 1 Peter and *2 Clement* may have made use of a loose tradition of Proverbs that has been cast into a more specifically ecclesiastical perspective. This second parallel to 1 Peter is highly suggestive in terms of any attempt to consider that writing as a source for our author. Indeed, the two phrases appear within the same passage of the New Testament text within only a few verses of one another. Furthermore, the context of the latter verse is that of prayer, the same setting in which the parallel in *2 Clement* is offered. Despite this quite limited evidence, however, it is difficult to make a strong argument for 1 Peter as a source behind *2 Clement.* Indeed, only these two phrases arise throughout the entire text of *2 Clement,* and they appear in widely disparate places, from chapter 1 to chapter 16.

Similar considerations arise with respect to potential Pauline parallels. Included here is a significant section in *2 Clem.* 2.1 (whose exact parallel in Gal 4:27 is borrowed from Isa 54:1), a pithy reference in *2 Clem.* 11.7 (whose rough parallel in 1 Cor 2:9 is reminiscent of Isa 64:4, as well as 52:15) that may actually find its completion in *2 Clem.* 14.5, and two brief phrases in *2 Clem.* 19.2 and 20.5 (with parallels in Eph 4:18 and 1 Tim 1:17,[7] neither of which is dependent upon Old Tes-

---

[7] Cf. 1 Tim 6:15–16.

tament sources). To these few references we might add *2 Clem.* 11.6, which offers a phrase parallel to Heb 10:23, which itself is a possible reflection of Ps 145:13. Two conclusions are immediately clear. Among these few scattered parallels, the longer instances may be grouped among the other references to the prophecies of Isaiah that the author of *2 Clement* employs throughout the text. The shorter instances are mere phrases that undoubtedly circulated widely among early Christian authors with no particular concern for attribution. In brief, then, the possible Pauline (and deuteropauline) parallels that appear here would seem to stand less as a witness to particular writings by the apostle and more as a testimony to the general verbiage of the second-century Christian situation.[8]

What is most telling for the situation of *2 Clement* is the way in which our author makes use of specific materials from the Gospels. The first instance of such a parallel within the text appears at *2 Clem.* 2.4, where the words "I have not come to call the righteous, but sinners" is recalled as an example of authoritative writing, namely, as "scripture" (γραφή).[9] It is perhaps telling that it is not to the authority of Jesus himself that the words are attributed, but simply to the authoritative text. Thus, in this instance at least, we see the distance that our particular author holds between the production of *2 Clement* and the authoritative tradition of ancient Christian texts themselves. To some extent, this suggests a somewhat late date for the composition of our writing.

To this first example we may quickly add further references to the Gospels. In *2 Clem.* 3.2 we find an approximate reflection of Matt 10:32;[10] in *2 Clem.* 3.4 we note a rough appeal to Matt 22:37;[11] in *2 Clem.* 3.5 there is an explicit citation of Isa 29:13 that has exact parallels

---

[8] Even Massaux, who can find parallels and dependences for every conceivable New Testament parallel in the apostolic fathers, agrees that Paul's works have had little influence upon *2 Clement;* see Édouard Massaux, *The Later Christian Writings* (vol. 2 of *The Influence of the Gospel of Saint Matthew on Christian Literature before Saint Irenaeus;* trans. N. J. Belval and S. Hecht; ed. A. J. Bellinzoni; NGS 5/2; Macon, Ga.: Mercer University Press, 1992), 17.

[9] An exact quotation of either Mark 2:17b or Matt 9:13b, and a rough parallel to Luke 5:32. It is quite likely that this is the earliest case of any New Testament passage appearing under the label "scripture" within our ancient Christian literature.

[10] There is no Markan parallel here, though an approximate equivalent appears in Luke 12:8.

[11] With parallels in Mark 12:30 and Luke 10:27, based upon Deut 6:4.

in Matt 15:8 and Mark 7:6b; and in *2 Clem.* 4.2 we find a close approximation of Matt 7:21, while *2 Clem.* 4.5 offers a very loose reflection of Matt 7:23.[12] In *2 Clem* 5.4 there appears to be a couplet of citations that have been laced together from clear allusions to Matt 10:16 and 10:28,[13] followed in *2 Clem.* 6.1 by a reference to Luke 16:13,[14] and in *2 Clem.* 6.2 by a rough citation of Matt 16:26.[15] In both *2 Clem* 7.6 and 17.5 there is a citation of either Isa 66:24 or its parallel in Mark 9:48; in *2 Clem.* 9.11 there is a very rough allusion to Matt 12:50;[16] and in *2 Clem.* 13.4 one finds an approximation of Luke 6:32 and 6:35.[17] Finally, in *2 Clem.* 14.1 there is a second reference to "scripture" that appears as a reference either to Jer 7:11 or its parallels in Matt 21:13, Mark 11:17, and Luke 19:46.

This conglomeration of various gospel citations and allusions, which are sometimes close in form to the New Testament manuscripts that we know and at other points are only vaguely reminiscent of the scriptural tradition, offer some intriguing insights into our author's access to and use of early gospel traditions. In the first instance, we see that the gospel traditions are consistently interwoven with Jewish Scriptures, especially texts that are drawn from the Major Prophets, most specifically Isaiah. This is to be expected, since it is typical of the approach of second-century Christian writers.

Second, the authority that stands behind each citation has been woven together into a tapestry of figures, some of which reflect the literary tradition and some the historical tradition. In other words, the authority of all citations from the Jewish Scriptures and many of the gospel references is variously attributed to the witness of God the

---

[12] In the first instance the text of Matthew would seem to have some preference over its parallel in Luke 6:46, though in the second instance the parallels of Luke 13:25 and 13:27 may offer the better choice. The value of a Matthean tradition as the source is that, like this passage in *2 Clement*, the two references fall within a single gospel context. The references are not exact, however, and they may indicate the citation of a loose tradition or a typically patristic recollection from memory. In any case, there is no Markan parallel to be considered.

[13] With parallels in Luke 10:3 and 12:4–5.

[14] Or Matt 6:24.

[15] With a parallel in Mark 8:36 and rough approximation in Luke 9:25.

[16] With the strong possibility of Luke 8:21 or, much less likely, Mark 3:35 as the source.

[17] There is a slim parallel to Matt 5:46 here, but it is only a partial equivalent.

Father or of Christ. It is not always clear with which voice of authority the citation is offered. At the same time, we find a specific reference to words that "Jesus spoke to Peter" (*2 Clem.* 5.4), with no apparently intended distinction between these citations and texts offered elsewhere in *2 Clement*. The best explanation for this unique phrase may be the author's desire to reveal gospel sayings within their presumed context. But if this is in fact the case, then this approach has been applied in this single instance alone for some indeterminate reason. Otherwise, the authority of the Father, Christ, and Jesus are intermingled throughout the work as the basis of inspiration for each citation, whether identified by source or otherwise. And, of course, as is typical of other early Christian texts, the phrase "the Lord" in used indiscriminately throughout the text in a manner that does not require the reader to distinguish between the nature of the first and second persons of the Trinity.[18]

Third, one is immediately struck by the choice of gospel texts that appear throughout. On the one hand, and as one might assume from common patristic usage, the Gospel of Mark receives no independent attestation as a source.[19] Though there are several instances in which a citation may have been drawn from this particular gospel, there is no single situation in which Mark alone must have stood as the author's only source. With respect to the Gospels of Matthew and Luke, the situation is somewhat more complicated. In most instances our author seems to have known either the wording or a combination of citations that favors the Matthean tradition as the source in question. In a few situations, however, either the wording or grouping of sayings seems to favor the Lukan tradition. The problem is aggravated further by the fact that in almost no circumstances does the author of *2 Clement* draw from the singular tradition that is attested by any one of these gospel sources, but virtually always employs a saying or passage that bears some parallel in yet another gospel tradition. Sometimes the parallels are between Matthew and Mark, sometimes between Matthew and Luke, and sometimes among Matthew, Mark, and Luke.

A number of conclusions thus may be drawn with respect to *2 Clement* and its view of New Testament images. There is a sound preference for the gospel tradition over against Pauline and other non-gospel

---

[18] This is an especially provocative trait in the text of the *Didache*.
[19] In agreement with Massaux, *Later Christian Writings,* 12.

literary sources.[20] Among these gospel sources there is a further preference for passages in which Jesus is seen to speak on behalf of his relationship with God, his relationship with his followers, or the way in
which he may serve as a mediator between God and humanity. Mixed
among these passages is the clear threat of apocalyptic judgment for
those who cannot accept the role of Christ as a figure of divinity or who
cannot respond to the teachings of Christ in faith. It is therefore all the
more intriguing that our author has not chosen to incorporate either
the language or imagery of the Gospel of John, which exhibits such a
pronounced concern for relationships between the Father and the Son,
between the Son and the disciples of faith, and the way in which the
Son mediates the relationship between the Father and the disciples.
One would assume that, had the author of *2 Clement* been aware of
either the Johannine tradition or the Gospel of John itself, then materials from those sources would have been widely utilized throughout
the text.

From the evidence at hand with respect to our author's use of gospel materials, it seems clear that *2 Clement* has been produced in a context that is unaware of the Johannine tradition and is the home of
various synoptic sources and trajectories, though not necessarily the
site of a single dominant gospel text. Such a context might immediately
suggest either an early date or an isolated location for the production
of the work. At the same time, however, the advanced ecclesiology
and theology of the writing seem to imply that our author has a well-
developed sense of such issues that might transcend early considerations of provenance. In either case, the text of *2 Clement* becomes a
particularly difficult work for analysis in this respect, since it features a
perspective that is noticeably late, and yet treats its sources in a fashion
that is typically reminiscent of early views of ancient Christian literature. The complexity of the situation suggests an active center of culture in which texts and traditions move freely, while, at the same time,
no particular gospel trajectory or specific manuscript has come to be
recognized as the bearer of inspirational authority in distinction to
other parallel works. Consequently, in this light one might question all

---

[20] This would seem to hold true for both canonical and noncanonical gospel sources to the extent that *2 Clem.* 4.5, 5.3, and 8.5 have been variously credited to the now lost *Gospel of the Egyptians,* while *2 Clem.* 12.2 has a clear
parallel in *Gos. Thom.* 22.

the more any attempt to assign the writing to Alexandria (home of the late Markan tradition) or to Rome (where use of the Gospel of Matthew predominated). Unfortunately, far too much of the Mediterranean world remains for consideration, and no certain parallels exist among other Christian literature by which we may detect a regional trend toward understanding the developing New Testament perspective that is replicated in the thought of *2 Clement.*

THE *SHEPHERD OF HERMAS*

An interesting situation arises with respect to the *Shepherd of Hermas.* The primary connection between the *Shepherd* and the bulk of New Testament literature comes not through specific citations or allusions to canonical themes, but instead through the incorporation of parallel literary genres. Three types of materials are of paramount concern here: those that contain apocalyptic imagery, those that feature aphoristic traditions, and those that are concerned with parables and parabolic teaching.

We start with the apocalyptic materials, since it is here that the *Shepherd* itself begins. The use of apocalyptic materials in the writings of the apostolic fathers is limited to only a few texts. As we have seen above, the author of *2 Clement* makes some scattered allusion to eschatological consequences for those who are unfaithful in several citations of the sayings of Jesus. Here, however, there is no general appeal to the last days or to future events in general. The *Didache* is that work which is best known for its so-called apocalyptic chapter (*Did.* 16), a collection of sayings and warnings that are reflections of similar materials in Mark 13, Matt 24–25, and 1 Thess 4:13–5:11. These passages are clearly reminiscent of a particular late Jewish and early trajectory of apocalyptic teachings that found a popular response among many early Christian groups. Many scholars believe that the author of the *Didache* has made use of these very materials from specific New Testament sources, but there is much disagreement here. We will explore this further in the section on the *Didache* below.

Despite the *Shepherd, 2 Clement,* and *Didache* being roughly contemporary parallels, however, the *Shepherd* does not reflect apocalyptic categories in the same manner as do the other two works. Instead, the *Shepherd* presents only limited imagery within a broader apocalyptic framework. With respect to that broader framework, it is entirely appropriate to see the *Shepherd* as an example of early Christian apocalyptic literature in two respects. On the one hand, the text is designed to reveal hidden truths to its readers, which is the primary purpose of late Jewish and early Christian apocalyptic materials. Such truths are presumably hidden to outsiders and are understood by the faithful through the interpretation of specific imagery. Thus, the primary narrators of the text, the "church" (in the varying forms of a woman) and the "shepherd," constantly provide the writing's hero (Hermas) with specific sayings and parables about the correct Christian lifestyle, together with an interpretation of the meaning of each teaching. It is clear that Hermas is ignorant of such wisdom, despite his role as a believer, and thus it is necessary that he be inducted into the deeper meanings of the faith.

On the other hand, the text seeks to engage in what is now seen as the expected task of ancient apocalyptic literature: to serve as an eschatological imperative for the living of an appropriate Christian lifestyle. Thus, Hermas finds himself entangled in a developing faith tradition that wrestles with questions of morality. Unlike texts such as Paul's Thessalonian correspondence and the Gospel of Mark, there is no evident concern for the imminent end of time in the *Shepherd*. Instead, issues of institutional structure and the role of the individual within that framework, evidenced elsewhere in the Gospels of Matthew and Luke and the Pastoral Epistles, clearly are the concern of our author.[21]

The specific images that appear in the *Shepherd*'s apocalyptic framework are actually quite limited. The most commonly recognized topos is exemplified in the figure of the great beast that Hermas encounters as he travels along the Campanian Way in chapters 22–24 (= *Herm.* 4). This creature is highly reminiscent of comparable images from Daniel and Ezekiel in the Old Testament, and especially Revelation in the New Testament. The beast raises a cloud of dust that suggests a cattle stampede, and it has the features of a mythological sea monster from whose mouth a swarm of locusts comes forth.

---

[21] As a result, one must even question the extent to which the apocalyptic genre in the *Shepherd* represents the Jewish tradition reflected elsewhere in New Testament literature; see John J. Collins, *The Apocalyptic Imagination: An Introduction to the Jewish Matrix of Christianity* (New York: Crossroad, 1984), 205–15.

Its colors of black, red, gold, and white are distributed across its head, and its powerful attributions suggest an ability to destroy cities. And yet, trembling before this onrushing creature, Hermas is saved because he is not "double-minded." Indeed, the creature merely lies down by the side of the road and permits him to pass, much as a friendly watchdog might turn away from the master of the house. As a conclusion to this episode, a woman who prefigures the church appears and explains the significance of the beast's individual colors and the importance of leading a spotless and pure life before the coming of the great tribulation.[22]

Numerous authors have suggested that this image of the beast has been drawn specifically from the materials of Revelation, but it seems much more likely that our author has tapped into a more commonly recognized topos of Mediterranean cultures. It is certainly conceivable that Revelation does indeed serve as the source for the image in the *Shepherd*, but there are precious few other indicators within our text that the author has used this particular text. Instead, other materials within the *Shepherd* suggest a widespread dependence upon the common storehouse of oral and, perhaps, written traditions that were incorporated into the New Testament and apostolic fathers alike.

This takes us to our second genre, the category of parables. An entire section of the *Shepherd* has been dedicated to this particular genre: chapters 50–114, which forms the second half of the work. Some scholars consider these chapters to have been derived from a separate source that an editor has incorporated into the larger work, but this is by no means certain. The use of the term "parables" immediately suggests some association with the parables of Jesus that are identified with the broad teaching tradition of the New Testament gospels. But, curiously enough, there is nothing within these chapters to indicate any hint of association with the canonical tradition. The ten so-called parables that appear here are often long and complex in form, and they are always accompanied by a specific allegorical interpretation. Unlike most of the parables of the Gospels, there is little here to suggest a background of oral tradition and much to indicate the conscious work of a literary mindset.

---

[22] For a thorough discussion of this material see Carolyn Osiek, *Shepherd of Hermas: A Commentary* (ed. H. Koester; Hermeneia; Minneapolis: Fortress, 1999), 89–97.

At the same time, an examination of the parables in the *Shepherd* reveals a wealth of images that are likewise scattered throughout the gospel tradition. Of particular note are vines and mighty trees (*Herm.* 51.1–60.4; 67.1–77.5), masters and slaves (*Herm.* 55.1–59.8), shepherds and sheep (*Herm.* 61.1–66.7), and stones and towers (*Herm.* 78.1–110.3). In the midst of such imagery there appears to be a clear link to the idea of the coming of the Messiah as the Son of God (*Herm.* 55.1–60.4), a concept that is clearly supported within early Christian literature, especially among the longer parables of the Gospels. Otherwise, the images do not suggest any clear source of origin that could be specifically identified with individual religious traditions or cultural contexts. The concepts of planting and growth, family and work relationships, and construction projects reflect Mediterranean society in general.

What is suggested by this wealth of common imagery and any lack of concern to utilize specific parable materials from the known sources of early Christian literature is the probability that our author, or perhaps our author's sources, has tapped into a broad storehouse of parable images that were widely known in the Roman world. Such images are universal in scope, but the specific ways in which any particular author or religious tradition may have manipulated them are truly varied. It is certainly true, for example, that Jesus of Nazareth drew upon such imagery in the construction of the parables of the Gospels, while the rabbis of late Judaism and the Christian authors of the late-first- and early-second-century church used them for their own purposes.[23] What is most remarkable about the situation of the *Shepherd* is, first, that this second-century text with such a large section devoted to "parables" does not make use of any specific New Testament parallels; and second, and perhaps of more particular interest, there is nothing in these parables that we might be able to identify as "Christian" in theology or essence. The author of the *Shepherd* clearly reflects the growing tendency of evolving Christian consciousness in these parables. Like

---

[23] For comparative approaches, both Hellenistic and Jewish, see Charles W. Hedrick, *Parables as Poetic Fictions: The Creative Voice of Jesus* (Peabody, Mass.: Hendrickson, 1994); Harvey K. McArthur and Robert M. Johnston, *They Also Taught in Parables: Rabbinic Parables from the First Centuries of the Christian Era* (Grand Rapids: Academie Books, 1990); Clemens Thoma and Michael Wyschogrod, eds., *Parable and Story in Judaism and Christianity* (SJC; New York: Paulist Press, 1989).

the authors of the New Testament gospels, the key to parable interpretation is seen to be the process of allegory.[24] At the same time, like the concerns of the second-century church, a primary emphasis is the nature of the Christian lifestyle, demonstrated through the daily observance of ethical norms and acceptable standards. The parables of the *Shepherd* continually demonstrate both of these features: allegory and ethics.

The final genre that appears within the *Shepherd* is that of aphorisms, or sayings. As with the case of the parables above, what appears here includes only general sayings of a typically ethical tone. The sayings form a collection of twelve "mandates" (chapters 26–49), which are focused upon correct lifestyle, primarily in the form of appropriate response to the will of God and the assiduous avoidance of all things that are evil. The themes covered by these teachings are primarily general and ethical in nature, including warnings for the appropriate Christian lifestyle on the topics of faith, purity, patience in suffering, grief and cheerfulness, and so forth.

Though the majority of these sayings would seem to reflect the general attitudes of the late-first- and second-century church, curious reflections of New Testament teaching appear throughout. The opening call to respect God first above all things (*Herm.* 26) is reminiscent of the famous teaching from Matt 22:34–40 and its synoptic parallels. So too, the admonition to be sincere and innocent, and thus to be "like little children" (ὡς τὰ νήπια) (*Herm.* 27.1), sounds curiously like Jesus' teaching on entering the kingdom of God as a child from Matt 19:13–15 and its gospel parallels. A more specific didactic genre is revealed in the *Shepherd*'s use of virtue-vice lists in *Herm.* 2–12. These lists are primarily in the form of virtues and are impersonal in nature, unlike similar examples that appear in *Herm.* 16 and *Herm.* 92, where the virtues become specific characters, namely, the women who assist in the construction of the tower (= the church). All of these examples are only general reflections, of course, and do not betray certain knowledge of any single biblical source.

---

[24] The authors of the Gospels offer an opening allegory with the parable of the Sower as a clear key to how the remaining parables of each text should be interpreted. The author of Matthew adds a second allegory to the parable of the Wheat and Tares, of course, undoubtedly to stand as a second witness to the validity of this method.

Ultimately, we must conclude that, though general early Christian themes permeate the *Shepherd* and have various parallels in New Testament literature, there is nothing to suggest that our author has made use of specific sources from the Gospels or from the letters of Paul. Scholars may argue that the *Shepherd* reveals an awareness of books such as Hebrews and James, but there is little evidence to support the use of other biblical texts.

THE *MARTYRDOM OF POLYCARP*

Our witness to the death of Polycarp is particularly intriguing with respect to Scripture for two reasons: it is a later witness to the impact of specific images from the Gospels within developing ecclesiastical literature, and its use of New Testament elements is unique to the collection of the apostolic fathers.

It seems most reasonable to assume that the text of the *Martyrdom* as we now have it is derived from a careful process of editing. On the one hand, we find preserved here an eyewitness rendering of the events associated with the arrest, trial, and execution of Polycarp. On the other hand, we detect the clear handiwork of an early Christian tradent who wishes to preserve the blessed memory of the bishop within the framework of imagery that has become associated with the passion narrative of the New Testament gospels. I assume that what remains in the *Martyrdom,* then, is a combination of historical event and interpretive perspective that is highly reminiscent of ancient historiography. Clearly, our author offers specific reflections of biblical themes that were well known in the early Christian world.

New Testament imagery is found in two different forms in the *Martyrdom.* The best known and most easily recognized comes in the specific parallels with the Gospels. I have already indicated the most obvious parallels elsewhere.[25] Polycarp enters into Smyrna riding on a donkey (*Mart. Pol.* 8.1; cf. Matt 21:1–11), offers a prayer on behalf of the church (*Mart. Pol.* 5.1; cf. John 17:1–26), finds himself betrayed from within his own circle of support (*Mart. Pol.* 6.1–2; cf. Matt

---

[25] See Clayton N. Jefford, with Kenneth J. Harder and Louis D. Amezaga Jr., *Reading the Apostolic Fathers: An Introduction* (Peabody, Mass.: Hendrickson, 1996), figure 5–B.

26:47–49), serves as the host of a final meal (*Mart. Pol.* 7.2; cf. Matt 26:17–29), and prays once more before his arrest (*Mart. Pol.* 7.2–3; cf. Matt 26:36–46). Thereafter, a government official by the name of Herod interrogates Polycarp (*Mart. Pol.* 9.2–3; cf. Luke 23:6–12), during which the bishop is instructed by a voice from heaven to "be a man" (ἀνδρίζου) (*Mart. Pol.* 9.1; cf. John 19:5). Then the local proconsul puts Polycarp on trial (*Mart. Pol.* 9.1–10.1; cf. John 18:28–19:11), and with the encouragement of the Jews who call for the bishop's death (*Mart. Pol.* 12.2–13.1; cf. John 19:12–16) he orders that Polycarp be crucified, an event that occurs on a Friday (*Mart. Pol.* 7.1; cf. Luke 23:54). Finally, his followers come to remove his bones for safety (*Mart. Pol.* 18.2–3; cf. Matt 27:57–61).

These literary parallels to the passion narrative of the Gospels are highly instructive in at least three different ways. In the first instance, the parallels are not precise in nature, thus to indicate perhaps that not all of the facts of the bishop's arrest, trial, and death have been altered to form a precise fit with the biblical account. To this extent, then, we must assume that the core of the account is somewhat historical.

Second, no single gospel source serves as the foundation for the parallels. Indeed, there is a curious blend of parallels that come from the synoptic "triple tradition" intermingled with episodes that have rough equivalents in the Gospel of John and with passages that are known only from either the Matthean or Lukan sources. This suggests that, as with Tatian's *Diatessaron,* the editor of the *Martyrdom* is working with a rich tradition of scriptural sources that reflect several gospel perspectives.

Third, the *Martyrdom* stands as one of our earliest Christian efforts to shape historical remembrance in the light of the authority of ancient literary tradition through the use of specific biblical imagery and themes. In this effort the image of the revered Polycarp gains a certain degree of sanctity through its comparison to the image of Jesus of Nazareth. As the Messiah has suffered and died on behalf of the people, so too his follower has endured a similar fate. The perspicacity of this insight ultimately foists the martyrdom of Polycarp to the forefront of Christian tradition over the previous, and by tradition earliest, martyrdom of Stephen, as known from Acts 7. The death of Stephen, which is couched in the imagery of Israelite history and tradition, is no longer seen to serve as a suitable model for subsequent Christian martyrdoms, the ultimate form of what becomes recognized in the tradition as "imitation" (μίμησις) of a master by the disciple.[26] Instead, Polycarp now assumes this role for the second-century church, and his death, as preserved in the *Martyrdom*, comes to serve as a model for the construction of most subsequent martyrdoms that are recorded by the tradition well into the early medieval period.

Beyond this somewhat patent illustration of gospel imagery that has been preserved in the depiction of the death of Polycarp, the author of the *Martyrdom* reveals yet another way of engaging New Testament literature. There is a decidedly Pauline strain of interpretation that stands at the beginning of the narrative in the form of two quotations. So, at *Mart. Pol.* 1.2 the narrator states that Polycarp, in imitation of "the Lord," waits for betrayal in order to serve as a marker for other would-be followers who are "not looking only toward their own interests, but also toward those of others." The wording is a very close parallel to Phil 2:4. Shortly thereafter, our author praises those who have suffered martyrdom for Christ, stating in *Mart. Pol.* 2.6 that their patient faith has permitted them to see eternal visions, a clear reflection of 1 Cor 2:9 (or possibly its root text of Isa 64:4). The entire section, which provides the essential framework by which we are meant to come to understand the personal sacrifice of Polycarp, offers a unique faith vision of personal discipleship for those who would follow in the path of the bishop. In this respect, our author has drawn upon two decidedly New Testament images: the faithful obedience of Jesus as the willing Son of God, capable of sacrificing his life to the will of the Father, and the persistent devotion of Paul of Tarsus as the ultimate disciple, choosing to give himself in service to God, ultimately to his own death as the perfect follower.

It is not surprising that these images are so closely welded together in this text, particularly given the significance that the gospel passion narrative maintained in ancient Asia Minor and Syria, and in light of the reverence that the Pauline mission commanded in these same regions. A similar devotion will be seen from the hand of Ignatius of Antioch in the discussion below. In the case of Polycarp, a

---

[26] See Elizabeth A. Castelli, *Imitating Paul: A Discourse of Power* (Louisville: Westminster/John Knox, 1991); Paul Hartog, *Polycarp and the New Testament: The Occasion, Rhetoric, Theme, and Unity of the Epistle to the Philippians and Its Allusions to New Testament Literature* (WUNT 2/134; Tübingen: Mohr, 2002), 216–22.

faithful follower of the bishop illustrates that these same biblical influences continued to mold the early Christian perspective in the late second century.

THE *DIDACHE*

A completely different situation awaits us as we move from the *Martyrdom of Polycarp* to the *Didache*. This altered state of affairs is enabled by the early date that now is assigned, if not always to the final form of the *Didache*, at least to the early nature of its sources and traditions. Past reviewers of the text often argued for a late date with respect to the *Didache*, sometimes even placing the work into the fourth century. This view was based primarily upon what were seen to be idiosyncratic liturgical rituals that were attributed to some now lost backwater Christian community and the apparently clear dependence of the author upon the circulating writings of the New Testament, especially the Gospel of Matthew. By the middle of the twentieth century, however, many scholars had come to see these elements in a different way. The liturgical vagaries of the text became identified as extremely early rituals of nascent Christianity that either were subsumed into or were replaced by the gradually accepted norms of tradition that characterized the evolving universal church. At the same time, it seemed less likely that the *Didache* was so firmly dependent upon written gospels and more probable that its author was in contact with the highly fluid oral traditions of a specific region of early Christian development. It is with this change of consciousness in mind that I offer the following review of how the Didachist—that is, the author and/or editor of the text—received and understood biblical materials.

From the outset, there is little question that the Didachist was in intimate contact with what is now called the Matthean tradition. Debate continues with respect to the question of whether our author knew the text of the Gospel of Matthew itself, but at least this individual knew the traditions that went into that particular gospel.[27] This is evident from the numerous parallels to Matthean materials that are spread

---

[27] For an argument that the *Didache* actually served as a source for the Matthean author see Alan J. P. Garrow, *The Gospel of Matthew's Dependence on the Didache* (JSNTSup 254; London: T&T Clark, 2004).

throughout the *Didache,* including texts such as the call for a consideration of the famous "two ways" motif that appears at the beginning of the work (*Did.* 1.1–2; cf. Matt 22:34–40; 7:12), the Lord's Prayer in the middle (*Did.* 8.2; cf. Matt 6:9–13), and the warnings about the approaching end times in the final chapter (*Did.* 16.1–8; cf. Matt 24:10–13, 22–24, 30–31; 25:13, 31). These are but a few examples of what is clearly a broad trend throughout the *Didache* that seems to support the Matthean tradition as a foundational concept behind the work.[28]

But because the *Didache* is what might be called "evolved literature,"[29] the text also illustrates the influences of other New Testament traditions. This seems most evident in the famous secondary insertion at *Did.* 1.3b–2.1, a supplement into the work (either by the Didachist or a somewhat later hand) that reflects some knowledge of the famous Q source or, perhaps, the Gospel of Luke itself. These materials include sayings in the strictest sense, which does not help us to date the text in general, since sayings circulated quite early and varied widely as individual units among churches. Otherwise, certain limited sections of the text share an affinity with the theology and language of the Gospel of John and the letters of Paul. But the parallels to these texts are limited and highly debated. So too, there seem to be individual parallels to materials known elsewhere only from the book of Acts, as is illustrated by the brief allusion to the famous apostolic decree of Acts 15 (see *Did.* 6), though here again there is much discussion about the implications of such limited references.

What is perhaps most important about the *Didache* with respect to its association with New Testament literature and traditions is what is different or missing from our text. For example, if one may accept the lack of comment upon the nature of Christ as a mark of the Didachist's theology, the *Didache* appears to endorse a very low form of Christology. There are no references to the salvific nature of the crucifixion or to the soteriological significance of the Eucharist (if this is in fact the liturgical event to which the "thanksgiving" materials of

---

[28] For a more complete listing of parallels between the *Didache* and Matthew see John M. Court, "The Didache and St. Matthew's Gospel," *SJT* 34 (1981): 109–20; Jefford, with Harding and Amezaga, *Reading the Apostolic Fathers,* 48; Garrow, *Matthew's Dependence,* 158–243.

[29] So Robert A. Kraft, *Barnabas and the Didache: A Translation and Commentary* (AF 3; New York: Thomas Nelson & Sons, 1965), 1–3.

chapters 9–10 make reference). There is no focus upon the ministry of Jesus, the parables or miracles, or any other element typically associated with our New Testament gospels. In this respect, then, the *Didache* has been constructed to serve some role other than what was intended for our Gospels.

The particular aspect of the *Didache* that most closely links the text with the imagery of the New Testament faith is best discovered in the common roots that it shares with the biblical authors. To some extent, this will be addressed in the next chapter, but for the moment, we may identify this element as the Jewish background of the Didachist. Of course, we must take some care in any attempt to identify what "Jewish" might mean in this context. But in the broadest sense we may detect what are classic elements of Jewish literature and thought scattered throughout the *Didache,* factors that appear variously among the numerous writings of the New Testament. Here I will list only a few of the broadest indicators.

The text of the *Didache* opens with the traditional warning about the two ways—that is, the need to choose between the path of life and the path of death. This motif is universal in scope, of course, but is most eloquently stated in numerous early Jewish writings from the Hebrew Bible to Qumran, and is featured by the author of Matthew at Matt 7:13–14. The theme becomes the foundational background behind the materials of *Did.* 1–6, which are offered as a commentary on the motif. The primary focus is on the way of life, which is covered in chapters 1–4; the secondary focus is on the way of death, which is featured only briefly in chapter 5. The framework for understanding these ways is offered in a loose recollection of the Decalogue. A semiformal statement of this rule is provided in *Did.* 2.2–3, followed by a list of regulations designed to help the listener to avoid breaking any of the Decalogue's prohibitions. This, in essence, is an oral Torah that stands as a fence around the written Torah.

In chapter 6 we find a bridge between the explication of the two ways and the liturgical and ecclesiastical materials that follow. This passage focuses briefly upon the debate that arises in Acts 15 concerning the question of which laws of Jewish tradition should be observed by Christians. The audience of the *Didache* is counseled to do whatever is possible, but in any case to avoid foods that have been sacrificed to false gods. This, of course, must surely be considered the most minimal observance of the tradition, and is noted both in Acts and among the writings of Paul.

In chapters 7–15 one discovers a broad collection of materials that have been variously examined as formulated either upon Jewish perspectives within the evolution of early Christian consciousness or in debate with those perspectives. Thus, chapter 7 offers insights into baptism that reflect contemporary codes for Jewish baptisms, yet, as with chapter 6, permit for a broader interpretation of those rules. Chapter 8 is directed toward fasts and prayer, with noted departures from early Jewish practices. The code that is offered here is highly reminiscent of the materials that come to form the early didactic materials of Matt 6:1–18, whose rules of piety on alms, prayer, and fasting undoubtedly have been drawn from an independent source. With chapters 9–10 we find prayers of thanksgiving that often have been categorized as typical of early Jewish meal prayers in the *berakah* tradition. It remains uncertain as to whether these prayers represent a rival tradition to the formal Eucharist that arose within the universal church at large or, instead, were meant to supplement that particular liturgical practice. In any case, the Jewish nature of their structure and theology is clearly evident.

Chapters 11–15 of the text are particularly interesting as a potentially unique insight into the developing structure of the late-first-century church. One finds several elements of the early Christian lifestyle featured here, particularly with respect to issues of authority and community structure. In chapters 11–13, for example, the listener is counseled on the activities of "apostles and prophets," with special concern for the value of their teachings and consideration of the length of time that such people may stay within the community. There seems to be a particular focus upon the productivity of such individuals, suggesting that the true follower of Christ must not simply be a "Christ merchant" (χριστέμπορος) (*Did.* 12.5), but rather a contributing member of the larger people of faith. Such a clear and concise consideration of early Christian preachers carries us beyond the mere warnings against false prophets that threaten the church, as seen in the Synoptic Gospels and within the concerns of the author(s) of 1–3 John. In these biblical texts one finds warnings against those whose purpose is clearly to deceive the body of Christ. But in the *Didache* the listener is warned specifically against testing such prophets in order to avoid any possibility of making an errant judgment against true prophets (*Did.* 11.7). Indeed, final judgment is the prerogative of God alone. In the meantime, those who come to the community are evaluated by their contribution to the life of the common fellowship.

Chapters 14–15 are even more specific with respect to community activities. Here we are told that the gathered community should not bring with it any interpersonal quarrels or complaints, much reminiscent of Matt 5:21–26. Those who lead the gathered assembly—bishops and deacons—are to be appointed and accepted with honor. Their desired traits of humility and generosity are somewhat suggestive of similar descriptions in the Pastoral Epistles, though this same New Testament literature is not paralleled elsewhere in the *Didache.*

Finally, chapter 16 is a concluding collection of apocalyptic materials that is extremely difficult to date by the very nature of the genre. One might say with some reassurance, however, that what appears in this section is clearly reflective of similar materials in the Synoptic Gospels (see, e.g., Matt 24 and its parallels) and 1–2 Thessalonians. There is less of a parallel to Revelation, though the spirit of that text certainly is present.

1 CLEMENT

The imagery of *1 Clement* is particularly difficult to analyze, since the exact origins of the work are unclear. This is not to question Roman authorship for the work, of course, but rather to recognize the difficulty in dating the production of the text. I offer this comment with the recognition that many scholars have argued for the author's knowledge of the book of Hebrews and the Pastoral Epistles. I am prone to argue for just the reverse hypothesis, however, that the authors of Hebrews and the Pastorals had some knowledge of *1 Clement*, or, perhaps less likely, that they had shared sources.

A series of New Testament parallels may be discovered throughout *1 Clement*, though these are somewhat limited in scope. What appears here may be classified into three forms: attributions, words and phrases, and thematic elaborations. Let us look to these in order.

With respect to attributions, we find that in *1 Clem.* 2.1 our author describes the recipients of the letter—the church at Corinth—as people who are "more gladly giving than receiving." The famous parallel to this idea—"it is more blessed to give than to receive"—is preserved in Acts 20:35 from Paul's speech to the Ephesians, a saying that is attributed there to the teachings of Jesus. It is most curious that this saying does not appear in any of our New Testament gospels, thus making it difficult to place specifically within the catalogue of teachings that tradition attributes to Jesus, though similar ideas certainly abound.[30] We are left to wonder whether the author of *1 Clement* likewise understood the roots of this saying to lie within the teachings of Jesus and thus thought of the phrase as a quotation. This is certainly possible, though it would be unusual, since otherwise there is no particular appeal to the authority of Jesus or of his teachings.

Naturally, the question of quotations of the sayings of Jesus is raised once more with parallels to specific gospel materials. So, for example, in *1 Clem.* 13.2 we find a quotation, attributed as "the words of the lord Jesus," that is a rough approximation of the sayings found in Matt 5:7, 6:14, and 7:1–2 about the need to show mercy and forgiveness in order to receive the same.[31] A second attribution to "the words of Jesus our lord" appears at *1 Clem.* 46.8, which is a warning against those who would foster schism within the community of believers. Once more, the gospel reference here is not exact, but it does find a reflection in Matt 18:6–7 and its synoptic parallels.[32] For those who would argue that our author has made use of a specific canonical gospel in these two citations, one is hard pressed to argue why so little has been used in this process. It seems much more likely that we find here specific citations of a free-floating tradition of teachings that have been attributed to Jesus prior to their inclusion into any particular literary work.[33]

The use of similar words and phrases is somewhat more common throughout the text. For example, in *1 Clem.* 2.7 our author describes the Corinthians as those who were "ready for every good work" in the service of God, a phrase with a close parallel in Titus 3:1, where it is offered to Titus as advice for the Christians of Crete. In *1 Clem.* 60.4 we find the petitions of a prayer in which our author calls for God to give harmony and peace to the church, as were given to the fathers when they called upon God "in faith and truth." This same phrase appears in 1 Tim 2:7 as a self-description of the author, who considers himself to

---

[30] Loose parallels are found intermingled within the Gospels, but also in Sir 4:31 and *Did.* 1.6.

[31] Parallels are found for the latter materials in Luke 6:31, 36–38.

[32] As valid here are the parallels of Mark 9:42 and Luke 17:1–3a.

[33] Koester (*Synoptische Überlieferung,* 4) attributes both of these references to the author's use of the Old Testament.

have been appointed to be a teacher of the nations "in faith and truth." Shortly thereafter, in *1 Clem.* 61.2 and as part of the closing of the same prayer, our author makes reference to God as "king of the ages" (βασιλεῦ τῶν αἰώνων), an expression that likewise is used to conclude the thanksgiving prayer of 1 Timothy at 1 Tim 1:17. These three examples are perhaps significant in that they are all found within the Pastoral Epistles.

Other words and phrases are paralleled elsewhere, especially among the authentic Pauline letters. In *1 Clem.* 5.2 both Peter and Paul are identified as the "pillars" (στῦλοι) of the church, a term that Paul himself uses of James, Cephas, and John, whom he identifies as "those who are believed to be pillars" in Gal 2:9. Another Pauline parallel is seen in *1 Clem.* 37.3, where the Corinthians are informed that each official of the government executes commands "each in his own order," much as Paul identifies those who will rise with Christ in 1 Cor 15:23. In a much more intriguing parallel from Phil 4:15, the author of *1 Clement* makes explicit reference to Paul's phrase "the beginning of the gospel" (*1 Clem.* 47.2) as an idea with which the Corinthians should be intimately familiar. Though Paul never explains this phrase, it undoubtedly is a reference to the message that he preaches throughout his missionary journeys.

Apart from Pauline parallels, we find the expression "your servant" (or "child") in reference to Jesus throughout the prayer of *1 Clem.* 59–61. This same phrase is used in Acts 4:27, where it appears in the prayer of Peter after his release by the Sanhedrin in Jerusalem. This phrase undoubtedly was used very early in the Christian tradition, as is evidenced by its appearance in the ancient prayers of the *Didache* as well.

Most noticeable about these various words and phrases is their consistent association with the Pauline tradition, either through the authentic letters of Paul or through the Pastoral Epistles. The single exception is perhaps the expression from the prayer of Peter in Acts, though the antiquity of this term suggests that it was widely employed among the various Christians of the Mediterranean world.

The most important of our categories is that of thematic expressions, illustrations of which are found in two key examples. The first consideration is the relationship of *1 Clement* to the book of Hebrews. Scholars have long observed the likelihood of a historical relation between the two works. To state the situation in brief: on the one hand, the descriptive characteristics of Christ that appear in Heb 1:3–13 find clear and orderly parallel in *1 Clem.* 36.1–6; on the other hand, the list of Israel's faithful heroes portrayed in Heb 11 are closely paralleled in *1 Clem.* 10–12 and 17–18 with a similar purpose, namely, to portray the history of faith that was expressed among Judaism's founding patriarchs and leaders.

One is free to argue that both of our authors have drawn upon a similar listing of historical witnesses to faith that is evidenced primarily within these two early Christian sources alone. Or, instead, one might suppose that one of our authors has drawn upon the other as a source. Traditionally, most scholars have argued for Hebrews as the source of *1 Clement,* primarily through the assumption that *1 Clement* was written at the turn of the first century and thus somewhat after the writing of Hebrews. But to argue the reverse situation seems possible as well, particularly if one places *1 Clement* during the period of the 60s–70s and gives due consideration to the highly developed Christology of Hebrews. To be fair, this same Christology seems to be shared by *1 Clement,* but it is hardly the focus of our author. One might easily imagine a situation in which both authors have shared similar materials within a common ecclesiastical situation, such as that of Rome, or at least have agreed to a well-developed theological understanding that circulated within the same community. In consideration of this common christological link, of shared concerns for order and structure, and of similar considerations for obedience, faith, and holiness, it seems entirely likely that our two authors have worked within a common historical context, perhaps with one having drawn from the other.

The second consideration is that of our author's knowledge and use of Paul's correspondence to the Corinthian church as suggested specifically in 1 Corinthians. A number of passages in *1 Clement* seem to reveal specific knowledge both of Paul and of the situation in Corinth. We find in *1 Clem.* 13.1 a quotation from Jer 9:23–24 that is likewise quoted in part in 1 Cor 1:31, and perhaps is reflected later in 1 Cor 15:31. The primary issue in each instance is that of boasting with respect to wisdom and the need to avoid such behavior, seeking humility instead. Since this is such an integral aspect of Paul's argument with respect to the Corinthian situation, it seems entirely appropriate that the author of *1 Clement* should pursue it as well.

Somewhat later, in *1 Clem.* 34.8, our author draws from a second Old Testament text, Isa 64:4, which is also cited by Paul at 1 Cor 2:9.

This text about the unknown secrets that God has prepared for those who offer love and obedience is a curious citation for two reasons. In the first instance, it continues the theme of wisdom that our author employed in chapter 13. Second, whereas the two citations are widely separated in *1 Clement,* they are quite close in 1 Corinthians, perhaps to suggest that the Corinthian text, rather than random Old Testament sayings, may have served as a source for the author of *1 Clement.* Elsewhere, in a quest for the reestablishment of order at Corinth, *1 Clem.* 37.3 employs the wisdom of rank and status, arguments that clearly have been drawn from Paul's own line of reasoning in 1 Cor 15:23. The theme of wisdom reappears in this particular passage as part of the author's view that the church is best led by those who are older and have lived blameless lives, whose experiences and knowledge should serve the community better than the impetuousness of youth.

The theme of wisdom, then, is a clear link between *1 Clement* and 1 Corinthians. But broader themes certainly are present as well. For example, it is not by accident that both *1 Clement* and Paul make specific reference to the imagery of games and struggle,[34] an illustration of life that would have been well known to the Corinthians. Further, the very idea of division within the church, the role of suffering and sacrifice as an inevitable component of faith, and the presence of repugnant sins within the church that need to be washed away through repentance are concepts that stand as primary considerations of both texts.[35] We might also include a concern for the body of faith having many interdependent members[36] and the theme of Christ as the first fruits of the resurrection.[37] But most specifically, of course, the author of *1 Clement* refers directly to 1 Corinthians in *1 Clem.* 47.1–7 when he recalls the work of Cephas and Apollos in the church of Corinth, as well as the division and factions that their ministries brought to the faithful there (see 1 Cor 1:10–17).

What seems to be resolutely clear in any comparison of the imagery between *1 Clement* and the New Testament is that, despite the

---

[34] See *1 Clem.* 7.1; cf. 1 Cor 9:24–27.
[35] Compare these themes in *1 Clem.* 1.1–3.4, 4.1–6.4, and 7.1–8.5 with their parallels in 1 Cor 1:10–17 and 3:1–15, 1:18–2:5, and 5:1–10:22.
[36] See *1 Clem.* 37.4–5; cf. 1 Cor 12:12–31.
[37] See *1 Clem.* 24.1–5; cf. 1 Cor 15:12–28.

inclusion of a few sayings of Jesus and various scattered words and phrases that find parallels in the Pauline and Pastoral Epistles, our author is heavily dependent upon the witness of 1 Corinthians as a resource for the Corinthian situation. Furthermore, quite specific imagery that is paralleled in Hebrews suggests the presence of a theology at Rome that supports a markedly high Christology and stands as somewhat unique within the New Testament. All in all, *1 Clement* is a text that provides a gateway for understanding much of the historical and doctrinal background behind much early Christian theological development.

THE *LETTER OF POLYCARP TO THE PHILIPPIANS*

Polycarp's single preserved letter to the Philippians offers evidence of his knowledge of a variety of passages from the New Testament.[38] This seems especially reasonable in light of the late date of his writing and his close geographical proximity to so many of early Christianity's important communities in Asia Minor and Greece. Indeed, one of the stated purposes of his writing is to provide the Philippians with copies of the correspondence of Ignatius of Antioch (see Pol. *Phil.* 13.2). This naturally suggests that he was a preserver of contemporary Christian manuscripts and, undoubtedly, a student of their theological perceptions.

A quick survey of Polycarp's letter indicates a wide knowledge of the authentic letters of Paul,[39] the so-called Pastoral Epistles,[40] and both

---

[38] We are fortunate to have two relatively recent studies for support here; see Hartog, *Polycarp and the New Testament;* Kenneth Berding, *Polycarp and Paul: An Analysis of Their Theological Relationship in Light of Polycarp's Use of Biblical and Extra-Biblical Literature* (VCSup 62; Leiden: Brill, 2002).

[39] See the following texts in Polycarp, *Philippians,* and compare the parenthetical texts: 1.3 (Eph 2:5, 8–9); 2.1 (1 Cor 15:28; Phil 3:21?); 2.2 (2 Cor 4:14); 3.3 (Gal 4:26); 4.1 (2 Cor 6:7; Rom 6:13?); 4.3 (1 Cor 14:25?); 5.1 (Gal 6:7); 5.3 (1 Cor 6:9); 6.1 (2 Cor 8:21 [based upon Prov 3:4]); 6.2 (Rom 14:10; 2 Cor 5:10); 10.1 (1 Cor 15:58?); 10.2 (Eph 5:21?); 11.1 (1 Thess 5:22); 11.2 (1 Cor 6:2); 12.1 (Eph 4:26 [based upon Ps 4:5]); 12.2 (Gal 1:1); 12.3 (Eph 6:18?).

[40] See the following texts in Polycarp, *Philippians,* and compare the parenthetical texts: 4.1 (1 Tim 6:10 and 6:7 consecutively); 5.2–3 (Polycarp's household comments upon the role of deacons clearly reflects that of 1 Tim 3:8–10); 5.2 (2 Tim 2:12); 6.3 (Titus 2:14?; 2 Tim 3:5–6?); 9.2 (2 Tim 4:10); 11.1 (1 Tim 3:5?).

1 Peter and 1 John.[41] To this collection of texts we may also add some knowledge of materials that have been preserved within the tradition of the Synoptic Gospels and Acts,[42] though what appears here certainly is limited and suggests that Polycarp employed individual sayings from the teachings of Jesus rather than specific texts of the Gospels. With such a broad knowledge of early Christian literature, it is somewhat surprising that he does not employ broader images from the authors of that literature. Nor does he employ the arguments of either the evangelists or Paul, but rather seems to remain restricted to brief words and phrases from their writings or, in the case of the authors of the Gospels, from their sources. This leads us to some fairly interesting observations about Polycarp with respect to his use of New Testament literature early in the second century.

From the outset, we can readily see that Polycarp witnessed the circulation of numerous ancient texts and accepted a number of them as authoritative and worthy of collection. He respects the authority of the apostle Paul and of those who have written in his name (the Pastoral Epistles), as well as of teachings attributed to Jesus. Polycarp's use of 1 Peter indicates, presumably, that he assumes that text to have been written by the apostle Peter and, thereby, holds some respect for the Petrine tradition, too. All of this is as we would expect from a bishop in his position early in the second century, and it is somewhat gratifying to see that he is exposed to such a broad survey of materials.

What is particularly intriguing is Polycarp's use of key words and phrases versus the primary imagery and ideas of his presumed sources. It is somewhat puzzling, for example, that he has not made any broader appeal to a specific gospel text in his writing. By way of example, since the primary focus of the bishop's letter is to explain the concept and application of "righteousness" (δικαιοσύνη) for the

---

[41] See the following texts in Polycarp, *Philippians*, and compare the parenthetical texts: 1.3 (1 Pet 1:8); 2.1 (1 Pet 1:13 [based upon Ps 2:11] and 1:21 consecutively); 2.2 (1 Pet 3:9); 5.3 (1 Pet 2:11?); 6.3 (1 Pet 3:13?); 7.1 (1 John 4:2–3; 3:8); 7.2 (1 Pet 4:7); 8.1 (1 Pet 2:24 and 2:22 consecutively); 10.1 (1 Pet 2:17); 10.2 (1 Pet 2:12).

[42] See the following texts in Polycarp, *Philippians*, and compare the parenthetical texts: 1.2 (Acts 2:24); 2.1 (Acts 10:42? and Luke 11:50–51 [paralleled in Matt 23:34–36] consecutively); 2.3 (Matt 7:1–2 [paralleled in Luke 6:37–38] and Luke 6:20 with Matt 5:10 consecutively); 5.2 (Mark 9:35?); 7.2 (Matt 6:13 [or Luke 11:4] and Matt 26:41 [or Mark 14:29] consecutively); 12.3 (Matt 5:44 and Luke 6:27).

Philippians (Pol. *Phil.* 3.1–12.1), one might expect him to have employed the useful words of the Gospel of Matthew that are illustrated in the Sermon on the Mount (Matt 5–7), if he actually knows that particular gospel. Indeed, he quotes occasionally from sayings within the Sermon on the Mount, but he makes no use of those materials that employ the concept of righteousness or that may in fact be the product of Matthean editorial work.[43] So too, one might expect Polycarp to make use of Paul's discussion of this theme in Romans,[44] particularly since he knows Pauline literature so well. But once again, no such material is used.

The words and phrases that Polycarp chooses to employ are primarily related to cosmological and eschatological concerns of Christian salvation. The language is largely confessional in scope and is indicative of a certain theology that focuses upon the hope of salvation and the threat of judgment. Thus, we find comments about Christ "whom God raised up against the woes of Hades" (Pol. *Phil.* 1.2), having been raised from the dead and glorified and who is "judge of the living and the dead" (Pol. *Phil.* 2.2), who became "a servant of all" (Pol. *Phil.* 5.2), before whose "judgment seat" we must all stand (Pol. *Phil.* 6.2), who has come in the flesh (Pol. *Phil.* 7.1), whose body bore our sins despite his sinless nature (Pol. *Phil.* 8.1), and who stands as our "high priest" (Pol. *Phil.* 12.2).[45] It is clear that Polycarp is firmly steeped in the language and thought of a future eschatology, a view that was so typical of the early Pauline writings, Mark 13, Jude, and Revelation. It is perhaps all the more remarkable that he has not drawn from these last three sources for his language, suggesting perhaps that they were unknown to him.

Yet, his words and phrases obviously are not offered simply for the purpose of a personal expression of his theology. He has instead intermingled this "indicative" of doctrine with an "imperative" of ethical concerns. In other words, he has formed his theology to serve as the motivation behind the ethical challenges that he wishes the Philippians to confront. And it is primarily here that he appeals to the teachings of Jesus about resisting the temptation to judge others and the need to

---

[43] Indeed, of the six usages of the term "righteousness" in Matthew (having only one parallel in Luke [Luke 1:75, here drawn from a Q parallel in Matt 3:15] and none in Mark), four are found in the Sermon on the Mount. This suggests that we find here a theme that is more at home with the view of the Matthean author than, perhaps, with the specific teachings of Jesus.

[44] See scattered references and discussion throughout Rom 3–10.

[45] This, of course, is a clear reflection of the unique theology of Hebrews.

show mercy, passages that are known primarily from the Synoptic Gospels. Of course, the demonstration of such traits is illustrated by the use of standard virtue-vice lists (passim) and household codes (see Pol. *Phil.* 5.2–6.3), culminating ultimately in very specific advice in chapter 11 about how the community must engage the situation of Valens. To this we must add the constant call for faithfulness to true doctrine and the necessity of avoiding false teachers, a theme that both the *Didache* and Ignatius, not to mention the authors of the Johannine letters and Jude, had raised previously.[46]

Finally, it seems especially important to acknowledge the heavy dependence of Polycarp upon the writing of 1 Peter. On the one hand, as with the Pauline materials, the materials that are incorporated by the bishop are primarily confessional in nature. They are the representation of doctrinal positions that were held by the author of 1 Peter. At the same time, however, one might be tempted to argue that Polycarp has chosen to base his own epistle upon the progression of themes that appear in 1 Peter. This is not necessarily a strict dependence, it would seem. Similar analogies may be made between Polycarp's epistographical style and that of Ignatius, upon whom, I would also argue, Polycarp is highly dependent. Yet when one scans through the bishop's use of passages from 1 Peter, a certain sequential consistency is determined based upon the progression of Petrine texts (1 Pet 1:8; 1:13; 3:9 [2:11?]; 3:13; 4:7) followed then by a reversal of themes (1 Pet 2:24; 2:22; 2:17; 2:12).[47] The materials that Polycarp uses from the text are, once more, primarily confessional in nature. But it is perhaps especially instructive that he has used Petrine authority to produce his own letter and to provide a certain foundation to the arguments that he provides for the Philippians.[48] This is a technique that is borrowed also by Ignatius, who seems often to have used Paul's letters as the framework for his own correspondence, as will be demonstrated below.

---

[46] Cf. *Did.* 6.1–2; Ign. *Eph.* 7.1–9.1; Ign. *Magn.* 8.1–9.2; Ign. *Trall.* 6.1–11.2; Ign. *Phld.* 2.1–3.1; 6.1–7.1; Ign. *Smyrn.* 4.1–6.2; Ign. *Pol.* 3.1; 1 John 2:18–27; 3:4–10; 4:1–6; 2 John 7–10; Jude 8–16.

[47] The single break in this pattern is the appearance of 1 Pet 2:11 in Pol. *Phil.* 5.3.

[48] See the following texts in Polycarp, *Philippians,* and compare the parenthetical texts: 1.3 (1 Pet 1:8); 2.1 (1 Pet 1:13, 21); 2.2 (1 Pet 3:9); 5.3 (1 Pet 2:11); 6.3 (1 Pet 3:13); 7.2 (1 Pet 4:7); 8.1 (1 Pet 2:24, 22); 8.2 (1 Pet 2:21); 10.1 (1 Pet 2:17); 10.2 (1 Pet 5:5; 2:12).

LETTERS OF IGNATIUS

This final analysis will address the situation of Ignatius and the nature of New Testament imagery and its influence upon his letters. Scholars have long recognized that Ignatius holds the apostle Paul as something of an inspiration and hero of the faith. This may be easily gleaned from the numerous Pauline phrases and allusions that appear throughout the Ignatian correspondence, whose frequency make it too difficult to list in this brief consideration.

There seems to be a variety of reasons why Ignatius holds Paul in such high esteem. In the first instance, many of the Ignatian letters are directed toward early Christian communities that Paul himself had encountered some half century previously. Included here, at least as we know it from the written record of Paul's own writings and Acts, are Ephesus and Rome. The remaining churches at Magnesia, Tralles, Philadelphia, and Smyrna undoubtedly are locations that either were known by Paul or were influenced to some degree by his missionary activities. Thus, it is useful for Ignatius to recall Paul's influence and approach to Christianity as the bishop addresses those same churches.

Second, Ignatius finds Paul's theology of freedom to be a welcome opportunity to expand his own influence within the church at Antioch, primarily in refutation of the more foundational form of Jewish Christianity that undoubtedly already existed in the city. This approach helps Ignatius to fend against false teachings that pummel the church in the form of Docetism and attempts to turn emerging Christianity into what it had previously been, namely, simply a form of messianic Judaism.

Perhaps what is most important for our current consideration, however, is the third reason for the Ignatian acceptance of Paul. Simply stated, Ignatius borrows constantly from Pauline literary style. We see this at various points throughout the Ignatian letters. The most obvious instance is in the greeting of the Ignatian letter to Rome, a passage in which Ignatius seeks to influence the Roman church through an expression of his doctrine of God and the sharing of his understanding of the true faith. This is never the bishop's approach in his remaining letters, and clearly it is patterned upon Paul's own expression of doctrine and faith as stated in Rom 1:1–6. Each author is fully aware that his future is to some great extent dependent upon the actions of the church at Rome. And so both the apostle and the bishop approach the Christians there with an epistolary format that is atypical of their other letters.

Another example of the way in which Ignatius is dependent upon Pauline style is reflected in his letter to the Ephesians. Of course, for those who consider the New Testament text of Ephesians to be deutero-pauline, what we find here is the bishop's faithful replication of a work that stems from the so-called Pauline school. In either case, the Ignatian letter to Ephesus is truly unique in its faithful replication of its Pauline exemplar. With respect to the New Testament text, we find a unique movement from comments about the spiritual blessings that are available through Christ (Eph 1:3–14), to a prayer for wisdom in governance (Eph 1:15–23), to a plea for unity in Christ (Eph 2:11–21; 4:1–16), to instructions for living the Christian life (Eph 4:17–5:2; 5:21–6:9), to warnings against a lifestyle of deceitful ways and teachings (Eph 5:3–20), to a recognition of the divine power that protects all believers (Eph 6:10–17), and finally to closing greetings and instructions (Eph 6:18–24). With Ignatius we find a similar pattern: comments about the blessings of Christ that come through the role of ruling authorities (Ign. *Eph.* 1.1–3.2), a plea for unity based upon the ordered nature of ecclesiastical hierarchy (Ign. *Eph.* 4.1–5.3), instructions for Christian living (Ign. *Eph.* 6.1–2), warnings against those who would teach falsely against such unity, particularly in view of the end times (Ign. *Eph.* 7.2–16.2), comments upon the mystery of God as expressed in a collection of creeds (Ign. *Eph.* 18.1–20.2), and finally, closing greetings and instructions (Ign. *Eph.* 21.1–2). Throughout both letters there are scattered comments and allusions to the chains of the author and the significance of a life offered in service to Christ. Ignatius makes specific mention of Paul as a faith link between his own journey and that of the apostle (Ign. *Eph.* 12.2). Of special interest here is the bishop's development of the idea of the body of Christ, though not expressed explicitly in such terms. Whereas Paul envisioned the body as the collected members of the church, it is clear that Ignatius now sees that image through the hierarchy of the church's leadership, around which all unity and faith expression must conform. This is a significant reflection of the ecclesiology that developed among Christians at the end of the first century, attested both by Ignatius and by the Pastoral Epistles.

Another interesting way in which Ignatius makes use of early Christian literary materials is found in his employment of the Gospel of

Matthew. A careful reading of the Ignatian correspondence reveals that the bishop is very familiar with this particular gospel in comparison with remaining texts. Though he makes only rare reference to passages from the text of Matthew itself, he uses the work as the springboard for a variety of comments, thus to reveal a close familiarity with Matthean concerns and the ideas that are characteristic of the Matthean mindset. We can easily find a number of these usages.

In the first instance, we see that Ignatius makes reference to gospel materials that find their focal point in Matthew. Thus, while he notes that "the tree is distinguished by its fruit" (Ign. *Eph.* 14.2), a text shared by Matt 12:33 and Luke 6:44, he shortly thereafter refers to the anointing of Christ's head (Ign. *Eph.* 17.1), an episode known from Matt 26:6–13 and Mark 14:3–19.[49]

Second, we find that Ignatius makes use of Matthean phrases and ideas. Thus, in his letter to the Trallians he proclaims that those who hold a docetic vision of the nature of Christ are evil sprouts that the Father has not planted (see Ign. *Trall.* 10–11). It is in Matthew alone that we find the words of Jesus, "Every plant that my heavenly Father has not planted will be rooted up" (Matt 15:13). Of course, Ignatius has not cited this text specifically, and furthermore, the Matthean context is applied directly to the situation of the Pharisees. Ignatius has adopted the saying to a more contemporary setting and problem, thus to make it his own in essence.

Another example of a similar usage of Matthew appears in the Ignatian letter to the Smyrnaeans, where the bishop insists that John's baptism of Jesus was undertaken "so that all righteousness might be fulfilled through him" (Ign. *Smyrn.* 1.1). This view of Jesus' baptism is found only in Matt 3:15, of course, and indicates that Ignatius understands this troubling event for the church through the eyes of the Matthean tradition. Of particular interest for our consideration is the fact that the bishop presents this interpretation as part of a longer creedal statement (Ign. *Smyrn.* 1.1–2). While there is much speculation about the source of the Ignatian creeds, one might likewise turn the question around in this particular instance to ask whether the Matthean author did not draw this interpretive comment from some creed that was endorsed locally (in Antioch?), a creed that Ignatius simply presents to us in its entirety.

---

[49] The Lukan and Johannine parallels indicate that it is the feet of Jesus that are anointed, of course; cf. Luke 7:36–50 and John 12:1–8.

Elsewhere, Ignatius makes use of phrases that appear to be unique to the text of Matthew. One might refer, for example, to the observation of "the one who accepts this, let him accept it" (Ign. *Smyrn.* 6.1), which appears to be a reference to the parallel in Matt 19:12 about those who are eunuchs for the kingdom of God. So too, Ignatius counsels Polycarp with wisdom that clearly reflects Matt 10:16 about the need to be as shrewd as serpents yet as innocent as doves (Ign. *Pol.* 2.2). The Matthean context is related to the missionary assignment on which Jesus sends the apostles, a passage that has related parallels in both Mark and Luke. Ignatius, however, applies this same wisdom to the role of the bishop in his struggle against those who teach strange doctrines.

The potential parallels between Ignatius and the Gospel of Matthew would seem to be endless.[50] The important insight to be drawn here is the recognition that Ignatius feels free to make use of the gospel text without the need to identify it in each case as some literary authority. Furthermore, the images that he draws from the Matthean tradition are widely varied, sometimes presented as elements of creedal statements and often given as random comments in support of his own theological and ecclesiastical insights.

The Ignatian focus upon Pauline and Matthean texts represents only the most obvious use of early Christian literature by the bishop. One might easily indicate other themes that stand as reflections of the theology of Hebrews or the faith insights of the Johannine tradition. In any case, it is clear that the close proximity of Ignatius to the living experience of evolving New Testament literature makes his letters a most valuable reflection of nascent Christianity before the general adoption of our canon into the broader church of the Mediterranean world.

CONCLUSION

The apostolic fathers provide a divergent reflection of New Testament images and biblical faith. With respect to later documents within

---

[50] Elsewhere, we might consider the following texts: Ign. *Eph.* 5.2 (Matt 18:19–20); 6.1 (Matt 10:40; 21:33–41); 10.3 (Matt 13:25); 11.1 (Matt 3:7); 15.1 (Matt 23:8); 16.2 (Matt 3:12); 19.2 (Matt 2:2, 9); Ign. *Magn.* 5.2 (Matt 22:19); 8.2 (Matt 5:11–12); 9.1 (Matt 27:52); Ign. *Trall.* 9.1 (Matt 11:19); Ign. *Rom.* 9.3 (Matt 10:41–42, 18:5); Ign. *Phld.* 2.1–2 (Matt 7:15); 6.1 (Matt 23:27); 7.2 (Matt 16:17); Ign. *Smyrn.* proem (Matt 12:18); 6.2 (Matt 6:28); Ign. *Pol.* 1.1 (Matt 7:25); 1.2–3 (Matt 8:17).

the collection, one tends to find the quotation of quite specific biblical texts. These are rarely provided as word-for-word equivalents to modern New Testament translations, but instead reflect the more common oral recitation of materials that were known from popular writings. The advantage for the student of early church history is that texts such as *Diognetus,* the *Martyrdom of Polycarp,* and *2 Clement* consistently provide "quotable" materials that clearly reflect their biblical sources. For the most part, these sources are drawn from the narratives of the Gospels, the Johannine tradition, the Pauline letters, or deuteropauline writings. But in any case, they indicate an author's knowledge of quite specific biblical sources and thus give us some idea of which texts from the earliest church literature circulated throughout the Mediterranean world. Primarily, however, they provide us with some idea of which texts were the more popular writings among certain theologians and larger church communities. And further, they indicate which materials had begun to gain some status as canonical standards for the early patristic community.

With respect to our earlier writings, the situation is somewhat different and certainly more complicated. The letters of Ignatius, the *Didache,* the *Epistle of Barnabas,* and *1 Clement* are sufficiently early in the process of Christianity's literary production to leave us regularly confused about the extent to which their authors knew specific New Testament writings. The themes of those writings are clearly evident throughout the apostolic fathers. But this is not always a clear indication that our earliest authors always knew and used every individual biblical manuscript. Instead, they often may have utilized many specific images that circulated widely among church communities. The source of those images would not always have been evident, particularly as imagery was adopted and adapted to fit new contexts and ecclesiastical situations.

What seems to be particularly clear about the use of New Testament images by the authors of the apostolic fathers may be summarized somewhat succinctly. In the first instance, it is clear that the Gospel of Matthew, both as a literary source and as a foundation for faith, gained an early status as the most widely known and utilized of our gospel texts through the churches of the early Christian world. The apostolic fathers attest to this fact on a wide scale. Connections to Matthew are evident in the *Didache,* the *Epistle of Barnabas,* throughout the letters of Ignatius, in *1–2 Clement,* and in the *Martyrdom of Polycarp.*

This suggests that the text of Matthew circulated quickly around the Mediterranean and gained an authoritative status quite readily among disparate churches in different locations.

Second, the teachings and letters of Paul were widely known and cited early in Christian literature. Even though he fell out of favor with many Christian writers during the second century, primarily because of the stigma that Marcion gave to the Pauline corpus through his gnostic interpretation of the epistles, Paul's authority and imagery were broadly recognized and employed by individual authors. Several of our writers—Ignatius, Polycarp, and the author of *1 Clement*—mention Paul by name, and the remaining authors tend to make extensive use of Pauline images and ideas.

Finally, though not widely quoted among our materials, the themes and ideas behind the Johannine literature seem to have gained a gradual acceptance and influence among the apostolic fathers. The quest to identify Johannine trajectories within early patristic literature has presented a continuing frustration for modern students. For the most part, individual authors rarely quote directly from the Gospel of John or 1–3 John. Instead, it is only the themes that those materials preserve that appear in various texts within the apostolic fathers—the letters of Ignatius, the *Martyrdom of Polycarp,* the *Epistle to Diognetus,* and perhaps the *Didache*—suggesting that the influence of the Johannine tradition was more profound than a simple survey of biblical quotations might imply.

As one might expect, the texts of the apostolic fathers are full of New Testament imagery and themes, some of which are quoted consciously with knowledge of their source, and others of which are employed in an almost haphazard manner as a reflection of common usage. Indeed, the connection between New Testament literature and the apostolic fathers is extremely close in this respect. Their authors breathed the same literary air and shared the diverse memories of the evolving, ancient Christian faith.

FOR FURTHER READING

There are numerous studies of the use of New Testament texts and images in patristic literature. Most of these tend to be directed toward specific authors:

- Berding, Kenneth. *Polycarp and Paul: An Analysis of Their Theological Relationship in Light of Polycarp's Use of Biblical and Extra-Biblical Literature.* Supplements to Vigiliae christianae 62. Leiden: Brill, 2002.
- Brown, Charles T. *The Gospel and Ignatius of Antioch.* Edited by H. Gossai. Studies in Biblical Literature 12. New York: Lang, 2000.
- Draper, Jonathan A., ed. *The Didache in Modern Research.* Arbeiten zur Geschichte des antiken Judentums und des Urchristentums 37. Leiden: Brill, 1996.
- Garrow, Alan J. P. *The Gospel of Matthew's Dependence on the Didache.* Journal for the Study of the New Testament: Supplement Series 254. London: T&T Clark, 2004.
- Hagner, Donald A. *The Use of the Old and New Testaments in Clement of Rome.* Supplements to Novum Testamentum 34. Leiden: Brill, 1973.
- Hartog, Paul. *Polycarp and the New Testament: The Occasion, Rhetoric, Theme, and Unity of the Epistle to the Philippians and Its Allusions to New Testament Literature.* Wissenschaftliche Untersuchungen zum Neuen Testament 2/134. Tübingen: Mohr, 2002.
- Massaux, Édouard. *The Influence of the Gospel of Saint Matthew on Christian Literature before Saint Irenaeus.* Translated by N. J. Belval and S. Hecht. Edited by A. J. Bellinzoni. 3 vols. New Gospel Studies 5/1–3. Macon, Ga.: Mercer University Press, 1990–1993.

Chapter 5

The Question of Christians as Jews

In recent years there has been a concerted effort to explore the nature of early Christianity with respect to the ways in which it can best be understood within and against the parameters of first-century Judaism.[1] This is not a new quest, of course. But within the last century of New Testament scholarship there has been a marked evolution in understanding about the faith and theological consciousness of early Christian authors and their relationship to the mother faith of Judaism that spawned and, for the most part unwittingly, nourished the rise of a living "messianic consciousness" that developed into a major world faith.

The worlds of the New Testament authors and apostolic fathers provide an overlapping view of numerous perspectives into this evolution. Indeed, the close relationship that the apostle Paul[2] and the author of the Gospel of Matthew[3] share with their Jewish roots reveals a marked and singular contrast with the positions of Ignatius of Antioch and the author of the *Epistle to Diognetus,* neither of whom indicate any hint of sympathy for Jewish perspectives of faith or hold any appreciation for the contribution of the Jewish heritage to Christian principles.

---

[1] See, for example, the recent volume of conference papers in Simon C. Mimouni and F. Stanley Jones, eds., *Le judéo-christianisme dans tous ses états: Actes du Colloque de Jérusalem, 6–10 juillet 1998* (LD; Paris: Cerf, 2001).

[2] See Alan F. Segal, *Rebecca's Children: Judaism and Christianity in the Roman World* (Cambridge, Mass.: Harvard University Press, 1986), 96–116.

[3] See Anthony J. Saldarini, *Matthew's Christian-Jewish Community* (CSHJ; Chicago: University of Chicago Press, 1994).

Recent investigations into the variegated forms of late Judaism out of which such diverse opinions developed have contributed greatly to our understanding of how such strong and contrasting views arose among the writers of the apostolic and postapostolic periods of the early church. In the following pages I offer a broad survey of those contrasting perspectives, primarily as their roots are found in the New Testament literature and subsequently developed in the writings of the apostolic fathers.

NEW TESTAMENT PERSPECTIVES

As has been noted by those who take a sociological approach to the rise of religious movements, the roots of nascent Christianity undoubtedly took hold in a fairly predictable manner. From the outset, those earliest Christians who felt that they had a faith to share, whatever its form and scope, clearly found ways to express their beliefs to persons who were sympathetic to them.[4] And, as the so-called parable of the Sower that is preserved in the Synoptic Gospels suggests, those beliefs fell upon a variety of surfaces, including both fertile soil and landscapes that were inhospitable to the gospel message. But unlike what the parable suggests—that is, that the gospel message was either accepted or rejected—the situation surely was much more complicated. Indeed, by the nature of human interaction, undoubtedly there were many people who heard the message and responded to its hope in various private and personal ways. Perhaps they showed no change in their lifestyle but secretly believed in their hearts; perhaps they chose to reshape their daily patterns of living according to new faith-based ethical guidelines. The response to the spread of Christianity's earliest message is extremely difficult to ascertain. In fact, the only response of which we can be truly certain is that which caused hearers to break with their traditional ancestral customs and to become new voices on behalf of the gospel message. Such people produced the letters and homilies that have been preserved for us in part by the subsequent keepers of Christian literary tradition.

---

[4] This is the basic premise in Gerd Theissen, *Sociology of Early Palestinian Christianity* (trans. J. Bowden; Philadelphia: Fortress, 1978).

In summary, we might say that, though we know something of how a number of people responded to the hope of the earliest Christian preaching, most of those who responded have been lost to the witness of history. Those whose memories are preserved included the "squeaky wheels," the individual voices that spoke out on behalf of the new faith. But even the witness of these voices has been restricted by the values of later faith tradition and the vagaries of poor manuscript preservation. In other words, we have some idea of the views of Paul of Tarsus and of the unknown authors of the remaining New Testament literature. And we know the names of Christians such as Stephen, Barnabas, Apollos, "the Twelve," Aquila and Priscilla, Rufus, and numerous others, but their individual views on the nature of earliest Christianity have been primarily lost. Indeed, the best witness to which we can attach a specific name is that of the apostle Paul. And it is here that we must begin to understand how Judaism and Christianity became unraveled historically.

Paul and Jewish Consciousness

In the figure of Paul we find the focal point of what can be known about early Christianity's split from its Jewish roots. Paul himself has borne the brunt of much of the discussion that exists in modern secondary literature with respect to this situation and has in many respects come to influence contemporary Christian theology as it has attempted to understand itself apart from its Jewish heritage.

From the outset, we must begin where much scholarly speculation and traditional teachings about Paul finds its origin: at the point where he received a personal revelation of the risen Christ. This story is recounted for us no less than three times in the book of Acts,[5] and it has been used by Christian theologians ever since to define the nature of Paul's relationship to Judaism. Earlier commentators often were quick to label this event as Paul's "conversion," as though to suggest that in a single moment he chose to forsake his religious, ethical, and ethnic background to become some new type of individual within the ancient world: a religious enthusiast who was completely free from any previous aspect of his personal background. Indeed, much subsequent theology within the ecclesiastical tradition has built its understanding of conversion upon this precise moment in the career of Paul and has

---

[5] See Acts 9:1–19; 22:1–22; 26:2–23.

offered him as a model for similar transformations within the lives of later Christians.

In many respects, it is no longer realistic to hold this antiquated perspective. One need only look elsewhere in Acts, not to mention Paul's own writings, to find ample testimony to the contrary. When we trace the travels of Paul in Acts, for example, we witness his movement from synagogue to synagogue in an effort to find those with whom he shares a common background. His preaching to them is of a messiah who has come from among the Jews, someone to offer salvation to Israel. But, of course, it is not simply for Israel alone that the Messiah has come; rather, as the prophets Isaiah and Ezekiel foretold, it is for all the nations of the earth.[6] As the author of Acts attests, when certain listeners from within the synagogues heard this message, they believed what Paul preached, and they worshipped this messiah with him.

What happened after this point was the result of the division between those who followed Paul and those who rejected him. For the most part, it seems, it was the "God-fearers" within the synagogue—that is, those non-Jews who came to worship with the Jews themselves—who chose to accept Paul's message and, subsequently, began to form house churches in which they could worship the new Messiah. Most of Paul's listeners from among the Jewish people, as once more attested by Acts, typically rejected his message. Some, in fact, hounded him and his fellow evangelists as they moved from one city to the next (so Acts 13:44–14:7; 14:19; 17:1–15). In some sense, there is a certain irony here in that the author of Acts never suggests that it was Paul who rejected the Jews, but instead it was the Jews who rejected Paul.[7]

When we peruse Paul's own letters, we find materials that seem to support this same position. In his various directives to the Corinthian church, for example, he offers a certain perspective with respect to questionable moral situations that reflects both a realization of the new reality that the church experiences as the body of the risen Christ and a heavy dependence upon sound Jewish tradition and ethical guidelines. This latter viewpoint typically is supported by an appeal to the Jewish Scriptures.[8] The angle that Paul employs in this process is never typical

---

[6] See Segal, *Rebecca's Children*, 163–81.

[7] See William Horbury, *Jews and Christians in Contact and Controversy* (Edinburgh: T&T Clark, 1998), 111–26.

[8] See, as an example of Paul's ethical teachings, the following texts from 1 Corinthians and compare the parenthetical texts: 1 Cor 5:1 (Deut 22:30;

of contemporary and later rabbinic efforts in which the Scriptures are used because of their individual authority within the tradition. Instead, Paul appeals to these texts as the support for his view of who Jesus of Nazareth is as the Messiah and as evidence of how God has made this realization a reality of Judaism's historical consciousness.

Perhaps the best witness to Paul's Jewish consciousness can be found in his most famous correspondence, his letter to the church at Rome. This letter holds much of what often has been identified by subsequent Christians as Paul's basic theology. But more importantly for our purposes, one discovers that the letter can be read correctly only in the light of Rome's divided congregation, a church that was in part Jewish in background and in part non-Jewish. Thus, as one reads through the text of Romans, one finds Paul sometimes speaking to the Jewish community and sometimes to the non-Jewish community. He applauds the legitimate foundations of Judaism as a basis for faith (Rom 3:1–8; 9:1–13), but he warns those who have a Jewish heritage that this does not entitle them to special privileges (Rom 3:9–18). He supports non-Jews who have come into the church as though they were new grafts upon an ancient tree trunk (Rom 11:17–24), yet he also warns these believers, who serve as evidence of what God is doing throughout the world, that this does not justify any attempt to despise those of Jewish background, from which Christianity has developed (Rom 11:25–36). Indeed, it seems that Paul is the apostle not only to the nations but also to the Jews of the Diaspora.

At the same time, scholars often have emphasized the clear resistance that Paul offers to any Christian who would argue for the need to return to Judaism before becoming a follower of the Messiah. In his letter to the Galatians, Paul becomes rhetorically violent in his refutation of such people, the "circumcision party," offering the wish that they would "castrate" (ἀποκόπτω) themselves (Gal 5:12). He sees no justification for arguments that insist upon the merits of a Jewish background before seeking salvation in Christ. It is true that he himself is the product of just such a background. He does not, however, consider his own Jewish experience to stand as a prerequisite for the conversion of others.

The author of Acts attests to specific individuals within the rise of early Christianity who undoubtedly supported the very understanding

---

27:20); 5:8 (Exod 12:19; 13:7; Deut 16:3); 5:13 (Deut 17:7); 6:16 (Gen 2:24); 7:5 (Exod 19:15); 8:4 (Deut 6:4).

of Judaism behind Christianity that Paul himself rejected. We discover the names of Simon Peter (Cephas), James the Lord's brother, and presumably the remaining apostles of Jesus of Nazareth that the Gospels identify by name, even if no specific characterization of their views or personalities is offered. These were Palestinians by birth whose identification with the cause of their native heritage had been enlivened by the teachings of a single Galilean teacher, Jesus of Nazareth. But this was not Paul's own experience. Instead, he represents the new wave of believers who had come from outside these ranks and whose names included Apollos, Barnabas, Silas (Silvanus), and others. Many of these we now know only by name, and it is entirely unclear that their experience should be equated with that of Paul. Yet it is safe to argue that Paul stood somewhat apart from what the mainline views of early Christianity were seen to be, at least in the region of Jerusalem. As we see in Acts, the Jerusalem church was extremely nervous with respect to Paul. Explicitly, this was because of his reputation for the persecution of Jesus' early followers and their messianic teachings; implicitly, it was because Paul's own view of the early Christian message looked so utterly different from their own. And it was agreed, quite conveniently for all, that Paul would become the missionary to the unwanted; that is, he was to become the so-called apostle to the nations (at least by Paul's own account [see Gal 2:8]).

What happens in the New Testament world thereafter is largely a reflection of reactions to Paul and his teachings. Characteristic of Paul's work are his efforts to explain the value of the cross and resurrection for an understanding of what the church is supposed to be: the living body of Christ in the world. He is not bothered by stories of appearances of the risen Christ. Indeed, he spreads such stories himself and attests to his role as the least among those who have witnessed the living reality of Christ in the world (so 1 Cor 15:1–11). He undoubtedly attracts believers who are interested in such visions, and he offers a theological perspective that appeals to those who want to experience a new life beyond what is their common existence. Sometimes these very listeners misunderstand what Paul preaches and claim a special privilege for their new life in Christ, as is attested by the special "knowledge" that they have in their Christian experience. Paul roundly rejects such elitists, as is attested by his letters to the Corinthians. Yet, at the same time, it is clear that he is providing a theological foundation for such speculation among his listeners. In some sense he becomes his own worst enemy as he attempts to establish a living church body along his missionary travels. He offers a message that many hear and accept, many hear and reject, and many hear and evolve.

Reactions to Paul as Evidenced in the Gospels

Undoubtedly, many of Paul's listeners heard his message, found themselves in sympathy with what he preached, and attempted to organize into the body of Christ that he envisioned. There is no question that it was among just such audiences that the essence of Pauline theology was preserved in the collection of his letters and in the memory, if somewhat romanticized, of his activities as an evangelist. The testimony of these hearers is greatly attested in the latter two-thirds of the Acts of the Apostles and exists to a large extent within the history of the institutional church since the first century.

At the same time, however, there is sufficient literary evidence within the New Testament itself to suggest that many early Christians who came after Paul struggled to "circle the wagons" against the rising tide of unbridled enthusiasm that he seems to represent at the midpoint of the first century. A quick glance at the Synoptic Gospels offers just such evidence. The Gospel of Mark, though not in principle opposed to the theology of Paul, seems to make a specific effort to downplay the fantastic nature of the resurrection appearances that clearly circulated within early Christianity. The author of Mark does this in several different ways. Most conspicuously, Mark omits the closing resurrection scenes that later are portrayed by Matthew, Luke, and John. There is little talk in Mark about the nature of the activity of Jesus after his anticipated crucifixion, and the reader is left with little more than an empty tomb about which to offer some speculation.[9]

In yet another sense, we find the Jewishness that underlies the Gospel of Mark within the author's concern for the humanity of Jesus. Indeed, Mark's Gospel is somewhat suspect because of the low Christology that the text supports. Jesus seems to be fully human as he interacts with those who follow him and with those who oppose his teachings. His miracles inspire awe among Mark's readers, but they seem to make little impression among his literary opponents, the scribes and Pharisees. They undoubtedly identify him as yet another

---

[9] Assuming, of course, that the text originally ended with Mark 16:8, as the earliest manuscripts attest.

messianic pretender whose actions and teachings are typical of others like him in the first century.[10] Our author offers us a different angle on their distorted views of the messianic nature of Jesus, of course. As Peter confesses, Jesus alone is the true Messiah of God (Mark 8:9). But this messiah is not at all what the religious authorities of the Jews have anticipated. He teaches against traditional Jewish views of the coming of the Messiah and acts in the interests of outcasts. This messiah is very human and acts in very human ways. He has to perform certain miracles twice, as in the case of the healing of the man who was blind from birth (Mark 8:22–26). And he is beaten in a rhetorical debate by a Syrophoenician woman, a set of circumstances that would stand as a clear disgrace among the rabbinic teachers of Judaism—that is, to lose an argument before one's disciples to a non-Jew, and a woman at that (Mark 7:24–30)![11] He is a Jew among Palestine's Jews, and nothing at all like any description that Paul might have given to him.

It probably is true that the authors of the Gospels of Matthew and Luke incorporated Mark's view of the Jewish Jesus into their own perspectives, if we can accept either the two- or four-source hypothesis as a solution to the classic synoptic problem. And the Markan tradition certainly found a home in Egyptian Christianity, as is attested by the long-standing tradition of the Coptic Orthodox Church. Otherwise, however, we do not find the limited views of Jesus that the author of Mark endorses to have been particularly popular among the churches of the patristic period. Indeed, the Gospel of Mark clearly is the least quoted gospel text among early Christian theologians. What the authors of Matthew and Luke did with Mark's vision came to typify the ancient church perspective. Each author offered a view of the Jewishness of Jesus that, while different from the others, was much more palatable for early, non-Jewish Christian audiences.

In the case of Matthew, readers can still discern those elements of the gospel story that speak to a clear understanding of the Jewish context of the good news message.[12] Some fourteen times we are told that events occur within the life of Jesus "in order to fulfill the scriptures."

---

[10] Note the speech of Gamaliel in Acts 5:33–39; see Richard A. Horsley, with John S. Hanson, *Bandits, Prophets, and Messiahs: Popular Movements in the Time of Jesus* (San Francisco: Harper & Row, 1985).

[11] Matthew tries to put the blame upon the disciples here (Matt 15:21–28), while Luke omits the episode entirely.

[12] Saldarini, *Matthew's Christian-Jewish Community,* 194–206.

This is made all the more obvious by scenes that clearly cast Jesus within the traditional pattern of Moses, whether escaping the slaughter of the innocents and the threat of life in Egypt (so the birth narrative), or receiving the commandments on Mount Sinai (so the Sermon on the Mount), or standing with Moses and Elijah at the transfiguration scene after the confession of Peter. Indeed, even the most scripturally insensitive reader can detect that Matthew's Jesus has come first to the "house of Israel" with his message of good news. But after having been rejected by his own people, he sends his disciples outward from the land of Israel to the non-Jews on a second mission. In this way we see that Jesus, while Jewish with respect to expected messianic images, has a message that is pertinent to the entire world. To be sure, our author encourages us to see the rigid rejection of Jesus by the scribes and Pharisees as the motivation that leads to the cross, much as Mark has already said. At the same time, however, the Jewish people are responsible for their own lack of faith to the extent that they are misled by the rulers of the synagogues who insist upon "human philosophies" (Matt 15:1–20) rather than upon the righteousness of God.

The Matthean perspective is a clear reimaging of what it meant for Jesus to be the messiah of Jewish expectations. On the one hand, his teachings represent a call to a sincere practice of Judaism that is faithful to traditional ethics, but not for the reasons that are advocated by the acculturated Pharisees. Indeed, people of faith are called to follow the commandments of the law and the prophets out of a desire for a close relationship with God. In certain respects, this is a return to Paul's understanding of what it means to live the Christian lifestyle according to established Jewish principles, specifically defined by love of God and love of neighbor. At the same time, Matthew has elevated the status of Jesus as the Messiah beyond what Mark has suggested. Indeed, the Matthean Jesus is ultimately every bit of the Christ figure that Paul seems to suggest in his letters. He is at once both human and ultra-human in form and function. His purpose was both to live as an example of how believers in his message should live, and to die as the means by which human salvation could be realized. Matthew is not as clear as Paul with respect to the way in which this salvation through the cross is made real to believers, but the veracity of the message is firmly in place. This is evidenced by the resurrection commandments for Jesus' followers to act as he has acted and to make disciples of faith in what he has done.

A similar process may be seen within the development of the Gospel of Luke. Though history has insisted that the author of Luke was a non-Jewish physician who gained insights about early Christianity primarily from his relationship to Paul and from the incorporation of early faith traditions, the observant reader finds that there is much within this particular gospel to signify a reimaging of Jesus as the Jewish Messiah. It is true that in Luke, unlike Matthew, the imagery of Judaism is not so obvious to the casual reader. Indeed, one does not find Jesus in the guise of Moses delivering the law of God in a recreation of the scene at Mount Sinai. Nor do we find the more obvious references that actions within the gospel text have been undertaken in order to fulfill specific predictions from the Old Testament. Instead, the author of Luke is somewhat more sensitive to Jewish concerns, as is illustrated by the trial of Jesus before the Sanhedrin, which has been moved from nighttime to morning in order to be in compliance with rabbinic law. So too, the sequencing of elements at the Last Supper now includes not just the bread and cup, but two cups, which is much more in line with traditional Passover ritual. Most surprising of all is the strong likelihood that the famous "travel narrative" of Luke has been patterned to follow events that occur in the text of Deuteronomy, thus to illustrate a missionary journey of Jesus that is in accordance with Judaism's "second law."[13]

Yet, in the midst of this subtle Jewish perspective that permeates the background of Luke, it is clear that Lukan theology is strongly linked with Pauline perspectives, especially as these ideas continue to be played forth within the Acts of the Apostles. As viewed by the author of Luke, early Christianity's success was dependent primarily upon the work of the Holy Spirit, particularly as that force had influence upon the primary figures of Peter and Paul, our author's twin heroes. At the same time, the Gospel of Luke, much like Matthew, has moved a long ways back toward Pauline concerns for the formation of the universal church and away from Mark's primarily Jewish image of the "divine man" Jesus.

A quick examination of our final New Testament gospel, the Gospel of John, reveals the extent to which a Pauline perspective on Ju-

---

[13] First suggested in C. F. Evans, "The Central Section of St. Luke's Gospel," in *Studies in the Gospels: Essays in Memory of R. H. Lightfoot* (ed. D. E. Nineham; Oxford: Blackwell, 1957), 37–53.

daism serves as the foundation for a split in Christianity's historical and theological perspectives.[14] We find that the author of John, quite in distinction from the Synoptic Gospels, offers us an image of the historical Jesus that stands in sharp contrast with late-first-century Judaism. As has traditionally been argued, this is most clearly in evidence with our author's use of the phrase "the Jews" throughout the text, an anachronistic suggestion that both Jesus and his followers were not associated with the tenets, rituals, and history of Judaism itself. There is no similar suggestion in the Synoptic Gospels, of course, where Jesus and the apostles find themselves in conflict with the scribes and Pharisees, not with the Jewish people. And, needless to say, this stands in distinct contrast with the perspectives of Paul, who works foremost among the Jews of the Diaspora as he gradually comes to bring non-Jews into the framework of the church of the mid-first century. Indeed, it is clear that the Fourth Gospel has opted to separate itself completely from its Jewish heritage. This is evidenced through an emphasis upon the responsibility of the Jewish people for the eventual fate of Jesus, an act in which the Romans seem to have been somewhat excused. So too, it is suggested by the claims of Jesus' Jewish opponents, who insist that their covenant with God through Abraham and Moses is sufficient to justify their relationship with God's mercy. The implications of this transition in perspective will be most clearly seen in a number of texts from the apostolic fathers below.

Reactions to Paul as Evidenced in the Epistles

Among the remaining texts of the New Testament that serve as some sort of reflection of Pauline theology there tends to be a clear division between those authors who have accepted the vision and those who have not. Most of the former are difficult to distinguish from Paul himself, and often they are classified as works from the hand of the apostle. These include the letter to the Colossians, the letter to the Ephesians, the second letter to the Thessalonians, and the Pastoral

---

[14] This is not to suggest that the author of the Gospel of John is directly dependent upon Pauline teachings, but rather has inherited a Christian tradition that was greatly influenced by Paul's ideas. One might consider, however, the intriguing suggestion that the "beloved disciple" was a literary attempt to work Paul into the gospel narrative; so Michael Goulder, "An Old Friend Incognito," *SJT* 45 (1992): 487–513.

Epistles. The text of 2 Thessalonians is somewhat unique within this grouping, of course, since its style and themes are almost exactly those of 1 Thessalonians. Indeed, the authenticity of the writing is denied by a number of scholars primarily because of its exact duplication of the parallel work.

In the case of the remaining letters there is a marked degree of development from the other Pauline works. This seems to be true in several ways. One detects, for example, the evolving image of what it means to be the body of Christ. In Paul's letters to the Romans and Corinthians it is clear that he envisions all members of the church to form the basic components of the body of Christ imagery. To function on behalf of Christ is to serve as a portion of the larger body. Paul does not see the role in which a believer functions to be the primary issue of concern, of course. There are apostles and prophets, teachers, and other leaders. All who function on behalf of Christ are important. Indeed, the activity of Christ in the world is seen precisely in the actions of those who believe.

In texts such as Colossians and Ephesians, however, this image is significantly developed. The church continues to be seen as the body of Christ, but Christ himself stands as the head of that body. In some sense, then, the image of the Lord is separated in form from those who would serve as the body. This development is highly significant because it represents the foundation of what late-first- and second-century theologians came to believe about the nature of the church and the role of those believers who formed its membership. For early Christians, there quickly developed a consciousness of difference between the ordained and the laity that becomes associated with this anthropomorphic imagery of the head and body.

Indeed, hints of this are found in the Pastoral Epistles, which are writings that focus upon the nature of ecclesiastical offices and the characteristics of those who function in those roles. As is suggested by those texts, at least by a surface reading, the primary leaders of the developing church body were men who already held traits of honor within the community. These traits may have included either political or social prominence, but certainly they were defined by moral characteristics that served as valid reflections of Jewish ethics. Indeed, the very standards by which such leaders were to be identified may be readily traced back to the standards of Jewish tradition.

At the very least, we can find within the writings of the so-called deuteropauline authors a clear tendency both to support Paul's theology and to expand upon its implications within the development of late-first-century ecclesiology. The nature of Paul's Jewish background, whether expressed theologically or in terms of ethical standards, however, gradually pales in this process. On the one hand, we see less of a Jewish foundation for the arguments that are offered in this material because the debates that these authors address are less deeply involved with Jewish issues, such as concerns for food rituals and debates over what is ritually clean, for questions of circumcision, and for situations in which believers must consider the validity of Jewish authorities. On the other hand, we find more concern for questions of distinguishing Christian standards and ideals over against pagan practices, for the establishment of roles within church hierarchy that are not defined by Jewish models, and for respecting the authority of the risen Christ as a model for imitation.

The issues that the Pastoral Epistles address are oriented around the realization that the church has a role within the world that undoubtedly will persist for many years to come. The original Pauline concern for an imminent Parousia has been largely abandoned. The vibrant missionary vision of early Christianity has been gradually transformed into the reality of a settled faith situation. Traveling prophets and teachers are less the normative standard for the first-century Christian faith witness, having been replaced by the presence of settled church communities that serve to support the diminishing number of these itinerant Christians. The role of the church, fashioned in some sense upon Paul's own teachings and activities, is to establish the boundaries of the living faith communities: to determine who may serve as the leaders of the community; to set the boundaries of right behavior and appropriate liturgical practice; to determine who may be accepted into the body of Christ and who must be excised from it. Such values are clearly demonstrated by the texts of the deuteropauline authors.

At the same time, however, the New Testament attests to the late-first-century rise of authors who were concerned to temper Paul's teachings. This is not to say that such authors were in opposition to Paul, but merely to note that they witness to a widespread reaction against extremist interpretations of Pauline thought. Such writings include the work of James, 1 Peter (and later, 2 Peter), Jude, and perhaps

Hebrews. What typically is true about these texts is that they are concerned to address Paul on two levels: theology and ethics. With respect to theology, the authors of these materials clearly have accepted Paul's insistence upon the value of the cross and resurrection for the development of a valid Christian self-understanding. The theological speculation that follows among early Christian authors explores this reality beyond Paul's own writings.

At the same time, there is a concerted effort to reestablish the Jewish concern for "right actions" in daily living as a necessary requisite of Christian identification over against the single criterion of "faith." This is traditionally recognized in the book of James, of course, a text that Martin Luther once identified as "a right strawy epistle" for what he saw as a denial of Paul's insistence upon salvation by grace. But in reality, the authors of our so-called Catholic Epistles do not seek to deny Paul's arguments for grace and faith at all, but rather insist that there is sufficient merit in correct actions to envision an appropriate Christian lifestyle as an acceptable standard of judgment within the faith community. And that lifestyle is measured largely by Jewish standards of satisfactory living.

The concern to reinstitute Jewish canons of authority into Christian imagery is found prevalently in the book of James, as is often recognized, but is clearly evident in works such as Hebrews and 1 Peter as well. In these particular writings, however, it is the evidence of Jewish traditions of faith that come primarily into play. In Hebrews, for example, the ultimate image of the one who offers the sacrifice to God and who also is the sacrifice is presented as the final production of a long history of those who have sought to confess to and prophesy for God within Israel's history. As the author of Hebrews notes in the first four chapters of the work, God has spoken through angels and through Moses and Joshua but has chosen to speak ultimately through the Son and great high priest, Jesus. This priesthood, which is conformed to that of the ancient priest Melchizedek, stands as the mediation between God and the righteous elect ones, and it has been witnessed by Abel and Enoch, Noah and Abraham, and the judges of ancient Israel.

What is particularly intriguing here is the recognition that, while our author represents the typical movement of the late-first- and early-second-century church to distance itself from various forms of Jewish structure and ritual, there is likewise a typical insistence that the history of ancient Israel's witness to God is a sufficient testimony to justify the role of Jesus as the Messiah of Christianity's faith. In this process we witness the adaptation of the materials of Judaism's ancient tradition for use as a justification for a specific faith perspective that gradually breaks from the development of mainline, formative Judaism.[15]

In a similar manner, 1 Peter offers an understanding that parallels Hebrews in this respect. Although the theology of 1 Peter clearly is not as explicitly revealed, the situation is analogous. In this particular case, our author is concerned to state that believers have been "ransomed" (λυτρόομαι) from the futility of ancient Israel through the blood of Christ and have been called to be a holy priesthood that will offer "spiritual sacrifices" to God through Christ. This has been established through the theological imagery of the living stone, a cornerstone that once was rejected but now has become the foundation for faith and righteousness (1 Pet 2:4–8).

The author of 1 Peter then makes a transition that is not pursued in Hebrews by indicating the practical ramifications of this theology for the correct lifestyle of believers. This lifestyle is oriented around the imagery of sacrificial suffering, in the same way that Jesus suffered, and in the call to act righteously as good stewards of God's grace (1 Pet 4:1–19).

Here we can see the practical application of the theology that the late-first-century church developed in response to Paul's previous teachings. Whereas Paul confronted the practical issues of daily Christian existence from a moderately Jewish perspective and correspondingly built his theology of God's grace and human faith upon that reality, much of the later New Testament epistolary literature fashioned a theology of the high christological nature of God's Son and shaped its understanding of correct Christian lifestyles based upon that theology. In these two processes, Paul was forced to argue against the parameters of Jewish traditions in order to validate his theology, while the Catholic Epistles chose to include Jewish ethics and traditions as a means by which to support their theology. It is this second trend that is most evident throughout the writings of the apostolic fathers.

---

[15] We find, for example, that the image of Christian priesthood is borrowed from views of the ancient Jewish priesthood as envisioned in the Hebrew Scriptures; see Ray Robert Noll, *Christian Ministerial Priesthood: A Search for Its Beginnings in the Primary Documents of the Apostolic Fathers* (San Francisco: Catholic Scholars Press, 1993).

PERSPECTIVES AMONG THE APOSTOLIC FATHERS

The various writings of the apostolic fathers show a curious response to the question of Christianity's Jewish roots. To some extent, this is influenced by the presumed dating of the materials. At the same time, however, there are clear trajectories of New Testament perspective that either radiate throughout the perspectives of the early second century or are absent entirely. Presumably, much of what appears in the apostolic fathers with respect to Judaism and the church's response to Jewish traditions and ideals has been shaped not only by the individual perspectives of the authors of each text, but also by the communities served by those authors. The following survey attempts to keep each of these three aspects in mind—date of literary production, influence of New Testament trajectory, and community background—as the parameters by which a review should be directed.[16]

Literature That Is Close to Judaism

Within the apostolic fathers, a collection of texts defined to a great extent by its distance from the Jewish roots of the Christian faith, two writings clearly reflect a close affinity to Jewish traditions and concerns. The first of these is the *Didache,* whose author has compiled a variety of teachings and traditions squarely rooted within a living Jewish milieu. The second is the text of *1 Clement,* which is not as obviously dependent upon a Jewish background but is replete with Old Testament citations that are used in sympathy with the Jewish tradition. We turn to each of these texts in order.

Didache

The *Didache* is clearly unique within the apostolic fathers by virtue of its sympathetic view of Jewish perspectives and materials. Scholars of an earlier generation viewed this sympathy as a sign that the work was the product of some lost, isolated church of late-second-century Jewish

---

[16] At the same time, of course, it is acknowledged here that these elements are in some respects determined by a process of circular thinking about the nature of each writing and the purpose of its author. Unfortunately, however, this type of thinking is made necessary by the murky circumstances of certain texts and their situations.

Christians, but the more accepted view now is that such marks are characteristic of the work's ancient nature.[17]

The longer, formal title of the writing (*The Teaching of the Lord to the Gentiles by the Twelve Apostles*) suggests that the materials have been handed along from Jesus (?) through the apostles to the churches. But this suggestion surely is misleading in certain respects. On the one hand, the title itself is most likely secondary to the work; on the other hand, the materials that are transmitted are themselves only secondarily Christian in nature. In this regard, the *Didache* stands as a work that is utterly Jewish in scope, having as its basis certain sayings and teachings paralleled in the New Testament gospels. Of course, the materials are now Christianized in their presentation. However, this process is not as explicit as many students seem to assume, since the teachings typically are attributed to "the Lord," a title that may be heard either as a referent to Jesus as the Christ or to God as the Father. So too, nothing specifically Christian appears within the teachings that are found throughout the work. Indeed, the *Didache* often is accused of supporting a very low Christology and of preserving a facet of early Christianity's religious heritage that is not very progressive, even within the bounds of the late-first- and early-second-century church.[18]

What is particularly curious about the *Didache,* and what often has caused some considerable concern with respect to any attempt to place the work within some historical trajectory, is that the views of the author are so indelibly associated with what much of ancient Christianity must have looked like before it came into contact with Pauline theology. Indeed, to the extent that Paul found himself in conflict with early Christian missionary competitors who supported a preservation of traditional Jewish values and a concern for the importance of the Torah, the perspective of the *Didache* seems to support many of those same values.

The formational teachings of the *Didache* are oriented around the ancient Deuteronomistic principle of life's "two ways," a theme that was continued in the writings of Isaiah and Sirach, the *Community Rule*

---

[17] See, for example, the perspective of Jonathan A. Draper, "Torah and Troublesome Apostles in the *Didache* Community," *NovT* 33 (1991): 347–72.

[18] In some respects, then, the Christology of the *Didache* might be seen as a loose parallel to that of the Gospel of Mark.

of the Dead Sea Scrolls, the Gospel of Matthew, and Paul's own letter to the Galatians, in addition to the letter of *Barnabas,* the *Apostolic Constitutions,* and the *Rule of Benedict.* Around this principle, which appears as the leading idea of the text, are collected a variety of teachings that are associated with the Decalogue and with traditional Jewish wisdom (*Did.* 1.2–5.2). In the materials that follow these teachings are instructions on the correct form of baptism (*Did.* 7.1–4), prayer (*Did.* 8.1–3), the holding of communal meals (*Did.* 9.1–10.7), the acceptance of prophets from outside the community (*Did.* 11.1–13.7), and appropriate ways by which to observe holy days and honor religious leaders (*Did.* 14.1–15.4). Indeed, at the core of the *Didache* there is little that is not Jewish in perspective or intention.

At the same time, however, it is clear that our author has offered a variety of editorial comments, additions, and alterations that indicate a predominant "messiah consciousness." Thus, in the very first chapter one discovers the addition of teachings that have clear parallel in Matthew's Sermon on the Mount with allusions in the Gospel of Luke. In chapter 6 there is an oblique reference to the laws of appropriate food etiquette that are demanded by the so-called apostolic decree of Acts 15, a text in which Christians are required only to keep away from foods that have been sacrificed to idols and to bear the "yoke of the Lord." And yet, the Didachist is careful to observe that such standards are primarily guidelines and are not designed to oppress those who are unable to keep such prohibitions. By the same token, in the next chapter the rules of baptism are offered with recognition that one cannot always meet the requirements of "cold, running water" and therefore may use "warm, stagnant water" to the extent that the baptism is conducted in the name of the Holy Trinity. Readers are counseled not to fast with those hypocrites who observe the fast days of the Jews (Monday and Thursday) and are advised to pick leaders whose titles ("bishops and deacons") indicate that their status is not associated with the tradition of the synagogue.

In the final analysis, the Didachist presents us with an early Christian community that presumably would have been of significant support to the opponents of Paul in Galatians, or even to the positions of Cephas when he entered into debate with Paul at Antioch. There is no particular reason to think that the materials preserved in the *Didache* could not have been easily adopted and adapted for the purposes of the sect of the Ebionites that later patristic authors so often condemned.[19] The focus upon Jewish customs and traditions that the followers of the Ebionite sect cherished could have easily found its roots in the same sort of perspective that the Didachist presents. Whether the *Didache* was actively in use in ancient Syria or, more specifically, in Antioch itself remains a matter of some limited debate. In either case, however, it seems clear that the living roots of Jewish Christianity were to be found scattered around the Mediterranean basin well into the second century.

1 Clement

This brings us to the question of *1 Clement.* There is no doubt that the text was written from the church in Rome and intentionally directed toward the church in Corinth. The primary issue is the question of the date of the correspondence, with traditional, majority views in support of a late-first-century date over against less widely supported positions that place the text more toward the 60s or 70s. With respect to the author's relationship to Judaism, however, this issue certainly is less important.

The context of the church in Rome throughout the first century is suggested somewhat by Paul's correspondence to that community in the 50s and to some limited extent by the Ignatian letter directed there after the turn of the century. Paul's letter to the Romans stands as the preeminent statement of his theological ideas and as his clearest expression of what it means to live as the "body of Christ." His arguments throughout the letter are complex and intriguing, and they have drawn the attention of biblical scholars and theologians for centuries. But it remains particularly true that those same arguments cannot be adequately understood until the reader comes to realize that Paul continually shifts between two segments of the Roman church audience: those who have become Christians from a Jewish background, and those who have joined the faith apart from such a backdrop. Apart from this understanding, much of what Paul says in the letter remains strained and opaque.

For reasons stated below, it seems reasonable to assume that this same split-community perspective remains by the time of the letter of Ignatius. Of course, as we will also see, Ignatius maintains staunch

---

[19] Irenaeus, *Haer.* 1.26.2; 3.21.1; 5.1.3; Hippolytus, *Haer.* 7.22; Tertullian, *Praescr.* 33; Origen, *Cels.* 2.1.

opposition to the Jewish roots of Christianity.[20] And he makes this clear throughout his various letters to those churches that he visits along his route, or from whom he himself has received visitors. What then becomes quite significant is that the single exception to this vocal opposition occurs in his letter to Rome. I suggest that there are two reasons for this omission. The first reason is based upon the likelihood that he anticipates the active intervention of the Roman church upon his behalf after he arrives in the city.[21] With this as his primary concern, he finds no particular reason to pursue his standard issues of anti-Judaism and anti-Doceticism. The second and more important motivation is that the church community in Rome remains divided between Jews and non-Jews. And, for this specific reason, he discontinues his traditional themes in order not to aggravate any sensitive situations that may remain there.

The resulting conclusion therefore is that, regardless of how one chooses to date *1 Clement* within the historical trajectory of the development of Roman ecclesiastical history, the milieu most likely remained roughly the same throughout the first century. It was a church that remained strongly within a Jewish environment yet included numerous non-Jewish believers.

This environment seems quite reasonable, then, when one comes to consider the perspective of the author of *1 Clement*. The primary concern of the letter is to reestablish order and harmony within the church community at Corinth, a city whose troubles and concerns were already readily apparent through Paul's various letters to the church there. The response of our author appears to be most intriguing, as there are at least two primary approaches that could have been taken. The first avenue of consideration is already suggested by the writings of the deuteropauline texts of Colossians, Ephesians, 1–2 Timothy, and Titus, as well as those of 1 Peter, the letters of Ignatius, and the letter of Polycarp of Smyrna. This well-considered and widely reasoned view was to call upon the traditional structures of ancient Roman society as

---

[20] For an informative discussion of the Ignatian view of Judaism see Judith Lieu, *Image and Reality: The Jews in the World of the Christians in the Second Century* (Edinburgh: T&T Clark, 1996), 23–56.

[21] See the discussion of this idea in Clayton N. Jefford, "Ignatius of Antioch and the Rhetoric of Christian Freedom," in *Christian Freedom: Essays by the Faculty of the Saint Meinrad School of Theology* (ed. C. N. Jefford; AUS 7/144; New York: Lang, 1993), 25–39.

a pattern of authority and organization that could have served to guide the Corinthian situation. As Paul had already indicated in his letter to Rome, all people are to be subject to the authority of government, which itself serves through the authority of God (Rom 13:1–7). The context for such a statement was most appropriate, of course, with Rome standing as the capital and center of political influence within the empire. But on a subtler basis, the New Testament texts and examples from Ignatius and Polycarp that are referenced here employ the conventional household codes of contemporary society as a significant portion of their arguments for order. Indeed, the various authors who wrote these texts and employed such codes are giving more than tacit approval to the structures of society as the foundation for their understanding of the nature of the church as a living community. And that structure, at least according to this particular vision, was primarily non-Jewish in concept.

However, the author of *1 Clement* did not choose to take this approach with respect to the Corinthians. Instead, we find in *1 Clement* a consistent appeal to Jewish imagery and references to Old Testament texts. What the author of the text offers is very much in line with the approach of Israel's ancient prophets, who themselves confronted the development of a society both in the northern kingdom and in Judea and Jerusalem that had a tendency to seek after foreign alliances and the model of competing cultures. In this task, *1 Clement* makes an appeal to traditional Jewish values. The role of jealousy and its consequences are identified (*1 Clem.* 4.1–6.4), the need for repentance is indicated (*1 Clem.* 7.1–8.5; 51.1–58.2), and a call for obedience, faith, piety, hospitality, humility, and peace is made (*1 Clem.* 9.1–20.12). Ultimately, the readers at Corinth are enjoined to follow a virtuous lifestyle that is pleasing to God (*1 Clem.* 21.1–23.5) and to accept holiness as the foundation of daily living (*1 Clem.* 29.1–36.6). With this in mind, the promises of a welcomed future with God are issued (*1 Clem.* 24.1–28.4). But more importantly for the present situation, the order of the ecclesiastical community would be restored under the reign of love and apart from the contentious nature of those who are wicked (*1 Clem.* 40.1–50.7).

This appeal to the ancient standards and traditions of Israel are clear from the beginning of the text to its end. At the same time, one can see the distinguishing marks of Jewish traditions and texts throughout. Our author draws from materials in Genesis, Numbers, Deuteronomy,

Joshua, 1 Samuel, Esther, Job, Psalms, Proverbs, Isaiah, Jeremiah, and Ezekiel, not to mention the books of Judith, Wisdom of Solomon, and Sirach. It is entirely possible that these materials have been borrowed from collections of texts for specific liturgical use, the so-called *testimonia,* and not from the Old Testament itself. But the matter remains that our author is very much in direct linkage with a Jewish environment, as a standard both by which to understand daily church life and by which to regulate ecclesiastical affairs. To some extent, *1 Clement* represents a loose parallel to the perspective of the *Didache,* at least as the latter text has been described above. Here is a witness to the living heritage of Judaism that was at work within the late-first-century church, a heritage that had influence upon ethics and structure, and that spanned the Mediterranean church from Italy to Syria.

Literature That Reflects the Pauline Argument

A large segment of literature within the apostolic fathers seems to reflect some form of interpretation of Judaism according to the Pauline tradition. This is a particularly curious phenomenon in early Christian literature. As has been demonstrated in the works of the New Testament referenced above, early responses to Paul's teaching and theology are clearly split in their interpretations of Judaism. Those who produced the deuteropauline literature and the Pastoral Epistles advanced the apostle's understanding of Judaism away from its heritage and traditions in favor of a non-Jewish perspective of what it meant to be the body of Christ. Reactions to this are evident in the writings of Hebrews and James, texts in which Jewish understandings of the priesthood and covenant, sacrifice and ethics, and God's bond with an elect people of faith were redefined back into the evolution of Christianity's development.

In the apostolic fathers a similar movement developed that was to have a profound influence upon subsequent patristic views of Judaism well into the third and fourth centuries. Two authors in our collection come into special consideration here: Ignatius and the author of *Barnabas.* We begin with the situation of Ignatius and the impact that he had upon second-century thought with respect to the impetus that the situation of Judaism played for the later church.

Ignatius

Ignatius is clearly a devoted disciple of Pauline thought and imagery. It seems somewhat evident that, as he was taken along his way from

Antioch to Rome and toward what he envisioned to be his martyrdom in the capital city, he came to see himself as a loyal disciple of Christ who was following in the footsteps of the tradition of the apostle Paul.[22] In this respect, he seems to have chosen a variety of themes to address as he wrote to various churches and ecclesiastical leaders along the way. As was typical of late-first-century Christian authors, he argued vehemently against the rise of Docetism among the churches, reflecting the tendencies of 1 John and Revelation, as well as the arguments of his younger contemporary the bishop Polycarp. And also typical of other authors of the period, he was concerned for the development of a stable structure of church governance, represented for him specifically in the threefold hierarchy of the bishop, presbyters, and deacons.

What is particularly interesting in the case of Ignatius, however, is the theme that he adopted most prominently from the perspective of Paul: the need to resist those who wanted to return Christianity to a faith of Jewish traditions. What Paul considers to be the "circumcision party," Ignatius labels as "Judaizers." The specifics of each group's perspective have been the focus of much speculation and are not clearly understood, but we may generally assume that each author is addressing roughly the same perspective, namely, a movement to return to the church's Jewish roots. Ignatius is zealous in the effort, making an extended use of the Gospel of Matthew's rhetoric against the false teachings of Judaism's leadership, the "philosophy of men." He offers creedal fragments to his readers that emphasize the role of Judaism's opposition to the coming of Jesus of Nazareth as the Messiah (Ign. *Eph.* 7.2; 18.2; Ign. *Magn.* 11.1; Ign. *Trall.* 9.1–2; Ign. *Smyrn.* 1.1–2). In addition, he highlights the discord that a return to Jewish norms would bring to the faith of an evolving Christian tradition (Ign. *Magn.* 8–10; Ign. *Phld.* 6).

Ignatius represents what the majority of later Christianity was destined to be. His values and understanding of the faith are inherently non-Jewish. Indeed, not only does his very name betray no influence of Judaism, but also he basically ignores the use of Jewish Scriptures throughout his writings, preferring instead the thoughts and imagery

---

[22] A strong case has also been made that Ignatius drew largely upon the imagery of 4 Maccabees for his vision of martyrdom; see O. Perler, "Das vierte Makkabäerbuch, Ignatius von Antiochen und die ältesten Märtyrerberichte," *RivAC* 25 (1949): 47–72.

of the evolving Christian tradition. In this respect, Ignatius, like Marcion of Sinope a short time later, establishes an understanding of Paul's teachings and theology that led to a general suspicion of the apostle's works among second-century authors. And though it is certainly true that, unlike Marcion, Ignatius is very much opposed to the teachings of Docetism that came to threaten the patristic church both in its ruminations about the nature of the divinity of the Messiah and in its speculation about the role of the Holy Spirit, he is every bit as guilty for having distorted Paul's views of Judaism and its influence upon the foundation for the church's understanding of itself. Indeed, for Ignatius, there appears to be no place within the church for anything that had its essential roots within Judaism. This is in large part due to the fact that Ignatius clearly is not dependent upon any Jewish background for his own views of the faith. And in that regard, like many of his followers, he finds no need to retreat to such roots for his understanding of a Christ-centered theology.

This perception of the Ignatian influence upon the development of patristic thought and theology does not necessarily argue that the bishop rejects Judaism itself. It certainly may be that this was the case, of course. Nevertheless, his primary concern is to combat Christianity's return to its Jewish roots and background, not to condemn Judaism per se. In many respects, it is unfortunate that we possess only the Ignatian correspondence from his travels to Rome, a time when he is under the duress of his forthcoming martyrdom and attempts to address the needs of individual churches along his route. What would be more helpful would be to possess some sample of his writings during his service as bishop of the church in Antioch, since this would help to place him more securely within the evolving tradition of that city.

The role of the church in Antioch certainly was complex, especially to the extent that the missionary activities of Paul, the partial witness of the Acts, the perspective of Ignatius, and possibly the writings of the Gospel of Matthew, the *Didache,* and the Epistle of James may all have found their origins within the Christian circles of the local area. This does not even include the influence of authors such as the author of the *Gospel of Peter,* the great gnostics Saturninus and Basilides, and ultimately even Tatian.[23] In the scattered writings of two late-second-

---

[23] See Clayton N. Jefford, "Reflections on the Role of Jewish Christianity in Second-Century Antioch," in Mimouni and Jones, *Le judéo-christianisme,*

century Antiochean bishops, Serapion and Theophilus, we see a tacit return to Jewish influences upon the church within the city. Thus, we must conclude that what Ignatius represents as a growing movement in the church at Antioch did not ultimately come to serve as the dominant perspective of the city. Indeed, in the fourth-century works of John Chrysostom we find yet again a strong reaction against Judaism and Jewish influences in the Antiochean church, thus to suggest that the pendulum of the debate continued to swing to and fro over the centuries.

Barnabas

We turn next to the text of the *Epistle of Barnabas*, a tractate that now appears in the form of a letter. Though some scholars have suggested an origin within Antioch for this writing as well, there seems little specific reason to make such an argument. Indeed, the way that our author makes use of the Jewish Scriptures is in complete contrast to that of the bishop Ignatius and contrary to the spirit of either Matthew or the Didachist, both of whom show some sensitivity to Jewish causes and concerns.

The curious aspect of *Barnabas* with respect to its understanding of Jewish tradition is the hostility that the author exhibits in the use of Hebrew Scripture.[24] This is a significant departure from the approach of Ignatius himself. Whereas Ignatius clearly has constructed his beliefs upon Paul's own struggle against those who wanted to return Christianity to its Jewish roots, the author of *Barnabas* has actively sought to deny the significance of those roots for the Jewish people themselves. In some sense, of course, *Barnabas* is a return to the Pauline approach to Scripture as a source. Ignatius virtually abandoned any use of Jewish texts in his own writings, but *Barnabas,* like Paul, has made use of those very sources in the quest to establish the work's primary themes.[25]

147–67; Robert M. Grant, "Jewish Christianity at Antioch in the Second Century," in *Judéo-christianisme: Recherches historiques et théologiques offertes en homage au Cardinal Jean Daniélou* (ed. J. Moingt; RSR 60; Paris: Beauchesne, 1972), 97–108.

[24] See Horbury, *Jews and Christians*, 127–51 (esp. 140–46).

[25] So the recent dissertation of James Rhodes, who seeks to find Deuteronomic reflection behind the motivations of *Barnabas;* see James Norman Rhodes, "'They Were Not Found Worthy': The *Epistle of Barnabas* as Deuteronomic Reflection" (Ph.D. diss., Catholic University of America, 2003).

A quick survey of the argument of *Barnabas* indicates the close ties that the author has with Judaism's Scriptures and traditional techniques of interpretation that characterize the midrashic approaches that were in use in both late Judaism and early Christianity. The author of *Barnabas* offers "three doctrines of the Lord": life, righteousness, and love (*Barn.* 1.6). It is around these three precepts that the majority of the tractate is oriented. In the first four chapters our author emphasizes that these ideas were the hope of God when Israel was called forth from Egypt and journeyed through the wilderness on the way toward a promised land. In response, God expected some sign of virtue among the Israelites, the offer of a pure heart as a pleasing sacrifice, and a hunger among the chosen people to support one another in their needs. But what the author argues in the following chapters is that Israel, though chosen by God, did not meet those expectations and consequently forfeited the covenant that had been offered on Mount Sinai. And as a result, God chose to offer a new covenant for all peoples through the works of Jesus of Nazareth for anyone who would be baptized and would believe in the imagery of the cross of Christ (*Barn.* 5.6–9).

In the midst of this argument *Barnabas* draws upon a wealth of scriptural images, from the rite of circumcision as instituted through Abraham to the patriarchal blessing delivered to Joseph, from the offer of God's covenant through Moses to the knowledge of the precepts given to King David. But most importantly, our author returns repeatedly to the issue of God's covenant, given to Israel through the faith of Moses, abandoned by the elect people through their own hardness of heart. There is a constant recollection of Israel's disobedience with respect to the legalistic rigors of the covenant (*Barn.* 4.1–14). Indeed, it is this very disobedience against God's expectations that led to the need for a new covenant, a new law in Christ, and a new people to follow that law (*Barn.* 5.1–8.7). As the author of *Barnabas* states, the prophets of ancient Israel foretold this eventuality, and the apostles of ancient Christianity proclaimed it (*Barn.* 1.7; 5.9, 11; 12.1–11; 13.1–6).

In many respects, the scriptural imagery and specific sources that the author of *Barnabas* employs are reminiscent of those used by the apostle Paul. There is a decided emphasis upon the covenant that was offered and then neglected; there is a great focus upon the prophetic utterances of Israel's great visionary prophet Isaiah; and there is a marked progression of views that recognizes the shift of God's revelation from one chosen people to another. All these basic approaches, to one extent or another, were represented by a variety of early Christianity's authors, both within the New Testament canon and apart from it. The most distinctive difference between Paul and *Barnabas,* however, is the perspective that came to dominate much of later Christian theology. This is to say that, whereas Paul employed Israel's Scriptures and traditions in an effort to convert non-Jews to Christianity and, particularly in the letter to the Romans, to shame Jews back into a covenantal relationship with God through Christ Jesus, the author of *Barnabas* uses those same sources to distance the growing traditions of Christianity from its Jewish heritage. And in this process Judaism became a scurrilous threat to what the church came to consider the "true faith."

What the author of *Barnabas* represents, then, is the growing trend toward an alienation of Jewish traditions and beliefs within the evolution of Christianity's self-understanding. To some extent, ecclesiastical leaders such as Ignatius in Antioch, who never felt comfortable with or saw the need to nurture a Jewish consciousness within the faith, fostered this trend. And the followers of Ignatius and similar church leaders naturally came to accept Christianity as a new religion that was independent from its Jewish roots. In the case of *Barnabas,* however, we seem to find the developing hostility toward Judaism that comes from the experience of a "true believer"—that is, someone who has consciously chosen to change ideological allegiances. This is suggested both by the ferocity with which the author accosts the neglectful nature of Judaism and by the easy familiarity reflected in the use of Jewish traditions. Indeed, this type of attack upon the nature of Judaism through Jewish sources becomes progressively rare after the early second century within patristic literature, primarily because subsequent Christian authors lack any real familiarity with Judaism and its culture.[26] Those authors who chose to condemn Judaism, either as a heretical influence upon the true faith of Christian doctrine or as a straw opponent against whom local churches were summoned to renew their devotion to Christ, rarely made any significant use of Jewish sources through the lenses of rabbinic theology, but offered instead only a caricature of the threatening Jew.

Thus, with the letters of Ignatius and the tractate *Barnabas* we find the evidence of an evolving church tradition that moved quickly from

---

[26] Notice how unusual it was for Jerome eventually to seek out rabbinic assistance in his translation of Jewish Scripture from the Hebrew for the Vulgate.

attempts to woo Jews into the fold of a messianic faith toward sharp attacks upon Judaism itself. There is little reason to doubt that this movement was both initiated and almost concluded within a single generation. To some extent, this trajectory was the natural development of a Jewish messianic movement that was successful in its appeal to non-Jewish sympathizers. In other words, we might agree that Paul was triumphant in his cause to spread the gospel to all nations. At the same time, what became an anti-Jewish sentiment throughout the churches of the Mediterranean world undoubtedly was directed by the synagogue's rejection of this messianic movement, as is attested both in the imagery and theology of the Gospel of John at the turn of the century and by rabbinic Judaism's own desires to reformulate the Jewish tradition into a cultural movement that no longer had the temple around which to rally. Ultimately, Christianity found that it had no place to go ideologically except away from Judaism and out into the vagaries of Greek culture and Roman politics. The remaining texts of the apostolic fathers reflect a variety of views of Judaism within the literature of the early- to mid-second-century literature that were neither as greatly influenced by Paul nor particularly indebted to Jewish approaches to Scripture.

Literature That Stands Apart from Judaism

A handful of texts are yet to be discussed from among the apostolic fathers with respect to the development of Christianity and its views of Judaism. These may be divided into three categories: works that indicate no particular concern for the question of Judaism, works whose position is at best speculative, and works that are aggressively anti-Jewish.

Among those writings whose authors or themes reveal no particular interest in Judaism or Jewish traditions as they relate to the situation of the early church we should perhaps include only the *Shepherd of Hermas*. This work is classified as neutral for two reasons. First, the issue of Judaism is neither raised nor questioned by the author; second, there is no dependence upon Jewish sources or traditions in the construction of the narrative. It may be enough to note this lack of concern with respect to the *Shepherd* and simply to move along to the remaining texts, except that this omitted theme is particularly curious in the light of the work's historical and narrative background.

As suggested by the author of the *Shepherd,* the events and teachings of the text are in some sense related to the experiences of the church at Rome, a religious community that, as suggested both by Paul's letter to the Romans and by the author of *1 Clement,* was greatly influenced by its Jewish roots. The absence of any tendency by the *Shepherd* to utilize Jewish traditions probably does not disqualify the text as Roman in origin, of course. Indeed, we may be viewing within these pages the idiosyncrasies of a single non-Jewish author within the general Roman situation, someone whose individual perspective does not reflect the general positions of the local church community at all. Nor should we necessarily expect this author to reflect the broader views of an entire church community. Nevertheless, it does remain strange that there is a total absence of Jewish concerns and sources. What are found in the *Shepherd,* instead, are images and teachings that more generally appear throughout the broader cultures of Greece and Rome. Included are parables that employ common themes and teachings that reflect the broad standards of righteousness and virtue, much as one would expect to find within the fables of Aesop or the teachings of Seneca or Epictetus.

In the second category—those writings whose perspective could be the subject of considerable debate—we probably should include the text of *2 Clement* and the bishop Polycarp's *Epistle to the Philippians.* Each of these writings presents its own difficulties for our review, and so each will be addressed individually.

With respect to *2 Clement,* once again we find a writing that is often associated by tradition with the community at Rome, though there is much room for speculation here, as I have observed in chapter 1. In either case, we find within *2 Clement* an attitude toward Jewish sources that is much more in harmony with *1 Clement* than with the *Shepherd.* Most notably in this regard, our author employs materials from the Major Prophets (Isaiah, Jeremiah, Ezekiel) and makes a handful of scattered allusions to materials from Malachi, Genesis, and Proverbs.[27] On the surface, this would seem to imply an intimate association with Jewish materials and teachings, much as we have come to

---

[27] See, for example, the following texts from *2 Clement* and compare the parenthetical texts: *2 Clem.* 2.1 (Isa 54:1); 3.5 (Isa 29:13); 6.8 (Ezek 14:14–20); 7.6 (Isa 66:24); 13.2 (Isa 52:5); 14.1 (Jer 7:11); 14.2 (Gen 1:27); 15.3 (Isa 58:9); 16.2 (Mal 4:1); 16.3 (Isa 34:4); 16.4 (Prov 10:12); 17.4–5 (Isa 66:18, 24).

find in *1 Clement*. At the same time, however, the use of these sources reveals a decidedly Christian concern to wrap them into contemporary church interpretations of faith. In other words, though the author offers the framework of Jewish tradition, it is not offered with any particular Jewish sensitivity. Indeed, the author of *2 Clement* seems to understand the great prophets of ancient Israel within a strictly Christian agenda, thus to reveal the extent to which the early church adopted and adapted the prophetic and liturgical aspects of Judaism for its own use. In a sense, this is messianic Judaism taken to its ultimate conclusion from the perspective of the wider non-Jewish world.

The situation with Polycarp is somewhat different from that of *2 Clement*, even though there are marked parallels between the works of each author. For example, Polycarp offers some very few scattered allusions to Old Testament texts in his brief letter,[28] but these are not even as numerous in perspective as with *2 Clement*. Most prominent here are wisdom references to Proverbs or scant allusion to Isaiah or Jeremiah. But as with *2 Clement*, the majority of references are to contemporary Christian writings, particularly Pauline sources, as well as texts from 1 Peter. Of course, Polycarp offers us a letter written to meet the specific needs of the Philippian church. On the one hand, he needs to address the challenge to authority and lifestyle that has been raised within the community there; on the other hand, he wants to send along a copy of his personal letters from Ignatius. And it is with Ignatius himself that the second element of Polycarp's vision comes into question.

Because we only have one letter (or perhaps two joined together) from Polycarp, and because the issues that he addresses are not associated with the threat of Judaism itself, it is impossible to know the extent to which he was influenced by the theology and ideology of his elder colleague Ignatius. Are we to assume that, like Ignatius, Polycarp was interested in a form of Christianity that purposefully sought to distance itself from Jewish roots? Or, instead, should we argue that, like *2 Clement* or the *Shepherd*, Polycarp simply did not have such issues before him? In either case, it seems that the little evidence that we have from

---

[28] See Paul Hartog, *Polycarp and the New Testament: The Occasion, Rhetoric, Theme, and Unity of the Epistle to the Philippians and Its Allusions to New Testament Literature* (WUNT 2/134; Tübingen: Mohr, 2002), 199–202.

Polycarp suggests that the question of the church's relationship to Judaism was not of primary concern. To make any other case is, in effect, an argument from silence.

This brings us to our third and final category: those authors who reveal an explicit and overt hostility to Judaism. We must include the writings of the *Martyrdom of Polycarp* and the *Epistle to Diognetus* in this consideration. Both texts reveal those aspects of second-century Christianity that found itself in competition with the synagogue. With respect to the *Martyrdom*, we find Polycarp in his final days, pursued, arrested, put to the trial, and executed. The elements of the presentation clearly recall the gospel accounts of the passion of Jesus, including a marked similarity of names and, most especially important for our purposes, the presence of Jewish opponents who seem to be at work behind the scenes in their manipulation of events.

It is perhaps most important that it is this tableau—the faithful bishop Polycarp burned at the stake by his Roman persecutors amid the cheers of the spiteful Jewish unbelievers—that ultimately served as the prototypical backdrop for most later depictions of Christian martyrdoms through the patristic and medieval periods. Early Christianity could as easily have chosen to offer the death of Stephen from the Acts of the Apostles as the framework for later depictions, but clearly Polycarp became the preferred model. Undoubtedly, this was influenced to a large extent by the fact that Polycarp was a figure who revealed little dependence upon Jewish traditions and images, unlike Stephen, whose very speech about Israel's stormy relationship with God led to his demise.[29] And to that end, the pious followers of the evolving church found a decidedly anti-Jewish setting in which to envision the heroes of its own faith.

Our final text, the *Epistle to Diognetus,* also falls into this third category without question.[30] The presentation of the Jews as active participants in the death of Jesus of Nazareth is not the point of contention for this author, however. Instead, we find here that Judaism itself stands among the various "false religions" of antiquity, combined together with the pagan faiths of the Mediterranean world. Our author is

---

[29] See Acts 7:1–53, a text in which Stephen recalls the salvation history of Israel as the background to his stoning.

[30] See Judith M. Lieu, *Neither Jew nor Greek? Constructing Early Christianity* (London: T&T Clark, 2002), 171–89.

anxious to explain that Christianity is certainly not to be acquainted with those pagans who worship idols that are made of wood or stone, from gold or silver or bronze, or even of pottery (*Diogn.* 2). But at the same time, Christians are unlike the Jews, who believe that they can worship God through sacrifices of blood and fat, and who believe that they can be faithful to God through the observance of the Sabbath and circumcision (*Diogn.* 3–4).

Indeed, Christians are to be found everywhere throughout the world, and yet they are not of the world. Their concern is to live and work for the benefit of all peoples (*Diogn.* 5.7–13). And in payment for their patient and merciful efforts Jews and Greeks alike persecute them (*Diogn.* 5.14–17). According to our author, Christians represent a new sort of faith within the ancient world that is neither linked to ancestral customs and traditions nor rooted within set rituals and superstitions. Instead, Christians live according to an eternal spirit of truth that has been revealed in Christ and now is available to all who will believe in the Christ spirit (*Diogn.* 7.1–8).

In this way, the author of *Diognetus* has simply lumped Judaism into the world's ancient religions. And though Judaism admittedly must be acknowledged as the foundation of Christianity in terms of historical background, it is as false as any pagan religion. This is a curious development of perspective that is unique within the apostolic fathers. Here we find that Judaism, though separate from other religions, is at the same time no more of value than what those other false faiths ever were. It is now simply another inadequate option for finding God. We can clearly perceive the root that this perception took in later patristic literature, particularly among the heresiologists who, in their defense of specific Christian faith and doctrines, linked Judaism and Jewish practices with the numerous false beliefs of antiquity. As with the *Martyrdom,* in *Diognetus* Judaism had finally come to be seen as the enemy of true faith, as an understanding of God that not only was unworthy of the Creator, but also often stood over against what God had come to offer first- and second-century humanity through the image of Christ. Such views surely were a long distance from the apostle Paul's original concern for messianic Judaism and its appeal both to non-Jews and Jews alike. They are the views that permitted the church to rise up against its Jewish opponents and to become the servant of later emperors and kings of the Western world.

CONCLUSION

The ancient church's relationship to Judaism is not easily classified into simple categories of acceptance or rejection. From the outset, we must come to recognize the tensions that existed among the numerous Jewish factions of the first century. Judaism was a faith that already found itself in conflict during those years when early Christian convictions began to take hold. And, of course, Christianity itself arose as one of the numerous factions within Judaism, emerging as a messianic movement that ultimately came to be identified as a full-fledged religion. Within this mix the earliest followers of Christ were confronted with the question of how their new faith consciousness, whose teachings often challenged many long-accepted practices and perspectives within the synagogue, should be understood in relationship to its Jewish background.

Our primary guide for understanding this dilemma must be found in the writings of Paul. His personal thoughts on this issue came to form the foundation either upon or against which numerous later Christian authors fashioned their own perspectives. For Paul, Christian faith was obligated to enfold both Jews and non-Jews into the kingdom of God. For many Jews, this would have been an exceptional challenge to long-cherished beliefs that God would one day reward and elevate all faithful Jews to a place of prominence over the nations. But as Paul saw the situation, God's plan also was to include those who were righteous among the nations into that same promised kingdom. Thus, there would be a place for all who had received God's grace, Jew and non-Jew alike.

As the successful evangelization of various new believers among the non-Jews began to unfold by the late first century, the issue was even further complicated. Many of Christianity's second generation of leaders, themselves having no strong ties to Judaism, came to lose respect for the Jewish foundations of the church. At the same time, the synagogue had grown uneasy with the presence of messianic followers in its midst and gradually sought to remove such "heretics" from the fold. It is during this period that we find several New Testament writings that reflect the earliest figures of the faith—Jesus, the apostles, Barnabas, Paul, and others—as those who had already confronted the hostility of Jewish rejection. This is especially evident in the Gospels, Acts, and Revelation. The author of the Gospel of John is particularly concerned to cast Jesus in opposition to "the Jews," thus to indicate the likely struggle that had arisen between the church and synagogue by the end of the first century.

Many authors among the apostolic fathers fell into this trajectory of rejection. Ignatius and Polycarp, writing within the influence of a Pauline school of thought, believed that true Christianity had little to do with its Jewish foundations. As Paul had argued in his letter to the Galatians, there was no room for "Judaizing" within the church. The author of *Barnabas* is even more virulent in the debate, explaining that the Jews had forfeited their divine covenant, leaving Christians to become God's newly favored people. Further, the author of *Diognetus* flatly rejected Jewish practices as equivalent to pagan beliefs, neither of which met the criteria of true faith and sincere devotion to God's wishes. And the *Martyrdom* offered a particularly keen image of Jewish depravity, linking the people of Israel with Rome and the devil in persecuting the church's ancient hero Polycarp.

At the same time, many authors within the New Testament and apostolic fathers preserved a strain of Jewish sensibility, arguing from the Scriptures that God had remained faithful to the Jews even as a new nation of believers in Christ was arising. Thus, the authors of James, Hebrews, and 1 Peter temper anti-Semitic interpretations of Paul that many Christians had begun to champion. And the authors of *1 Clement* and the *Didache* were steeply oriented toward Old Testament imagery and ideas, finding the framework of early Christian liturgy, ethics, and ecclesiology within the very Scriptures that continued to serve the synagogue at the turn of the century. Here one finds the value of the heritage of Judaism as a bulwark behind the growth of Christian consciousness, an element of faith that was not to be despised.

The early struggle between the synagogue and church served as a focal point for many Christian debates. The role of Jewish ethics, rituals, theology, eschatology, governance, and lifestyle all came into question for the church, particularly as it evolved from an institution that was primarily Jewish in nature to one that separated from the synagogue completely. Ultimately, among the apostolic fathers, both sides of this conflict are clearly represented.

FOR FURTHER READING

There is a plethora of literature that speaks to the relationship of Judaism and early Christianity. Among the more helpful volumes for the apostolic fathers are these:

- Horbury, William. *Jews and Christians in Contact and Controversy.* Edinburgh: T&T Clark, 1998.

- Lieu, Judith. *Image and Reality: The Jews in the World of the Christians in the Second Century.* Edinburgh: T&T Clark, 1996.

- ———. *Neither Jew nor Greek? Constructing Early Christianity.* London: T&T Clark, 2002.

- Lieu, Judith, John North, and Tessa Rajak, eds. *The Jews Among Pagans and Christians in the Roman Empire.* London: Routledge, 1992.

- Sanders, E. P., ed. *The Shaping of Christianity in the Second and Third Centuries.* Vol. 1 of *Jewish and Christian Self-Definition.* Philadelphia: Fortress, 1980.

Other volumes that provide a clear view into the Jewish situation of the period include:

- Bickerman, Elias J. *The Jews in the Greek Age.* Cambridge, Mass.: Harvard University Press, 1988.

- Hengel, Martin. *Jews, Greeks and Barbarians: Aspects of the Hellenization of Judaism in the Pre-Christian Period.* Translated by J. Bowden. Philadelphia: Fortress, 1980.

- Smallwood, E. Mary. *The Jews under Roman Rule from Pompey to Diocletian: A Study in Political Relations.* Studies in Judaism in Late Antiquity 20. Leiden: Brill, 1981.

- Tcherikover, Victor. *Hellenistic Civilization and the Jews.* Translated by S. Applebaum. Philadelphia: Jewish Publication Society of America, 1959.

Chapter 6

The Question of Christians as Citizens

The earliest Christians found themselves torn among a variety of personal loyalties. From the outset, their world was primarily dominated by the traditions and imagery of Judaism. It does not matter whether one wishes to argue that the teachings of Jesus of Nazareth offered a traditional reflection of the Jewish thought of his times or, instead, that his sayings reflected a virulent reaction against it. In either instance, his earliest followers were Jewish in background, and their lives in faith required some specific decisions with respect to the question of loyalty.

The world of the first-century Jew already was defined by religious obligations and cultic requirements. There was the persistent call to remain faithful to the teachings of the Torah and to observe the ethical restrictions of its teaching. There was the annual obligation to pay the temple tax that supported the work of the priests in Jerusalem. There was the daily assumption that Jews, who defined themselves through familial ties and cultic activities, would live an existence that honored those boundaries and community functions. Indeed, even the civil government in Rome recognized that Judaism, as distinct from all other nonofficial Roman religions, had a right to exist in a certain quasi-legal state throughout the empire. The claim of any particular individual to be Jewish thus carried with it certain religious duties as well as specific legal rights.

As a consequence, the situation of Christians in the late-first-century church assumed a tone of decided tension as synagogues gradually came to identify and define the encroaching scourge of messianic Judaism and its followers apart from the broader Jewish community. On the one hand, those messianic Jews (or Christians, as they came to be known) found themselves outside the boundaries of their traditional religious values and legal protection. A choice was necessary for such believers, and the reaction from within the synagogues often was violent. Among those Christians who did not come from a Jewish background, including the bishops Ignatius and Polycarp, many found themselves with no real concern for any particular Jewish loyalties, of course. Indeed, such leaders often took theological positions that were at odds with Jewish leaders and those who wished to influence the development of Christian theology and liturgy toward Jewish sympathies. At the same time, however, their position was likewise perilous in the light of Rome's eventual recognition that Christians held a distinct cultic faith that was not part of broader Judaism and therefore bore no specific legal rights.[1] As the literature of the late first and early second century indicates, civil authorities broadly categorized Christians as atheists—that is, atheists against the traditional gods of the Roman pantheon.[2]

In the midst of this process of early Christian growth, both Christian Jews and non-Jewish Christians found the need to identify the nature of their faith with respect to community and culture, as well as to decide in some conscious sense exactly where their loyalties lay. It is clear from the voices of our New Testament authors that the primary responsibility of any early Christian was to the lordship of the Messiah, Jesus of Nazareth. But a question naturally arose with respect to what the ramifications of such a loyalty were for community attachments and civic responsibilities. And in this process the ancient Christian record offers a broad perspective on the evolution of such concerns.

THE TEACHINGS OF JESUS

It is extremely difficult to know the perspective of the historical Jesus with respect to the question of personal loyalties and community

---

[1] See the discussion by Marta Sordi, *The Christians and the Roman Empire* (trans. A. Bedini; Norman: University of Oklahoma Press; London: Croom Helm, 1986), 23–37.

[2] So Pliny, *Ep. Tra.* 10.96–97. See W. H. C. Frend, *The Rise of Christianity* (Philadelphia: Fortress, 1984), 147–51.

responsibilities. This is not to say that our New Testament gospels do not contain a multitude of teachings on such issues. Indeed, we find that a primary theme of Jesus' parables in these writings is related to the kingdom of God (heaven) and the nature of that kingdom. And in the Gospel of John we hear the words of Jesus in his debate with Pilate in the passion narrative about the meaning of his kingdom and its implications for his followers (John 18:28–38). Furthermore, there are scattered specific scenes throughout the Gospels concerning the question of whether Jesus' followers had any need to pay the annual temple tax (Matt 17:24–27) or to fulfill their civil obligations to the Roman government (Matt 22:15–22; Mark 12:13–17; Luke 20:20–26). And clearly the most obvious struggle of Jesus within the gospel narratives may be found in the consistent call to ignore the hypocrisy of the scribes and Pharisees in favor of a more righteous observation of the law of God, an observance that explicitly respected the desires of God's kingdom.

The problem with this consistent presentation of the gospel teachings is that we can never be certain with respect to how much of this material was actually drawn from the views of Jesus himself and how much was actually a reflection of the struggles of the early church. Surely there must have been some debate between Jesus and the established religious and civil authorities of his day, whether Jewish or Roman. Otherwise, it is difficult to reconstruct a suitable explanation for the hostility that provoked the ultimate response that led to his crucifixion. At the same time, however, many issues that are related to taxes and questions of the kingdom of God within the Gospels have a secondary feel to them that suggests that the hand of the early church was at work in the construction of the narrative.

We must first focus, then, upon the idea of "kingdom" that seems to stand as a primary identifier of the message of Jesus as it permeates the Synoptic Gospels in general and arises variously in remaining New Testament and noncanonical literature. Significant debate ensues among students of biblical theology at this point, turning primarily upon the decision of whether the kingdom that Jesus envisioned was to be found as a reality of the first-century setting or, instead, was only to be seen in human history at the end of time. In scholarly terms, this is the decision between realized and future eschatology. This is not a debate in which I wish to engage here, except to say that any student's views on the subject ultimately lead to a vision of Jesus' theological message and the direction of his teachings as delivered to his followers.

In other words, if Jesus were "teaching to the moment," as many gospel texts seem to indicate, then much of his concern for his followers undoubtedly would have been directed toward their lifestyles and elements of social interaction. If Jesus were "teaching for the future," as many other gospel passages suggest, then he would have been focused primarily upon questions of faith and preparation for another time in the lives of his believers—that is, a moment that lay in some historical sense beyond the present. The Gospels clearly include both approaches to the views of Jesus (under the presumption that each is authentic). The question, then, is whether our non-gospel sources can illuminate our understanding of this theme apart from the literary presentation of Jesus' life and teachings as found in the Gospels.

EARLY NEW TESTAMENT CANON

The apostle Paul makes some limited use of "kingdom talk" in his known epistles. There is little question that his understanding of the concept is rigidly shaped by traditional Jewish views of kingship, royal power, and authority, and to a large extent by the Hellenistic imagery of those same ideas that had come to dominate the Mediterranean world. A primary question is the extent to which Paul's own views were influenced by the provocative, futuristic eschatology that dominated the early teachings of the church as he attempted to prepare his followers for the immediate end of time. And yet, we must ask whether there actually was some eventual change in his perspective that ultimately repositioned his outlook on what the kingdom meant for contemporary Christians and their lifestyles, such as we see in his letter to the Romans.

Among the clearly authentic letters of Paul, we find that he primarily warns his readers about the dangers of being omitted from the kingdom. The kingdom is characterized by the spiritual qualities of faithfulness that lead to the building of human relationships and not to the satiation of physical needs such as food and drink (Rom 14:17). The kingdom is realized in power, not in idle talk (1 Cor 4:20), and is not to be inherited by the unrighteous or those who act unjustly (1 Cor 6:9–10; Gal 5:21). Nor will it be inherited by "flesh and blood," but only by that which is imperishable (1 Cor 15:50). Otherwise, Paul in one of his earliest letters claims that God calls all people to lead a worthy life in order to enter "the kingdom and glory" (1 Thess 2:12), a kingdom that elsewhere he insists will be handed over to the Father by Christ at the end of time after every rule and authority and power has been destroyed (1 Cor 15:24).[3]

It is this last observation that is most intriguing, the idea that God's kingdom is somehow present within the world and yet a commodity that eventually will be transferred into another realm at the end of human history. Apart from the question of whether this material in 1 Cor 15 is truly an original composition of the apostle or, instead, a theological gem that he has adopted from some secondary source, the fact that it now exists within the epistle suggests that Paul was in sympathy with the concept. There is no similar depiction of the kingdom of God in the New Testament gospels. Even the language of Jesus as he characterizes the nature of his "kingship" before Pilate in John 18 does not progress so far as to offer the specifics of the kingdom's cosmic categories. Instead, the reader is left simply with the understanding that the dominion of Christ supersedes that of the world's temporal powers, whether those powers are manifested by Rome, by the temple authorities, or by some other worldly power.

  The deuteropauline epistles do not help to advance our understanding of kingdom language. Colossians 1:13 observes that the Father has transferred all believers from the kingdom of darkness to the kingdom of the beloved Son,[4] while Eph 5:5 simply repeats the Pauline assertion that sinners will not inherit the kingdom.

Elsewhere in the New Testament we discover an elevation of the language that is associated with the kingdom. The author of Hebrews, borrowing from Ps 44:7 (LXX), states that the kingdom of the Son is portrayed by a scepter of righteousness (Heb 1:8) and that this immovable kingdom that believers receive is worthy of appropriate worship to God through reverence and awe (Heb 12:28). Descriptive adjectives are applied to the kingdom in other contexts. In 2 Peter we find that it is the "eternal kingdom" (2 Pet 1:11), while in 2 Timothy it is the "heavenly kingdom" (2 Tim 4:18). Presumably these terms apply to the same idea of kingdom that has been expressed by Paul and

---

[3] One might also include here Phil 3:20–21, where Paul refers to heaven as that domain from which "we await a Savior, the Lord Jesus Christ," whose power enables him to subject all things to his authority.

[4] James 2:5 has a similar vision, utilizing the concept of "heirs of the kingdom" in a fashion that is likewise reflected by Paul.

elsewhere in the New Testament, especially since there is no particular reason to think otherwise.

This brief survey leaves us with an interesting set of circumstances. Though the early church clearly was aware of kingdom language and used, in some limited sense, the terminology of kingdom talk, what can be known from the canonical documents of the first century about the nature of the kingdom is severely limited.[5] The single exception to this premise is found in the Synoptic Gospels, which seem to share fairly common views on the subject. As noted above, the difficulty in this particular situation is that we remain in a perpetual struggle to understand the extent to which the teachings on the kingdom that appear here are those of Jesus of Nazareth versus the idealized speculation of the early church. To some greatly limited extent we can identify the secondary traits of ancient Christian speculation as we compare specific gospel perspectives. But for the most part, we remain uncertain about the originality of this vision of God's kingdom and, more important for our review here, about the question of loyalty to the kingdom that is demanded of each believer in the faith.

THE KINGDOM OF GOD (HEAVEN) IN THE SYNOPTICS

The Synoptic Gospel vision of the kingdom of God[6] seems to hinge on two factors. The first is the question of the manner in which the kingdom is initiated; the second is the issue of the final completion of

---

[5] Other instances of kingdom language may be found variously throughout the Acts of the Apostles and Revelation, though these references are hardly instructive on the nature of the kingdom itself.

[6] Of course, in the Gospel of Matthew the primary term is "kingdom of (the) heaven(s)." The actual phrase "kingdom of God" is used only four times, and it is uncertain whether the author intends two different concepts by using the two phrases, is dependent upon the reception of different sources for the materials in question, or simply has been inconsistent in presenting the materials. I will not review or critique the issue here, since it is beyond the scope of our consideration, except to say that most scholars attribute the change to the author of Matthew as an indication of the Jewishness of that writer. This has always intrigued me as somewhat disingenuous because Jesus himself was Jewish and presumably would have been as likely to have preferred such a phrase in his teachings. Consequently, the author of the Gospel of Mark (followed somewhat blindly by the author of the Gospel of Luke in this case) may have altered

the kingdom. The history of Christian interpretation behind the so-called kingdom parables has a decided tendency to focus on the outcome of the kingdom, however that may be interpreted. And yet, it seems highly likely that the parables themselves most often were intended to challenge the common first-century Jewish belief that the kingdom would appear in a dynamic, otherworldly way, an appearance that would be easily recognized by all the nations. Furthermore, believers typically assumed that this appearance of the kingdom would be a time in which the righteous and faithful among God's people would be rewarded in splendor for their sufferings, while the non-Jews and unrighteous would be punished. The characterization of that punishment varies widely throughout the literature, but always it is offered under the assumption that there was to be some separation from God (and hence from the kingdom itself).

Thus it is that we find consistent images throughout the Synoptic Gospels that run counter to this traditional view. The onset of the kingdom is compared with the small and unassuming and common elements of daily living. The kingdom comes into existence like a grain of mustard seed, the smallest of seeds (Matt 13:31–32; Mark 4:31–32), like a woman who hides leaven in measures of dough (Matt 13:33; Luke 13:20–21), like treasure that is only accidentally discovered on someone else's property (Matt 13:44). The nature of the kingdom is that it arrives unexpectedly, is often intermingled with the profane and unacceptable and thus ultimately must be sorted out by God alone (Mark 4:26–29; Matt 13:24–30), is typified by mercy and available to all who seek to find it in good faith, and is distinctive in its spiritual elements from the kingdom of this world. Most important, we read in the literature that one must receive the kingdom of God like a child (Matt 18:1–5; 19:13–15; Mark 9:33–37; 10:13–16; Luke 9:46–48; 18:15–17), that one may find the kingdom as a present reality (Mark 1:14–15), and that the trappings of worldly glory and success are not to be equated with the elements of the kingdom (Matt 19:16–22; Mark 10:17–31; Luke 18:18–23).

Despite the various descriptions offered of the kingdom in the Gospels, the single guiding principle for the idea is in essence Eastern in nature, at least by the standards of ancient Mediterranean societies. In other words, the kingdom of God is essentially a realm in which the

_____

the phrase to "kingdom of God" in order to meet the conceptual needs of a less Jewish audience.

single, true divinity of the universe is the ruler of all creation, and everything that has been created (humans included) by that divinity stands in subjection to that authority. It is certainly true that the New Testament offers optional visions of competing realms of power that are identified with the imagery of darkness, the evil one, worldly cares and concerns, and so on. However, these realms are temporary in nature and ultimately must fall to the ultimate glory of God's kingdom, as attested by Paul in 1 Cor 15 (see above). The resulting varieties of a dualistic cosmology that arise throughout the contemporary literature of the period have ancient roots and extend through patristic and medieval authors down to the present day. But the ultimate Christian vision insists that all final power is God's alone, envisioned through the glorification of the Messiah and the kingdom that is ruled by that reality.

What, then, is the situation of humanity? For those who respect the authority of Christ and the dominion of God "the Father" and who submit in obedience to that power, the blessings of the kingdom are theirs. As Paul so clearly assumes when he explains his gospel message to the various churches to which he writes, all of humanity must serve somebody or something. One is either a slave to the temporal powers of this world or a slave to Christ. There is no such thing as a "free person" who possesses self-autonomy and sole responsibility for his or her actions in the sense that modern humanity envisions, especially as seen through the eyes of Western culture.

Indeed, the Gospels themselves suggest this vision as well. Even Jesus is tempted by the power of Satan to switch obedience away from God, thus to inherit the worldly trappings of a temporal kingdom and to forsake any portion of God's eternal realm (see Matt 4:1–11; Luke 4:1–13). So it is that in a single setting the reader can see the Messiah himself at a point of decision, a choice between "entering into/ remaining within" the boundaries of a true kingdom or, instead, rejecting that authority for a lesser world. Jesus of Nazareth ultimately chooses to take his role in the true kingdom as the Son of God and, depending upon the theological perspective of subsequent early Christian authors, as the intermediary between humanity and God or, instead, as the judge of humanity who sits in the seat of God's divine power.

The choice for humanity is basically the same, though the role is essentially different. In other words, humanity chooses between life and destruction, a choice that is sometimes characterized as the selection between "two ways"[7] and reflects the option either for or against God's kingdom. At the same time, however, this choice contains a basic conceptual tension. On the one hand, the choice for life is in many respects a selection of personal glorification. This is illustrated by those texts that endorse the ancient idea of the so-called messianic banquet in which all of the faithful who are worthy of God's kingdom will share in the glorious bounty of divine grace, regardless of their status (Luke 14:12–24). The key idea here is that the kingdom is a setting of celebration and revelry that comes through an association with God's presence. On the other hand, the choice is also a decision to submit to God as a servant or slave. To be a part of God's kingdom is to turn one's will over to the Creator of the universe in a unified expression of subservience. There is no legitimate expression of desire except for that which matches God's own will. There is no true quest for personal satisfaction except for that which fulfills God's own intention.

The Gospel of John expresses a concerted attempt to address this "glorification-servitude" tension in the final teachings that Jesus offers to his disciples in chapters 14–17. These chapters were largely constructed to offer assurance to an early faith community for whom this particular gospel was written, a collection of early Christian believers who undoubtedly found themselves at a time of crisis. As John's Gospel suggests, the focal witness of the community was threatened, either through the anticipated death of the community's primary link to the life of Jesus (John 20:29–31) or even after that death had actually occurred (John 21:21–24). The rejection that the church experienced by the synagogue at the end of the first century is patently evident in the Johannine community's own disavowal of Judaism that permeates the entire narrative. In chapters 14–17 all believers are reassured with the instructions that they are not to be troubled (John 14:1), and that Jesus, even though no longer active in their midst as a historical personage, is present with them in the form of the Holy Spirit, who brings peace (John 14:16–17, 26). But this reassurance and peace are available only for those who respond in obedience: "If you love me, you will keep my commandments" (John 14:15). And the ultimate instruction is the commandment of love: "This is my commandment, that you love one another as I have loved you" (John 15:12).

---

[7] See Matt 7:13; *Did.* 1.1; *Barn.* 18.1.

For the author of the Gospel of John, then, we have a wedding of these two ideas of glorification and servitude through the medium of love. In the same way that the Son is glorified through his service to the Father by his sacrificial dying, the followers of the Son are glorified through their service to one another through their sacrificial living and, if necessary, death. As with Paul's own perception, there is no freedom within the kingdom of God here for anyone to act according to personal, selfish desires. Instead, all members of the kingdom are free simply to act according to the needs of others and, ultimately, according to the will of God. To be a part of God's kingdom is to be qualified to receive the glorification of service for the Creator of the universe, at least according to the general New Testament vision.

THE CONCEPT OF CITIZENSHIP

Against this somewhat Eastern view of kingdom and authority within the New Testament, one finds only a minimal glimpse into the more Western perspective of what it means to be the citizen of a larger community. In Acts 22 one discovers that Paul himself was a Roman citizen by birth, which carried certain legal privileges and rights for those who lived within the empire. Such citizenship could also be purchased, of course, and thus many of Rome's citizens ultimately rose to positions of honor and importance out of their original places of servitude or displacement (Acts 22:28–29).

But for the most part, there is no glorification of the idea of citizenship in the New Testament, nor is there any argument for the rights and responsibilities that such an image might hold for the followers of Christ. In the Gospels, all who live in service to Rome, such as Herod Antipas, are false rulers and are seen as vassals of a power that competes against God. The Gospels depict Jesus as essentially hostile to such powers, though the implication of that hostility is left to the hearer. No person can serve two masters (Matt 6:24; Luke 16:13), and authority comes from God alone (John 19:10–11). Yet, specific commands are given that indicate how the world distracts human allegiances away from God's kingdom. On the one hand, when Jesus was questioned about allegiances to civil authorities in the form of taxes paid to Caesar, we hear him saying, "Render to Caesar the things that are Caesar's, and to God the things that are God's" (Mark 12:13–17 pars.). The debate that is preserved here is designed specifically to leave the hearer with a basic choice to make between authorities: the kingship of God or the rule of Caesar. The choice is not between sacred and secular powers, as might be expected, but between the true God and the emperor cult of Rome.[8] To be a citizen of Rome, then, was not necessarily a claim to complete freedom, but rather an admission of servitude to a cultic power.[9]

On the other hand, when confronted with the question of paying temple taxes, Jesus and his followers are found to be the victims of a religious conundrum (Matt 17:24–27). It was a cultic duty for Jews to support the work and institution of the temple according to the dictates of religious obligation. At the same time, the teachings of Jesus suggest that all believers of the Messiah are justified through their obedient faith to God alone, not to those institutions that claim divine privilege while abusing their inherited powers. In this particular case the solution is once more disingenuous. It is only servants and workers of the empire, not royal family members, who pay tolls and taxes to human kings. So it is that God's spiritual family is not obligated to pay for the support of God's cultic servants. And yet, for the sake of good form, Jesus provides for such payment through the miracle of God's own grace: the provision of a shekel from the mouth of a caught fish to serve as payment for the temple tax.

This last story is particularly significant in our exploration of the notion of citizenship within the early church because it illustrates how Christianity's early authors came to understand the concept. Citizenship was not so much an expression of individual rights but of family privilege. This may be illustrated primarily by a single instance of the phrase "fellow citizens of the saints" (συμπολῖται τῶν ἁγίων) that appears within the New Testament at Eph 2:19. As the author of that epistle attests, those who were once wanderers and strangers in the world have become both fellow citizens and "members of God's household" (οἰκεῖοι τοῦ θεοῦ). As believers, they are to be counted among the rightful participants of God's gathered communities of the faithful,

---

[8] For the influence of the emperor cult see Robin Lane Fox, *Pagans and Christians* (San Francisco: Harper & Row, 1986), 39–41.

[9] We must assume here that the so-called "mark of the beast" that is raised in the book of Revelation is in some sense seen as a similar choice; see Rev 13:1–18.

the saints. Yet, also as believers, they are to be numbered as members of God's family. This is not the typical expression of citizenship that dominates classic Greek thought of the city-state society, nor is it typical of modern Western views of nationalism. Instead, it is an understanding of traditional kingship models by which a ruler possesses all power within the realm, and the members of the royal family subsequently are the heirs of both power and privilege. They are in essence "citizens" of family lineage, not "citizens" of the kingdom.

This idea ultimately seems strange in the light of traditional Western views of the rights and responsibilities that are incumbent upon those who live within the borders and boundaries of individual nations.[10] Indeed, as is suggested by Paul's situation in Acts 28, to be a part of the empire is to carry certain privileges that may not be violated by others within the realm. But we must observe that even within the setting of Acts, it is not Paul who lays specific claim to those privileges. On the contrary, it is his captor who recognizes the threat to his own security should he be caught in violation of another person's citizenship.

In his own writing Paul recognizes the power and authority of the empire as he instructs the Romans to "be subject to the governing authorities," for they rule under the divine approval of God (Rom 13:1–7). But we must remember that his audience was living at the center of Rome's jurisdiction, in the capital city itself, and that the church's existence in such close proximity to the emperor was perhaps directly threatened by its immediate response to questions of civil law and authority. Indeed, at no point in his instruction does Paul suggest that the church in Rome is in some sense composed of citizens of the empire who should be servants of the emperor. Quite the contrary! The church is a community that is responsible to God and thus to God's servants, the local civil authorities.[11] To the extent that Christians observe the daily laws of the empire, they are fulfilling their obligations to justice and right living. They are in support of a social structure that is acceptable to God. This is reinforced by the instructions that Paul offers immediately after his comments on governing authorities: all Christians

---

[10] Though it continues to be true that a similar idea persists among the royal houses of European monarchies.

[11] For a survey of how Christianity's reaction to Paul's teachings influenced the relationship between Rome and the church through the second century see Robert M. Grant, *Augustus to Constantine* (San Francisco: Harper & Row, 1990), 77–96.

should love one another, which itself is the fulfillment of the law (Rom 13:8–10). In this light, then, we find that Paul has suggested the very solution to the tension of glorification and servitude that ultimately is proposed by the author of the Gospel of John. And in both Romans and John the resolution is found in the concept of unity among the members of God's family.[12]

CITIZENSHIP IN THE APOSTOLIC FATHERS

The apostolic fathers offer a variety of views with respect to the New Testament concept of kingdom that is found in the Gospels and is reflected by the writings of Paul. In addition, there is a significant advance upon the idea of citizenship within this same collection of texts that propels the concept toward the view that ultimately became a linchpin for the unification of church and state under the emperors Constantine and Theodosius I in subsequent centuries.[13]

The *Didache,* one of the earliest writings among the apostolic fathers, makes some limited use of the idea of kingdom. But our author's witness is not particularly helpful, since the relevant passages are offered primarily in liturgical contexts. In *Did.* 8.2 the word "kingdom" appears in the so-called Lord's Prayer, which is preserved by the Didachist in a form virtually identical to that which is found in Matt 6:9–13. In *Did.* 9.4 there is a petition that the church may be collected from the ends of the earth into God's kingdom, a petition preserved as a prayer to be said over the broken bread within a liturgical moment. And as a final prayer in conclusion of the sharing of the holy meal, the "Lord" is petitioned once more to remember the church and gather it into the kingdom (*Did.* 10.5). Unlike many of the images that will be discussed below, it is difficult to assign any specific description of the kingdom of the Lord as understood by the Didachist apart from a

---

[12] This idea certainly is not unique to Paul, as it is likewise reflected in 1 Pet 2:17, where the hearer is enjoined to "fear God [and] honor the emperor." It is perhaps all the more interesting that, after this comment, the author of 1 Peter follows with an exposition of the "household codes" on the relationship between servants and masters, and between wives and husbands (see 1 Pet 2:18–3:7).

[13] See Agnes Cunningham, ed., *The Early Church and the State* (trans. M. Di Maio and A. Cunningham; Philadelphia: Fortress, 1982).

liturgical context in which the desires of the author are that the church be rescued from evil and drawn into God's realm of influence and protection.

The case is somewhat different with two of our other early writings, *Barnabas* and *1 Clement*, both of which offer several different usages of the idea of kingdom. In *Barn.* 4.4 we find a citation of Dan 7:24 that refers to ten kingdoms that will reign on earth, an example of earthly power that exists within a broad historical context.[14] Against this image we find a call to avoid being thrust out "from the kingdom of the Lord" (ἀπὸ τῆς βασιλείας τοῦ κυρίου), a kingdom that clearly stands in opposition to the power of evil (*Barn.* 4.13). As is typical of the general perspective of the larger tractate, the author of *Barnabas* evokes a sharp dualistic contrast here that pits the powers of evil, worldly kingdoms, against God's divine sovereignty. The hearer is warned to remain on guard because these are the last days, the age of lawlessness, which demand a true fear of God, a deep spirituality, and obedience to God's commandments in order to undertake deeds of righteousness (*Barn.* 4.9b–14). In many respects, this same type of perspective and dualistic contrast resonates throughout 1 John, and even more distinctively in the book of Revelation, of course. The Lord is once more called "king" in *Barn.* 11.5 (based upon a reading of Isa 33:16–18) as the author attempts to explain how baptism was foreshadowed within the Jewish Scriptures. And in *Barn.* 8.6–7 the author refers to the "kingdom of Jesus" (ἡ βασιλεία Ἰησοῦ) as he attempts to explain the significance of the cross in the light of ancient patriarchal images that appear throughout the Pentateuch.

Other than these few examples, the author of *Barnabas* does not seem to be particularly interested to explain the nature of the Lord's kingdom. The assumptions of the text are that the Christians of the late first and early second centuries lived within the last days, a time when the forces of good and evil were seen to be in struggle for the control of history. The author offers that all true believers are duty-bound to resist evil in this process and are beckoned to understand the imagery of the Jewish Scriptures as the tools by which to recognize the authority of the actions of Christ as essential for the salvation of the church. There is an essential eschatology at work here that is highly reflective of Paul's

---

[14] See also *Barn.* 12.11, based upon Isa 45:1.

own views, and undoubtedly of most other early Christians around
him, that continued to permeate the ideas of later theologians. The attempts of the New Testament gospels to explain the ways in which
the kingdom of God is alive and present in daily living are not to be
found. As with Paul's early writings in 1 Thessalonians and Galatians,
immediacy is the key![15]

Additional images of similar nature may be found in *1 Clement.* In
1 Clem. 50.3, for example, the author anticipates that time when those
who have been perfected in love and deserve a place among God's holy
ones "will be revealed in the arrival of the kingdom of Christ" (οἱ
φανερωθήσονται ἐν τῇ ἐπισκοπῇ τῆς βασιλείας τοῦ Χριστοῦ).
Unlike the situation in *Barnabas,* this is offered more as a promise of
hope for the future than as a depiction of the present struggles between
good and evil. At the same time, however, there is a clear expression
that the special kingdom of God over which Christ rules stands in opposition to the historical ages of earth's temporal kingdom. A similar
perspective is found previously in *1 Clem.* 42.3, a text in which the author recalls the authority of the apostles of Jesus Christ who received
the gospel message and were sent forth, full of faith in the resurrection
and with the news that the "kingdom of God" was soon to come. It was
from these apostolic efforts, according to our author, that bishops and
deacons were established in righteousness and upon whose authority
the rightful succession of authority must be perpetuated among the
churches. In neither of these cases, however, do we discover what the
specific role of the believer should be, nor what responsibilities and
rights the faithful have with respect to participation in the kingdom.

As we move about within the text of *1 Clement,* we find in the famous concluding prayer (see *1 Clem.* 59.2–61.3) a slightly different use
of the kingdom concept that is extremely intriguing in the light of
Paul's own exhortations to the Romans with reference to respect for
civil authorities. After an acknowledgment that the Lord is indeed the
Creator of the earth and has revealed the eternal structure of the cos-
mos, there is a call for God to provide peace and harmony to the
world's people so that "we" in turn might be obedient both to God "and

[15] As an aside, it does not seem that the apostolic fathers support the sub-
sequent rise of millennial thought among their eschatological views; see
Charles E. Hill, *Regnum Caelorum: Patterns of Millennial Thought in Early
Christianity* (2d ed.; Grand Rapids: Eerdmans, 2001), 75–103, 133–35.

to our earthly rulers and governors" (τοῖς τε ἄρχουσιν καὶ ἡγουμέ
νοις ἡμῶν ἐπὶ τῆς γῆς) (1 Clem. 60.4). The power and authority of
these human agencies is granted directly by God. Thus, to be subject to
the ruling authorities is to provide glory and honor to God as well
(1 Clem. 61.1–3). In many respects, this certainly is a direct reflection of
Paul's previously stated understanding in Rom 13:1–7, a teaching that
seems to have become popular with the Roman church and is offered
here as the expression of the type of harmony that is possible between
church and state when Christians envision that God's kingdom may be
achieved through both institutions. Of course, the primary assumption
is that God's eternal kingdom takes precedence over the world's temporal kingdom, and that the will of God may be worked through human
institutions as well as through divine means. Presumably, this is the
same assumption that the author of the Gospel of John holds when we
hear Jesus explain to Pilate that his kingdom lies beyond the reach of
Rome. The implication of this explanation is that, while Rome has no
control over the kingdom of God, the power of God has full jurisdiction over the movements of Rome.

In addition to these three texts, we also find that the bishop Ignatius
makes occasional use of kingdom talk in his own letters. In Ign. Eph. 19.3
he observes that with Mary's giving birth to the Messiah, all magic and
wickedness disappeared, and that the "ancient kingdom" (παλαιὰ
βασιλεία) was destroyed. This so-called ancient kingdom, which once
more clearly represents the power of evil within the world, is yet again
brought into contrast with the kingdom of God. In Ign. Eph. 16.1
Ignatius brings the discussion immediately into the Pauline perspective
with his comments that those who corrupt households with adultery will
not inherit God's kingdom. So too, those who create schism within the
community and are followers of such persons likewise will not enter the
kingdom, according to Ign. Phld. 3.3. It seems that Ignatius has drawn
both of these observations from Paul's instructions to the Corinthians, as
found in 1 Cor 6:9–10. And thus we find that, typical of Ignatius, he is
highly dependent upon his hero Paul for much of the language, imagery,
and theology that underlies his own understanding of what it means to
be a Christian. Unfortunately, much again like Paul, Ignatius does not
give us much material by which to define what the kingdom is or what
the role of the responsible Christian is within God's realm. Instead, he is
much more prepared to identify those shortcomings and failings that
would keep someone outside of the kingdom.

The situation of the bishop Polycarp is somewhat similar to that of Ignatius. In his letter to the Philippians he quotes from the Matthean and Lukan traditions that those who are poor and who are persecuted for the sake of righteousness will inherit the kingdom of God (Pol. *Phil.* 2.3).[16] But, like Ignatius, he returns to Paul in order to reject fornicators, male prostitutes, and homosexuals as unworthy of the kingdom (Pol. *Phil.* 5.3).[17] And so, Polycarp does little to advance our understanding of the Christian's role in the kingdom of God at all beyond the Gospels or the insights of Paul and Ignatius.[18]

Four texts remain among the apostolic fathers that must be considered in the question of kingdom and citizenship: the *Martyrdom of Polycarp,* the *Shepherd of Hermas, 2 Clement,* and the *Epistle to Diognetus.* Though some debate remains in this matter, it appears that all four are especially noteworthy for our discussion by virtue of their late date within the corpus of literature. In certain instances there is little to be added to the conversation, but in others the situation is quite different.

We turn first to the *Martyrdom.* References to the kingdom here are not found so much on the lips of Polycarp himself, but rather are offered by those who have composed the work and subsequently forwarded it to the church at Philomelium. Thus we find a closing blessing in *Mart. Pol.* 20.2 with respect to God's ability to bring all believers "into his heavenly kingdom" (εἰς τὴν ἐπουράνιον αὐτοῦ βασιλείαν) by grace and bounty. Afterward, in *Mart. Pol.* 22.1, a closing farewell is offered with the wish that all might follow Polycarp in order to enter "into the kingdom of Jesus Christ" (ἐν τῇ βασιλείᾳ Ἰησοῦ Χριστοῦ). Finally, in *Mart. Pol.* 22.3, we read the closing testimony of the scribe Pionius, who claims to have copied our known edition of the text and asks that he might be gathered "into the heavenly kingdom" (εἰς τὴν οὐράνιον βασιλείαν) by the Lord Jesus Christ.

These three witnesses are curious in that, even though they are in close proximity within the text, they clearly use different modifiers to describe the nature of the kingdom: two different words identify the

---

[16] See Luke 6:20; Matt 5:10 (cf. Matt 5:3).

[17] Again see 1 Cor 6:9–10.

[18] In Pol. *Phil.* 5.2 Polycarp makes a reference to becoming citizens worthy of Christ that would appear to be a clear reflection of Phil 1:27, in which Paul calls for a lifestyle that is worthy of the gospel of Christ.

kingdom as "heavenly," and one attributes the kingdom to Jesus Christ specifically. It is not presumed here that these phrases make reference to three different realities, even though those who would attribute the distinctions to the presence of different editors at work at different periods of time might make such an argument. Instead, however the kingdom is to be described and understood through these references, in each case the concept is of some future glory to which the believing church ascribes, a reality beyond the boundaries of common human experience. In no instance can we identify this idea specifically with the views of Polycarp himself, at least as a direct attribution of his role in the martyrdom sequence. And, furthermore, no comment is offered about the nature of this kingdom or the role of Christians within it.

Our second text is that of *2 Clement*. Here the situation is somewhat more interesting. In *2 Clem*. 12.2 our author makes reference to a situation in which Jesus, when asked about the timing of the coming kingdom, responded that it would occur "when the two become one, the outside like the inside, the male with the female, neither male nor female." Parallels to this saying may be found in the *Gospel of Thomas*[19] and in the writings of Clement of Alexandria.[20] And though the specific meaning of the teaching remains somewhat unclear in each instance despite the lengthy explanation of the author of *2 Clement*, two elements are worthy of note. First, under the assumption that the suggestion of the saying is actually possible, at least for individual believers, the kingdom of the Father (*2 Clem*. 12.6) may be envisioned as a human reality on earth, not simply as a future "heavenly" goal to be achieved through the magnanimous grace of God alone. Second, there are specific guidelines by which the kingdom may be achieved, defined in some sense by the ability of the faithful to blur the distinctions of sexuality and bodily partition that keeps believers separate from one another.

To make such a statement offers a significant advance beyond the Pauline commandments to avoid works of immorality and to accept actions of righteousness as the parameters by which to enter and enjoy God's kingdom. Indeed, it may in fact be true that Paul offered such comments to his readers merely as the surface distinctions of a deeper

---

[19] *Gos. Thom.* 22.
[20] Clement, *Strom.* 3.13.92. Clement attributes the saying to the *Gospel of the Egyptians*.

understanding of the reality of what it means to exist within God's realm. But the author of *2 Clement* expresses this reality in a much more explicit way and indicates that existence in the kingdom is better imagined as a transformational experience than as a position of honored service. There is more of a feeling of reformed vision than of reformed obedience in this saying.

Elsewhere, *2 Clement* speaks more of the kingdom as a future reality beyond the experience of worldly things. In *2 Clem.* 5.5 we hear that the kingdom will be a "resting place" (ἀνάπαυσις), and in *2 Clem.* 12.1 that we should wait for its coming. This interpretation does not seem to be as clear in two other passages. In *2 Clem.* 9.6 we hear that love of one's neighbor is a means by which to enter God's kingdom, and in *2 Clem.* 11.7 we are told that a lifestyle of patient righteousness leads to the same goal. In both cases one might well argue that a person may obtain the kingdom through human action. However, it is much more likely that our author once again has a future vision of the kingdom in mind. What is of particular interest here is that *2 Clement* seems to return to an understanding of the kingdom that is much more reflective of the general New Testament vision. In other words, it is through the believer's righteous obedience to the commandments of God as attested by the words of Jesus' own teachings that entry to the kingdom is obtained and life in that reality is experienced. Again, the "glorification-servitude" model seems to be at work in this understanding, though the overt expression of both elements—personal glory and individual service to God—seems to have been watered down. This general shift in emphasis appears to characterize the evolution of subsequent teachings about the kingdom of God that are associated with the later perspectives of Augustine and medieval theologians. It certainly is true of church teaching subsequent to that time, especially in the West, where individual rights and responsibilities eventually came to shape the typical Christian's expectations of future reward in eternal glory.

We now turn to the *Shepherd of Hermas*. It is a curious element of the *Shepherd* that the only expressed concern that the author seems to have for the kingdom appears in a single parable: *Similitude* 9. This so-called parable is one of the longest of the genre within the *Shepherd* and finds its focus in two primary images: the mountains and the tower. In essence, the parable is an extended allegorical interpretation of how the church (presented here in the form of a tower) is carefully constructed through time by the correct selection of stones from among the surrounding mountains so that ultimately it reaches its completion through the direction of Christ. It is only in this context that we find the *Shepherd's* use of kingdom imagery, which clearly equates the reign of God with the existence of the church. According to the parables, the stones of the mountains are carefully quarried and shaped by the holy spirits of God (represented here as virgins), who, clothed in the virtues of the kingdom, diligently labor to shape each stone that is appropriate to fit into the construction of the tower.

The author of the *Shepherd* appeals to typical kingdom language in chapters 89–90, 92–93, and 97 of the parable to indicate exactly which kind of stone (i.e., person) is suitable for entry into the tower (i.e., the kingdom). Those stones that are to be saved enter the kingdom of God through the new door that is included there, though even some of those who enter are rejected because they have not received the name of the Son (*Herm.* 89.3–4). In the midst of this process we discover that no person can enter the kingdom except through the name of God's Son (*Herm.* 89.5, 8). But even at that, it is insufficient to have received the name alone. Each person must likewise be clothed in the power of the Son of God that is given by the holy spirits (i.e., the virgins who shape the stones for the tower [see *Herm.* 90.2]). And it is their own names that a person must also bear—that is, the names of faith, self-control, power, patience, sincerity, innocence, purity, cheerfulness, truth, understanding, harmony, and love (*Herm.* 92.2). These names are offered in contrast to those virgins whose names are unbelief, self-indulgence, disobedience, deceit, grief, evil, licentiousness, ill-temper, falsehood, foolishness, slander, and hatred (*Herm.* 92.3), names that enable a "servant of God" to see the kingdom of God but not to enter it.

Furthermore, before the stones may enter into the construction of the tower through the door, first they must be brought through the waters of the lake that surround the building. This process represents the ritual of baptism, by which those who once were dead may now become alive and through which the seal of God's Son may be placed upon them so that they might enter the kingdom (*Herm.* 93.2–4). Thus it is that those who would be saved by the church—that is, the stones that are to be included within the walls of the tower—first must proceed through the waters of baptism, enter through the new door of Christ, be given the names of the Son of God and the holy spirits that serve as the seal of salvation, and be clothed with the garments of righteousness that only the spirits can provide. Only after all of this has occurred can anyone hope to enter the kingdom of God.

This characterization of the tower that the holy spirits, or virgins, construct is an interesting image that raises a number of questions about the evolution of the kingdom of God concept within early Christian theology. First, we see in this parable a clear understanding that the kingdom is the same as the institutional church. In Paul's own theology this is not stated so explicitly. Indeed, Paul argues that those who form the living, active church are themselves serving as the body of Christ. In the deuteropauline materials of Colossians, Ephesians, and the Pastoral Epistles we find a slightly different understanding whereby Christ now stands as the "head" of that body, while all other Christians serve the head in the role of the torso. But now in the *Shepherd* it is clear that those believers who come to form the body of the church form a monument to faith that itself stands as a structure that is the responsibility of the holy spirits, constructed to the glory of Christ through its existence as the kingdom of God. This is perhaps a considerably different perspective than that which Paul originally endorsed, namely, the idea that Christians served God as the body of Christ while in anticipation of a future coming of the kingdom of God.

At the same time, however, we find within the *Shepherd* a basic return to the arguments of Paul that insist upon the elements of righteousness as essential to one's entry into the kingdom (chapters 89–95). This continues to be a common trait among the apostolic fathers, as seen above, from its beginnings within New Testament faith right down through the mid-to-late second century. There is a universal insistence here that the appropriate participant in God's kingdom is someone who also bears the specific characteristics of righteousness. And as the *Shepherd* so aptly indicates, it is the holy spirits who give these traits (or garments) in order that adherents to the kingdom may be suitable for service (*Herm.* 90.5–9).

There is only a short step in the logic of this process between the acknowledgment that Christians who expect to be a part of the kingdom must be appropriate in character and the later argument that those who expect to serve in the church must be worthy to be anointed (i.e., ordained) in the eyes of God. In other words, the *Shepherd* stands among our earliest witnesses to early ecclesiastical attempts to define the standards by which priesthood and ecclesiastical offices should be determined. In this respect, the *Shepherd* offers some parallel to similar attempts within the Pastoral Epistles, 1 Peter, and the *Didache* to set guidelines for church leadership and appropriate lifestyle by employment of the so-called household codes. Yet, the *Shepherd* does not retreat to such well-recognized, ancient rules of behavior, which are based to a large extent upon the *paterfamilias* code. Instead, the *Shepherd* selects the approach of traditional virtue-vice lists, combining this particular standard with the sacrament of baptism and its imagery of the seal of confirmation as an approach to acceptability.

Finally, though it may indeed be accurate to say that the particular understanding of the kingdom of God that appears in *Similitude* 9 is assumed by the author of the *Shepherd* to hold true for the extended argument of the larger writing as well, the actual use of kingdom language seems to be restricted to this single segment. Are we then to presume that our writer, acting more as an editor and compiler than as a true author in this particular case, has incorporated the foundational perspective of some special source into the *Shepherd* here? In other words, we might question whether the view of the kingdom that is preserved in this parable may in fact have come from an older interpretation that either was well-understood and presumed in the church of Rome from ancient days or, instead, represented a broader point of view from around the Mediterranean. In either case, it is clear that the *Shepherd* offers some significant advancement upon the concept of kingdom suggested among our New Testament authors. Specifically, we find here that the notion of service clearly is wedded with the necessity of appropriate character, that the qualifications of entry into the kingdom are distinctly associated with specific sacramental rites, and that the right to stand in God's presence is associated with the work of the holy spirits and inclusion into the institutional church.

What is particularly interesting with respect to the concept of the kingdom of God that the *Shepherd* endorses, especially in the light of comments made by Paul in his letter to the Romans and in *1 Clement* itself, is the omission of any talk about the role of civil authorities who act under divine direction and guidance. If we are to place the *Shepherd* within the aegis of the city of Rome, then this seems to be a particularly important omission. Indeed, there is nothing in the language of the *Shepherd* to suggest any special concern for secular authority at all. In order to address this situation, we must turn to the *Epistle to Diognetus,* which offers language that seems to speak to this very question.

The *Epistle to Diognetus* is appropriately offered as the last text for consideration here for three reasons. First, it may well be the most recent of writings between the New Testament and apostolic fathers. In that respect, we would hope to see some development of thought with reference to questions about the role of Christians within the realm of God. Second, there is some specific, if limited, consideration of the concept of the kingdom of God within the text, thus indicating that the idea retained prominence within the theology of the mid-to-late second century. Third, our author moves the discussion forward with an additional consideration of the role of citizenship, an idea that eventually came to form a primary axis by which later theologians defined the role of Christians within God's reign, sometimes as a function of the civil authority under the so-called Christian emperors and feudal kings of medieval Europe and sometimes in opposition to civil authority in the subsequent years of Renaissance thought and post-Enlightenment nationalism.

The *Epistle of Diognetus,* which is the only true apology preserved among the apostolic fathers, is by definition directed to persons in political authority. If one accepts the name "Diognetus" as a genuine reference to an authentic historical individual, then we may place the location of that authority within a very specific setting. If, on the other hand, we are to assume that the name merely represents a straw character of literary construction that serves as a target for the author's argument, then we may argue that the text was intended to be read by a variety of people as a defense of ancient Christian values. In this second instance, the audience would not necessarily be restricted, but could conceivably include government officials.[21]

In the middle of the text (chapter 9) the author offers an explanation of the plan of God by which salvation for humanity was achieved. The focal point is the argument that God gave up the Son as a "ransom" (λύτρον) for the sins of humanity (*Diogn.* 9.2). God foresaw the need for this redemption as part of the divine plan. Indeed, as our author states, in the former time humanity was permitted to indulge in undisciplined impulses, in all manner of unrighteousness. The result was

---

[21] See the discussion by Robert M. Grant, *Greek Apologists of the Second Century* (Philadelphia: Westminster, 1988), 178–79.

humanity's clear demonstration of its inability to enter the kingdom of
God of its own accord (*Diogn.* 9.1).[22] Hence, it was necessary for God in
divine mercy and holy righteousness to make it possible, through the
death of the Son, for humanity to enter the kingdom. In essence, by virtue of its own unrighteous nature, humanity is incapable of entering
the kingdom. It appears that access to the divine realm is available only
through the holy activity of God, a process that humanity cannot ever
hope to imitate.

Within the text of *Diognetus,* and prior to this explanation of the
divine plan for human salvation in chapter 9, our author offers a description of Christians as they live within the common cities of the
Roman Empire (chapter 5). They are not easily recognized as different
from others who live either in Greek or in barbarian cities (a note presumably directed either toward contemporary Jews or extravagant cults
of an Egyptian or Eastern nature). And yet, they maintain their own
"citizenship" (πολιτεία) (*Diogn.* 5.4) in diverse countries, participat-
ing as "citizens" (πολίτης) (*Diogn.* 5.5) of those countries but living as
aliens and foreigners within them. They marry and have children, obey
established laws, share possessions with others and, though poor themselves, make everyone else rich. They are slandered and assaulted, persecuted and hated. Indeed, though they act as citizens of the earth (the
empire?), their true citizenship is in heaven (*Diogn.* 5.9).[23]

This is especially remarkable language, particularly in the light of
what our author intends to say about the presence of Christians as they
live and move within the cities of the empire. On the one hand, our author argues in chapter 9 that the kingdom of God has been made available to all humanity through the righteousness of the divine plan alone,
not through any particular righteousness that has been expressed by individuals; on the other hand, there is an acknowledgment that Christians are in fact "citizens" of this kingdom now. Specifically, their
"citizenship is in heaven" (ἐν οὐρανῷ πολιτεύονται) (*Diogn.* 5.9),
which is a realm of divine influence that clearly is already at work
within the world. As our author states somewhat later, God lives in
heaven, and believers will come to understand the nature of the true life
in heaven when physical death on earth is despised and the true death

---

[22] In anticipation of Augustine's theological opposition to the views of
Pelagius.

[23] Again in anticipation of Augustine's idea of "two kingdoms."

of the eternal flames of punishment is feared (*Diogn.* 10.7–8). The real
death that is to be feared certainly is a future threat. The real life that is
to be lived, however, is likewise clearly a present reality. In this sense,
then, Christians by nature hold dual citizenship. They are participants
in the life of earthly nations, and they are citizens in the life of the heavenly kingdom on earth.[24]

This matter of "dual citizenship" directs us back to two texts that
we already have discussed with respect to the question of the kingdom
of God: *1 Clement* and Polycarp's letter to the Philippians. In the first
writing, *1 Clement,* our author is concerned that the church at Corinth
conduct itself according to the standards of what is appropriate within
the tradition of God's authority. In this particular instance there is a
problem with upstarts within the community who have forcibly (?)
taken the place of their elders, members of the church hierarchy who
presumably represent the stability of apostolic tradition within the
community. Our author makes every effort to demonstrate the need for
obedience and humility in governing the gathered assembly. Indeed,
God's chosen leaders are called to demonstrate faith and to provide
peace among the members of the worshipping household.

The extended argument of *1 Clement* culminates in the last twenty-
five chapters of the work, a section that insists upon the divine origin of
ecclesiastical order, the wicked nature of contention, and the need for
love, repentance, and obedience among those who would be faithful to
Christ. In the center of this concluding argument our author offers a
description of those who may claim the right to stand before God with
a clear conscience and thus may assert the role of leadership. As we read
in chapter 54, those who recognize that they create rebellion and conflict within the community should abandon their positions of authority. Indeed, to do so is to gain great honor before Christ and to be
received in every place, since "the earth is the Lord's and all that is in it"
(*1 Clem.* 54.3).[25]

It is the statement that follows this instruction that is most important to us for the moment, however. As the author observes, "These
things are what those citizens who have no regrets in God's commonwealth [οἱ πολιτευόμενοι τὴν ἀμεταμέλητον πολιτείαν τοῦ θεοῦ]

---

[24] See Klaus Wengst, *Pax Romana and the Peace of Jesus Christ* (trans.
J. Bowden; Philadelphia: Fortress, 1987), 72–89.
[25] As drawn from Ps 24:1 (LXX 23:1).

have done and will do" (*1 Clem.* 54.4). In a text that undoubtedly is much earlier than the *Epistle to Diognetus,* regardless of whether one dates *1 Clement* in the 60s–70s or, instead, according to the more traditional dates of the 90s, one thus finds the idea of citizenship clearly associated with the concept of correct and honorable living. Indeed, our author has hinted at a lifestyle of honor and holiness throughout the letter, remarking that virtues are essential to God's desire for a faithful life within the church.[26]

Such comments upon the nature of what it means to live as a citizen within God's commonwealth are not only a foreshadowing of the kind of language used somewhat later in *Diognetus,* but also a significant advance upon the teachings that we have found in Paul. The question for *1 Clement* no longer seems to be related to the characteristics that one needs to personify in order to enter the kingdom of God, but instead is now to be associated with the traits that one must have to live within that kingdom. And those traits, though not unlike the qualities that Paul has already outlined in his letters, are especially related to issues of order and structure. It is only appropriate, therefore, that these elements should be associated with the perspective of citizenship and empire, much as they would be connected with family structure and hierarchy as demonstrated throughout the Roman Empire in terms of social and business etiquette. This focus upon hierarchy issues, honor and shame concerns, and relationships of power is clearly evident in the various "household codes" found in the deuteropauline letters, 1 Peter, the *Didache,* and *Barnabas.* It is not unreasonable, therefore, that we should expect to find the same type of language at work within *1 Clement.*

This leads us back to our second work, then, Polycarp's letter to the Philippians. We return specifically to chapter 5, which we have already examined above, because the issue that the bishop addresses here is very much the same as that which the author of *1 Clement* has addressed in chapters 42–45: the question of acceptable rulers for the assembly of God. In a certain sense, this concern for leadership and its association with righteousness directs the overall theme of the letter from the very beginning. Polycarp is concerned not about what traits are necessary for entry into God's kingdom, but about which elements

---

[26] See, for example, *1 Clem.* 2.8, 6.1, and 21.1.

are essential for those who would be leaders within the assembly. The discussion is directed toward deacons alone in this case, since it is with troublesome deacons that the bishop is most concerned. Such functionaries should be servants of all who are part of the congregation.

In the middle of this presentation Polycarp offers a most intriguing statement. He observes that those who please God on earth will receive the world that is to come, since God promised to raise the dead, and "if we prove to be citizens [ἐὰν πολιτευσώμεθα] worthy of him, we also will rule with him" (Pol. *Phil.* 5.2). This final clause is an intriguing combination of two scriptural references. The first phrase about "proving to be citizens" undoubtedly is intended to allude to Paul's previous instruction as found in Phil 1:27: "Only, live your life in a manner worthy of the gospel of Christ." The second phrase, about ruling with God, is an apparent reflection of 2 Tim 2:12, in which the hearers are encouraged to endure through suffering and in faith in order to obtain the prize of acting with the authority of the divine.

It is not entirely clear whether Paul in his letter to the Philippian church or the author of 2 Timothy in writing to Timothy intends for either of these phrases to be offered to their respective communities of faith as a whole. It is difficult, it seems, for us to know the extent to which such words of encouragement and hope are intended for average Christians or, instead, are purposefully addressed with special reference to the leadership of the community. In the case of Polycarp, who has written his letter to address specific questions associated with community authority and guidance, one might suspect that the latter audience (bishops, presbyters, and/or deacons) is intended.

In the parallel materials of *1 Clem.* 42–44 above, it certainly was to the leadership of the church that such instructions were addressed. Though the author undoubtedly meant for the entire congregation to hear the words written in the text, the implications of what appears there clearly were most important for the leaders—that is, those who had managed to gain control by removing their predecessors. This might seem to hold true for the words of Polycarp as well, at least with respect to questions of authority and rule within the structure of the community. In the case of Polycarp, however, there is the abiding promise of future resurrection and, for those who rule justly now, the hope of ruling with God in the kingdom that will come. But this promise is intended only for those who act as worthy citizens of God's realm.

CONCLUSION

Considerations of the nature of the kingdom of God and the role of the believer within that realm reveal a clear progression from the early presentation of Paul in the middle of the first century to the perspective of the author of the *Epistle of Diognetus* some hundred years later. The shift in this discussion occurs in tandem with the redefinition of the nature of the church that is assumed with each author along the historical trajectory.

From the outset, Paul assumes and addresses each church community under the rubric that the collected communities of God's faithful themselves form the "body of Christ." There are naturally a number of roles and "offices" that must be filled and respected within the living body, including the positions of elder (presbyter), apostle, teacher, and prophet. And yet at the same time, the body of Christ that this gathering of faithful believers represents is not itself divided according to rank and status, but rather finds itself to be a collection of workers each of whom is dependent upon the others. It is not at all clear, at least from what remains of Paul's correspondence, that this body should be considered as the kingdom of God itself. Indeed, Paul speaks of the kingdom as a reality that exists both in the present and in a more complete sense in the future. And his discussion of such issues is never attached to parallel considerations of the nature of the church.

With the deuteropauline authors and early apostolic fathers, a significant shift in perspective has begun to occur. In texts such as the Pastoral Epistles, *1 Clement,* the letters of Polycarp and Ignatius, and Revelation there continues to be talk about the necessary qualities that a believer must possess in order to enter the kingdom. At the same time, however, there is a distinct movement toward considerations of what is necessary "to live within" the kingdom. In many respects, this reflects a growing expectation that Christians, by virtue of their salvation through the church, are already either living the life of the kingdom or are assured of that life in the future. Of course, the boundaries of kingdom language are not so specifically defined within the process. There seems to be a shift toward the recognition that participation in the church in some sense serves as living within the kingdom on earth, and the promise of receiving the divine kingdom in its full glory is reserved for the future. This type of vision is particularly evident within the text of Revelation and may be assumed behind the liturgical language preserved in the New Testament gospels and the *Didache.*

In many of the remaining texts of the apostolic fathers, particularly *Barnabas, 2 Clement,* the *Shepherd of Hermas,* and the *Martyrdom of Polycarp* (and to this collection we surely should add the Gospel of John from the New Testament), there seems to be some evidence of the full evolution of the concept of kingdom as a realm of divine authority that stands apart from the influences of the world. In many respects within these texts there seems to be some understanding that Christians live as "citizens" within a divine empire that holds ultimate power over all other earthly authorities. In many of these texts, as already foreshadowed in Paul's letter to the Romans, there is a recognition that earthly leaders are themselves under the guidance of God and hold their power only with divine approval. In the later texts there is clear evidence that Christians are members of two worlds: they are at once members of a worldly order and citizens of a divine realm.

Most interesting within this particular collection of texts is the growing presumption that the leaders of the church themselves are particularly responsible for the salvation of believers. And in this role the promises of glory that previous authors offered to faithful Christians in general are now presented as encouragement for those who would seek to be the leaders of individual churches. It is clear that the shifting definition of Christian ecclesiology gradually moved from the idea of the church as the body of Christ, to the image of the church as the torso of which Christ rules as the head, to the view of the church as the leaders of the faith who served in the role of Christ as the head of the torso that is populated by the laity. The bishop Ignatius has already encouraged this movement in the threefold hierarchy of offices that he endorsed, a structure in which the bishop served in the role of the Father, and presbyters and deacons served in the role of the heavenly council and Christ. It is no wonder that the development of the institutional church often came to represent the perspectives of its leadership rather than those of the general populace.

In the middle of the progression toward specifically ordained leaders within the church there was a transition of definition for the place of Christians within the kingdom. In the beginning, the faithful seem to have been recognized as the children of God's own family. In the same way that the Messiah was the "Son of God," so too were the faithful to be recognized as the "children of light." As such, to be part of the body of Christ was to be part of the family of God. In the struggles that Christianity endured with its break from Judaism and in conflict with Roman authorities, the need for the church to define itself in more civil terminology became crucial. Thus it is that the later authors of the apostolic fathers came to recognize the members of the church as citizens of another empire, the reign of God. And the elements of citizenship that all people who lived within the boundaries of the Roman Empire knew and respected became the acceptable parameters by which later theologians came to define what it means to live as a faithful member of the institutional church. In many respects, then, the mentality of the apostolic fathers enabled early Christians to develop their self-understanding from the rudimentary views of Paul and his contemporaries to the well-developed ecclesiology of the church of the late medieval period.

FOR FURTHER READING

Several volumes offer helpful insights into the relationship between the early church and Roman ideas of empire:

- Benko, Stephen. *Pagan Rome and the Early Christians.* Bloomington: Indiana University Press, 1984.

- Fox, Robin Lane. *Pagans and Christians.* San Francisco: Harper & Row, 1986.

- Jeffers, James S. *The Greco-Roman World of the New Testament Era: Exploring the Background of Early Christianity.* Downers Grove, Ill.: InterVarsity Press, 1999.

- MacMullen, Ramsay. *Christianizing the Roman Empire (A.D. 100–400).* New Haven: Yale University Press, 1984.

- Sordi, Marta. *The Christians and the Roman Empire.* Translated by A. Bedini. Norman: University of Oklahoma Press; London: Croom Helm, 1986.

- Wengst, Klaus. *Pax Romana and the Peace of Jesus Christ.* Translated by J. Bowden. Philadelphia: Fortress, 1987.

Chapter 7

How Persons and Places Influence History

One of the most troublesome aspects of working with the materials of the apostolic fathers in general is the need to keep each text in context. To one extent or another, most researchers in the field are specialists in a few writings from the collection but have less familiarity with the structure, themes, or emphases of the remaining texts. This becomes painfully evident as students move from the apostolic fathers to the New Testament, a collection of works that themselves are not securely fastened in history. Indeed, though there is a general tendency to naively assume some general location and influence behind the majority of canonical writings, primarily based upon consensus opinions, the reality is that it is especially awkward to talk about the New Testament in relationship to the apostolic fathers when historical and geographical locales cannot be established.

What follows in this chapter is a cursory suggestion by which to link individual texts, their authors, and their ideas with specific geographical locations around the Mediterranean. This is by no means intended to be the last word on the question, of course. There are numerous issues that should be carefully considered but are not addressed here. The scenarios offered here may often raise more questions than they answer. Most troublesome of all, those students who have a particular interest in certain canonical texts or writings from the apostolic fathers undoubtedly will cling to arguments in support of other options and considerations that disagree with the following survey. Nonetheless, it seems appropriate to offer some insight into contextual matters that relate our texts, even if only in a cursory manner.

ALEXANDRIA, EGYPT

The most interesting aspect of New Testament views about first-century Egypt is that there are hardly any to be found within the corpus. The so-called flight into Egypt that appears in Matt 2 is a singular story that reflects Judaism's ancient resistance to the Nile delta's seductive attractions.[1] Egypt as a place and as a people represented an ever-present threat to the Jewish consciousness. The birth of Israel as a nation was clearly associated with its salvation by God through Moses away from the evil influences of the semi-divine hegemony of Pharaoh.

This reality is clearly recognized by both biblical and noncanonical authors, writers who depict an image of Egypt as the embodiment of what it means to be far from the glory of the God of Israel. The perspective is most noticeable in those places where the salvation history of the ancient Israelites has been recalled in Scripture. One finds examples in the speech of Stephen, as offered by the author of the Lukan tradition in Acts 7.[2] And various allusions appear throughout the letter of Hebrews (see, e.g., Heb 3:15–18; 8:9; 11:23–31). Outside of the New Testament, the so-called Hymn of the Pearl, preserved in the ninth act of the *Acts of Thomas,* provides a clear indication of the role that Egypt played for speculative theology among early semi-Christian sects. In the symbolism of this hymn the reader finds that the true treasure of divine knowledge can easily become misplaced in a world of corruption, a world identified with the land of Egypt.

Perhaps the most fascinating aspect of the fact that Egypt persists through third-century literature as a core antithesis to late Jewish self-identification and early Christian symbolism is the lack of attention that the area receives among the New Testament authors. This is most

---

[1] For parallels with the narrative of Jewish Scripture see Raymond E. Brown, *The Birth of the Messiah: A Commentary on the Infancy Narratives in Matthew and Luke* (Garden City, N.Y.: Doubleday, 1977), 113.

[2] And may be suggested by the inclusion of Jewish believers from Egypt who are present at the event of Pentecost as depicted in Acts 2:1–13; see C. Wilfred Griggs, *Early Egyptian Christianity from Its Origins to 451 C.E.* (ed. M. Krause; CS 2; Leiden: Brill, 1990), 14–16.

plainly evident in the accounts presented in the Acts of the Apostles. Though various scenarios of the lives of Peter and John are recounted both in and around Jerusalem, and though the various missionary journeys of Paul and Barnabas are detailed from Palestine to Greece to Rome, there is no mention of the spread of Christianity into northern Egypt. This is particularly intriguing in light of the history of the region, since it is well documented that nascent Christianity found an early foothold in Egypt and developed into a primary power during the great ecumenical debates of the patristic period. Further, the tradition of the influence of John Mark soon took hold and continues until the present in the living tradition of Egypt's Coptic Orthodox Church. We must wonder why the author of Acts has omitted so much from the historiographical reconstruction of ancient Christianity by offering no details about the Egyptian church. Was it because our author was uninformed about the Egyptian Christian tradition or, instead and much more likely, because there was a desire to omit it? We may never know with certainty.[3]

With such a minor witness to the first-century church in Egypt from the perspective of the New Testament, we are left with little literary assistance to elaborate on the supposition that the *Epistle of Barnabas* found its origins in the region.[4] What remains are broad comments about the situation in and around Alexandria in general.[5]

As is well documented, a thriving Jewish community existed in Alexandria from ancient times. It was quite logical, therefore, that the Hebrew Scriptures should find their monumental translation into the Greek Septuagint in that setting. In addition, Alexandria was broadly

---

[3] We might also observe that the evangelist Apollos had Egyptian roots, but his theology and influence are not widely known and apparently conflicted with the teachings of Paul as seen in Acts 18:24–19:7 and 1 Cor 1:12; see Griggs, *Early Egyptian Christianity,* 16–17.

[4] There are authors who have argued for a different milieu behind *Barnabas,* of course. Most often, the only other best option that is offered is somewhere in the region of Syria. As I have argued throughout this volume, this seems to be a far distant and secondary possibility. Yet, for arguments in favor of either Syria, Asia Minor, or Palestine see Robert A. Kraft, *Barnabas and the Didache: A Translation and Commentary* (AF 3; New York: Thomas Nelson & Sons, 1965), 48–56.

[5] Such efforts typically rely upon links between the rhetorical approach of *Barnabas* and Jewish exegetical techniques that were in use in Egypt; see, for example, L. W. Barnard, *Studies in the Apostolic Fathers and Their Background* (New York: Schocken, 1966), 57–85.

recognized throughout the Mediterranean world as a home of learning
and wisdom. This is evidenced by the great Alexandrian library housed
within the city,[6] and it is reflected in the philosophical and theological
speculation preserved in the writings of Philo. Thus the large and thriving Jewish community of Alexandria combined with the clear love of
learning and wisdom that the general population embraced and supported made the region a natural climate for the production of late
Jewish and early Christian theological tractates.

Traditional evaluations of *Barnabas* often have placed the text
within just such a setting. It makes little difference whether one considers the author to have been a Jewish Christian or, instead, a Christian
with a non-Jewish background but who clearly was familiar with Hebrew Scriptures and traditions. The locale of Alexandria would have
provided a most suitable setting for the themes and interfaith vitriol
that the author of the text reflects.

The primary emphasis of the text is directed toward "three basic
doctrines" that reflect the cross fertilization of Jewish piety standards
and early Christian categories: faith, righteousness, and joy (see *Barn.*
1.6–8). Such a pattern recalls the rules of piety from Matt 6 (alms-
giving, prayer, fasting) and Paul's own schema from 1 Cor 12–14 (faith,
hope, love). Clement of Alexandria, at some short distance in time
from the composition of *Barnabas,* offers his own developed consideration, which contains four elements: faith, hope, love, and knowledge.[7]
It is clear that Clement knows and utilizes this tradition of piety rules,
but he has expanded the pattern to include an element that was both
natural and typical of Alexandrian faith traditions: the consideration of
knowledge. While scholars traditionally observe that Clement is aware
of the text of *Barnabas,* as he is of many early Christian texts because
of his proximity to the famous Alexandrian library and his role as direc-
tor of the early catechetical school within the city, it is this focus
upon knowledge that most closely links Clement's views with those of
Barnabas.

For both *Barnabas* and Clement, knowledge of God is the ultimate
goal for valid aspirations of Christian faith. The difference between
these authors is that the context in which Clement writes is no longer

---

[6] See Luciano Canfora, *The Vanished Library* (trans. M. Ryle; London:
Hutchinson Radius, 1987).

[7] This, of course, is the basis of Clement's *Stromata.*

characterized by the struggle between Judaism and the rise of Christian claims to legitimacy. The author of *Barnabas,* however, clearly is in the midst of just such a struggle. On the one hand, *Barnabas* is truly focused upon those elements that the author considers to be legitimate aspects of true Christian living: virtues, the validity of baptism and crucifixion as the foci of the faith, and steadfast obedience to the ways of God. On the other hand, such claims are set forth as the tip of a theological spear that seeks to justify the claims of Christianity in specific contrast to the traditional elements by which Judaism defined itself.

This latter element of the Jewish-Christian struggle was by no means restricted to Alexandria, of course, but there are few texts within early Christianity that characterize the struggle in such a dynamic fashion. Within the New Testament, one might point to the letter of Jude as just such an example. Unfortunately, Jude is a letter that is extremely difficult to place within the history of ancient Christianity's evolution. In addition, of course, one may point to the letters of Paul for the apostle's concerted disavowal of those who would argue that the only true way to be a follower of Jesus as the Christ is to observe all the decrees of Judaism's Torah. In many respects, one finds that this is the very perspective that the author of Matthew may seek to preserve, at least in part. But after Paul, the pathway away from Judaism that the early church was destined to follow was foreshadowed by the author of the Gospel of John, who somewhat rather anachronistically offers Jesus in conflict with "the Jews," as though he himself had no similar Jewish background.

The interesting aspect of *Barnabas* when considered within the Alexandrian setting is that the author utilizes a basic midrashic technique by which to reinterpret the imagery of the Hebrew Scriptures into the Christian context. In this process the hearer is told that the ancient prophets of early Israel themselves emphasized that cultic sacrifices and fasting were not of real value for faith (*Barn.* 15.8). Instead, it is the inner sacrifice and desire to serve those who are oppressed that God wants from those who are genuinely faithful (*Barn.* 21.4–5). The use of Old Testament imagery here, as with, for example, the case of the redefinition of the "scapegoat" motif from Lev 16 (see *Barn.* 7) and the "red heifer" ritual of Num 19 (see *Barn.* 8), indicates that our author is aware not only of traditional Jewish imagery, but also of specific rituals that were ancient in origin and archaic in practice. And yet, in addition to this awareness of texts, our author is quite capable of redefining such imagery both to enhance the promises of God to the evolving Christian community and to deflect any importance away from Jewish claims to authenticity.[8]

In many respects, this midrashic approach is highly parallel to similar efforts within the materials of the Dead Sea Scrolls, which themselves presumably are attempts to redefine the traditional faith of common Jewish tradition within the light of a more esoteric and idiosyncratic understanding of what it meant to be a truly faithful and select Jew in the last days.[9] The presumptions of the Dead Sea authors that the last days had finally come upon God's faithful people were somewhat parallel to the same eschatological concerns of the early Christians, a feature that seems to exist also behind the mindset of the text of *Barnabas*. Of course, this attitude was typical of many, if not most, late Jewish groups and ancient Christian movements in the first century. It is easily recognizable in the writings of Paul, and it stands behind the emphatic message of Jesus preserved by the Gospel of Mark, with its focus upon "immediacy" and the need to make disciples quickly.

The addition of the "two ways" materials at the end of *Barnabas* (chapters 18–20) is difficult to access with respect to an Alexandrian provenance for the text. On the one hand, it is clear that some form of the two ways perspective was prevalent as far back as the witness of Deuteronomy and was quite common in both Jewish literature and Hellenistic philosophical traditions.[10] And, of course, it appears widely in first-century texts from the Gospel of Matthew, to Paul's letter to the Galatians, to the *Manual of Discipline* from Qumran, to the first and

---

[8] The author of *Barnabas* is careful to construct a repartee with the so-called wilderness narrative of ancient Israel as a means by which to transfer the old covenant between God and Israel to a new covenant between God and Christianity through the use of Judaism's own heritage of images. See specifically the imagery in chapters 4, 7–8, 12, and 14 as an illustration of this process.

[9] See M. Jack Suggs, "The Christian Two Ways Tradition: Its Antiquity, Form, and Function," in *Studies in New Testament and Early Christian Literature: Essays in Honor of Allen P. Wikgren* (ed. D. E. Aune; NovTSup 33; Leiden: Brill, 1972), 60–74; Jan Bergman, "Zum Zweiwegemotiv: Religionsgeschichtliche und exegetische Bemerkungen," *SEÅ* 41–42 (1977): 27–56; Jean Duhaime, "Dualistic Reworking in the Scrolls from Qumran," *CBQ* 49 (1987): 32–56.

[10] See the discussion by James I. H. McDonald, *Kerygma and Didache: The Articulation and Structure of the Earliest Christian Message* (SNTSMS 37; Cambridge: Cambridge University Press, 1980), 72 n. 23, 77, 95–97.

primary division of the *Didache*. In this respect, it may be possible to place the text of *Barnabas* at an early date because of the very presence of such material.

On the other hand, it seems much more likely that these few closing chapters represent an addition to the original tractate that has come to the work as a secondary component. As is evident from the later literary tradition of the *Apostolic Constitutions* and *Church Orders*, as well as texts such as the *Rule of Benedict,* the two ways continued to flourish in later Christian literature well into the medieval period. It certainly is conceivable that Alexandria, not to mention Egyptian Christianity in general, supported a culture whose religious values endorsed high ethical standards. This is clearly evident in the writings of Philo from the first century, and it persisted as the foundation of what eventually was to become the famous tradition of Egyptian monasticism under the leadership of figures such as Antony, Pachomius, and Schenute.

These two thematic elements—knowledge and ethical values—lead us, then, to a consideration of the *Epistle to Diognetus,* a text that might also be placed within the sphere of Alexandrian influence (see chapter 1 above). The text was not widely known in Christian antiquity, or at least was not widely employed, though Clement of Alexandria may offer some limited awareness of its existence.[11] But the two themes of knowledge and ethics, whose roots are readily apparent throughout the literature of the region, are likewise to be found within this particular text.

As the author of *Diognetus* emphasizes throughout the work, itself one of our earliest apologies from antiquity, the false idols of pagan worship and the incessant feasts and empty rituals of Judaism are useless as a basis for any true faith that is deserving of God. Christianity, on the other hand, is entirely different. Its members exist within the world in the same way that the soul inhabits the body. They work for the benefit of all nations, acting patiently to improve the lives of anyone who will heed their message and accept their graciousness. Yet, though they maintain lives of blamelessness and ethical moral purity, they are abused and persecuted by many whom they encounter. Christians are able to maintain their faith, however, because they are aware of their

---

[11] See Clement, *Protr.* 1.10.2; 4.50–52; 5.64–65; 10.97.3; 11.115.1–117.1; 12.118.4 (for these last two references see *Diogn.* 10.1–7).

role within the world: witnesses to the true knowledge of God that could not be known before the coming of the Christ.

As our author observes in *Diogn.* 10.1, anyone who desires this same kind of faith that enables believers in the Messiah to endure travail and persecution while living their lives in righteousness must first obtain "full knowledge of the Father" (ἐπίγνωσις πατρός). And that knowledge, at least according to our author, is an awareness of the love that God had for humanity, to whom was given both "reason" (λόγος) and "mind" (νοῦς), so that the only Son was sent for their salvation (*Diogn.* 10.2).

This mention of "reason" and "mind" offers a reflection of the two types of theology that were typical of early Egyptian Christianity. The first, the so-called Logos Christology that is so prominently featured in the Christ hymn in chapter 1 of the Gospel of John, seems to have been typical of Alexandrian theologians for centuries. It is reflected in the theological speculation of Clement and Origen, and it came to serve as a foundational premise of monastic thought throughout the region. Indeed, the essence of this view of the Son in relationship both to the Father and to the Father's created world became the avenue through which much christological debate ensued throughout the early ecumenical councils and around which various heretical teachings were organized, thus to draw the ire of the great heresiologists of the third and fourth centuries. In the final analysis, however, Logos Christology was deemed to be acceptable by the early church to the extent that it permitted the Son to share in an equal role with the Father and Holy Spirit as part of the Trinitarian formula of mainline faith. But when pushed to excess by those ancient Christians who wished to focus upon the divine nature of the Son to the exclusion of the remaining figures of the Trinity, it was quickly curtailed.

A second type of theology that developed throughout the Mediterranean world also found its center in the teachings of various Egyptian teachers: Gnosticism. Of course, Gnosticism was widely observed and practiced around the Roman Empire, and it continues to be a thriving perspective even today. On the one hand, the focus of many heresiologists was directed toward gnostic sects that either had their roots in ancient Egypt or were widely practiced there. Included here would be the school of Sethian Gnosticism and, if we are to believe the letter of Clement of Alexandria concerning variant renderings of the Gospel of Mark (the so-called *Secret Gospel of Mark*), Carpocratian Gnosticism was also prevalent. But this approach to early heterodoxy within the evolving Egyptian church certainly was prevalent within the monastic system of the third century and onward, as is suggested by various writings within the collected works of the Nag Hammadi Library.

The *Epistle of Barnabas,* with its early indication of the importance of knowledge, certainly may be a foundational text for coming to understand the rise of gnostic leanings within early Christian Egypt. So too, the author's concern for correct living and an appropriate religious lifestyle may also have helped to set the groundwork for the type of asceticism that most ancient gnostics practiced. An ascetic approach to living, with its abstinence from fleshly pursuits and lack of concern for material goods, was a typical characteristic of gnostic communities, despite the raging claims of the heresiologists that gnostics were primarily libertine in perspective and liberal in lifestyle.

The view of *Barnabas* is likewise supported by the arguments of the *Epistle to Diognetus.* At the same time, Alexandria was truly a region in which contrasting theologies and divergent ecclesiastical perspectives flourished. In the time of the great ecumenical councils and conciliar debates, the presence of someone such as Athanasius, with his support of Roman policies and theology, certainly would have stood out in Alexandria in contrast to the pervasive influence of Origenism and variations of the Logos Christology that was so popular among the Christians of the region. The keyword of the Egyptian Christian tradition clearly was "diversity." And such certainly was a troublesome concern within the early ecclesiastical tradition, a time when the primary quest of bishops everywhere was for unity in liturgy and theology. It is perhaps as a tacit acknowledgment of this reality that the author of the Acts of the Apostles chose to remain silent about the church of the tradition of Saint Mark.

ANTIOCH, SYRIA

Perhaps one of the most intriguing cities of the first- and second-century Mediterranean world was Antioch in Syria. In many respects, this was a region that betrayed certain aspects of the early Christian experience that also were to be found in Alexandria. History records that there was a strong Jewish community in the city from as early as the third century B.C.E. In addition, the long political, cultural, and religious background of Antioch helped to bring a variety of peoples and perspectives to the region in general. Like Alexandria, this variegated milieu helped in the development of gnostic schools in and around Antioch, and it nurtured a rich environment in which local churches were able to take root and evolve in a relatively short period of time.[12]

Though certainly there is much room for debate in the matter, it seems reasonable that we may place several early Christian texts within the general realm of Antioch's influence. With respect to the apostolic fathers, the last hundred years of scholarship has seen a growing recognition that the *Didache* should be interpreted within the influence of this particular community.[13] Because of textual and historical links to that text, it also seems reasonable to place the Gospel of Matthew and, perhaps, the letter of James there as well. And, of course, though none of their known letters are from the city itself, we must accept the fact that the apostle Paul and the bishop Ignatius were an important presence within the city, as might be expected from their dynamic personalities. Presumably, as is suggested by the Acts of the Apostles, illustrious Christian teachers such as Barnabas and the apostle Peter (known under the name of Cephas) were well-respected evangelists in the region as well.[14]

This is an unusually large number of writings to attribute to a single metropolitan area, at least from the corpus of literature that has come from the earliest authors of the Christian tradition. And yet, in addition to this number, one might easily add various writings and authors that the orthodox tradition ultimately rejected. Included in this category are texts such as the *Gospel of Peter* and the *Preaching of Peter*. So too, history records the presence of schools of thought such as those

---

[12] Among the best surveys of the situation of ancient Antioch are C. Kraeling, "The Jewish Community at Antioch," *JBL* 51 (1932): 130–60; G. Downey, *A History of Antioch in Syria from Seleucus to the Arab Conquest* (Princeton, N.J.: Princeton University Press, 1961); Wayne A. Meeks and Robert L. Wilken, *Jews and Christians in Antioch in the First Four Centuries of the Common Era* (SBLSBS 13; Missoula, Mont.: Scholars Press, 1978).

[13] See most recently Michelle Slee, *The Church in Antioch in the First Century C.E.: Communion and Conflict* (JSNTSup 244; London: Sheffield Academic Press, 2003); Magnus Zetterholm, *The Formation of Christianity in Antioch: A Social-Scientific Approach to the Separation between Judaism and Christianity* (London: Routledge, 2003).

[14] So Acts 13–15 for Barnabas and Gal 2:11–13 for Peter.

that were inspired by the great gnostic teachings of Menander, Saturninus, and Basilides. At the same time, we should not forget that this once was the home of the early manuscript collector Tatian, who compiled the famous *Diatessaron* in an attempt to standardize the various gospel narratives that were in circulation during his time.

The city of Antioch was truly an intellectual crucible for the distillation of late Jewish perspectives and the development of early Christian theologies. And yet, this variety and fertility actually provide some problem for understanding the nature of the city. There is a natural tendency to ask how a single metropolitan area was able to engender and sustain such a broad religious heritage in the midst of such an assortment of faith views. History indicates that this was indeed no easy task, since the political life of the community was greatly marred by the complaints of local Jews about encroaching faiths and political pressures, as well as riots by groups of citizens in response to the presence of competing religions within the cultural and religious life of the city.

There is some explanation to be found for the multiplicity of views within Antioch's religious life when one considers the widespread Jewish influence throughout the city. As was typical of most large Mediterranean communities, the Jewish community was extensively divided among different synagogues and cultural centers. One can hardly expect to find a broad uniformity of perspective throughout such a diversely scattered faith community. Some of these synagogues probably were quite conservative in perspective, perhaps functioning under the influence of the temple cultus in Jerusalem. Others quite naturally would have been progressive in orientation, responding positively to one degree or another to Hellenistic culture, just as many Jewish communities of the Diaspora did throughout the Mediterranean world.[15]

And, undoubtedly, it was just such contexts that provided fertile ground for the infiltration of the earliest evangelical efforts of ancient Christianity. For example, we see Paul at home in Antioch to the extent that he seems to have found the city to be a worthy base of operations for his various missionary journeys. He could hardly have felt comfortable in such a context had there not been a strong Christian community there to sustain and support him as he came to understand what it meant to serve as a slave for Christ. At the same time, however,

---

[15] So the thesis of Zetterholm, *Formation of Christianity*.

the influences of the Jerusalem church must have been great in Antioch, for we find Paul in dispute with Peter in the city over issues related to kosher restrictions. This is attested both in Acts and in Paul's
letter to the Galatians. And in Acts 15 we find that Jerusalem, under
the direction of Peter and James, felt that it had the authority to send a
brief list of moral restrictions to the church in Antioch as a guidepost
for following an acceptable Christian lifestyle, now known as the
"apostolic decree."

There is little wonder, then, that Paul ultimately seems to have
abandoned the city in favor of long stays in places such as Ephesus and
Corinth. On the one hand, he undoubtedly found communities in
those cities that were more convenient, at least to some extent, for the
purposes that he needed as he traveled around Asia Minor and Greece.
On the other hand, he may have found that the life of a Christian in
Antioch had become increasingly turbulent during the course of the
mid-first century.

This turbulence is actually suggested in the writings that the early
Christians produced in Antioch around the turn of the century. Indeed,
a community that could produce a text such as the *Didache* (which possesses a very strong association with the Jewish heritage of the Christian
faith), and that could produce a gospel such as the Gospel of Matthew
(which clearly clings to a basic respect for Judaism's traditions and heritage, while also affirming the need for a basic faith that surpasses traditional restrictions), and that could support the views of the bishop
Ignatius (whose letters take Pauline theology and views of freedom
from Jewish restrictions to a new level of awareness) is a community
that must have been sharply divided and full of fractures. It is little
wonder that the world of Christian Judaism that Paul first experienced
in his early missionary work in Antioch soon became too divided and
contentious to serve as his faith home.

As has been suggested above, the sharp divisions that existed
among the synagogues in Antioch with respect to the acceptance or rejection of theological trends and influences from outside of the city undoubtedly led to the same sort of variation of perspective among the
early house churches that grew up around those same synagogues.
Some of these churches perhaps were quite conservative with respect to
Jewish values (so the theology of the Didachist), while others were
more accepting of liberal interpretations of the Christian mission (so
the views of Paul). Still other churches would have welcomed a position

that fell somewhere in between the Didachist and Paul (so the stance of the author of Matthew).[16] But we must also keep in mind that to some great extent there were Christians in the city who possessed no Jewish background and held little sympathy for those who believed that the principles of Judaism should frame the essential structure of the faith (so the position of Ignatius). Though the author of Matthew ultimately produced a text that reflected the common views of the broadest majority of early Christians, as is evidenced by the wide acceptance of that text among later patristic authors and scattered church communities, the position of Ignatius with respect to the distance that Christianity sought to keep between itself and the synagogue and the structure of the ecclesiastical hierarchy that it chose to adopt eventually came to dominate what the church ultimately would become.

The struggle between the church and the synagogue in Antioch was not easily resolved. Even many years later at the end of the second century, the bishops Theophilus and Serapion found themselves in a constant dialogue with the Jews of the city. At the same time, the degree to which they found themselves in favor with Jewish desires certainly would have exasperated both Paul and Ignatius, who had served as leaders within the local church before them, as well as John Chrysostom, whose rhetoric against "the Jews" a century later was surely sharpened on the whetstone of Antioch's religious politics.

What is perhaps most important about the religious situation in Antioch is the degree to which the city's numerous perspectives led to a certain element of multiplicity in liturgical format and ecclesiastical hierarchy. Within a single milieu the modern historian may be able to find a context in which divergent practices were observed prior to a process of standardization.

One may consider the question of the Eucharist, for example. The *Didache* provides prayers for the time of "giving thanks" within the table fellowship of the community, but no words of institution (see *Did.* 9.1–10.7). The Gospel of Matthew, however, closely following the pattern of the Gospel of Mark, its basis, contains the words of institution, but no prayers. Students often have argued that this indicates that the two texts

---

[16] See the interpretation of Matthew's use of the Jewish ideal in Anthony J. Saldarini, "The Gospel of Matthew and Jewish-Christian Conflict," in *Social History of the Matthean Community: Cross-Disciplinary Approaches* (ed. D. L. Balch; Minneapolis: Fortress, 1991), 38–61.

must have come from different locations, or that they recognized two different rituals. However, it certainly is possible that these texts reveal two different ways in which various house churches within the same city observed the Eucharist before the ritual became standardized. It is even conceivable that the prayers, whose *berakah* structure suggests deeply Jewish origins, and the words of institution that have been attributed to Jesus may have been used together in some churches, though perhaps only for a short time. The situation simply remains uncertain.[17]

Or, as another example, one might consider the situation of ecclesiastical authorities as viewed from the different perspectives of our authors. The Didachist mentions the authority of apostles and prophets and of bishops and deacons. Though there may be some assumption that presbyters were present within the community, no such office is addressed. Ignatius, on the other hand, clearly advocates the roles of bishop, presbyter, and deacon, a threefold hierarchy that the mainline church ultimately came to accept. One might argue that these two authors reflect different approaches to ecclesiastical authority from the perspective of their own local churches before a standard system was institutionalized. Of course, the Gospel of Matthew makes no mention of any of these offices except to warn against the rise of false prophets, persons who were known to circulate widely by the end of the first century.[18] At the same time, however, it is within Matthew itself that one hears that Peter has received the keys to the kingdom. And as has been recorded by Eusebius of Caesarea, the apostolic lineage of the church in Antioch was broadly recognized to have the apostle Peter as its foundation.[19] All bishops in the city from the first century onward presumably assumed their authority from that source. It is all the more curious, then, that Ignatius never makes any particular attempt to justify his own authority by reference to the Petrine tradition.

As a third and final example, one should perhaps consider the role of literary authority within the Christian communities at Antioch. It seems clear that some collection of the teachings of Jesus that were somewhat unique to the local churches was in use. This is suggested by

---

[17] See John W. Riggs, "The Sacred Food of *Didache* 9–10 and Second-Century Ecclesiologies," in *The Didache in Context: Essays on Its Text, History, and Transmission* (ed. C. N. Jefford; NovTSup 77; Leiden: Brill, 1995), 256–83.

[18] So, for example, Matt 7:15–20.

[19] See Eusebius, *Hist. eccl.* 3.22.1; 3.36.2.

the so-called M source of materials that lie behind Matthew, a cadre of oral and written memories that are often paralleled within the *Didache*. So too, numerous texts from the Hebrew Scriptures and from traditional Jewish teachings are found both in Matthew and the *Didache*.[20] These two texts serve as fairly clear evidence that Antioch's Christians respected sayings traditions.

At the same time, however, Ignatius seems to run almost completely contrary to this trend of source utilization. He makes very few references to the Hebrew Scriptures throughout his letters,[21] and rarely does he base any of his comments upon the teachings of Jesus.[22] Instead, he is dependent upon short creedal statements as the authority for his pronouncements and upon vibrant cultural imagery as illustration of his theological ideas. To some large extent, his imagery is highly dependent upon previous parallel Pauline images, many of which have been preserved in Paul's own letters. Some of these ideas were naturally drawn from the common culture of the audiences to whom Ignatius wrote. But his creedal statements, which include some of the earliest creeds of Christian history, offer no suggestion as to their source. One must question the extent to which such creeds were the unique compilation of the church in Antioch or the individual compositions of Ignatius himself.

What is particularly intriguing about the literature produced by Antioch's Christians is the heavy dependence upon recent Jewish history, especially as the record of those events have been preserved in the writings of the Second Temple period. Most notably, one should give specific attention to Sirach and 4 Maccabees. A quick scan through the *Didache* and Matthew indicates that various sayings that appear in both texts are dependent to some degree upon similar teachings found in Sirach. It is clear that the wisdom of that ancient text influenced the sapiential sayings of these later Christian writings.

This may hold true in a different sense for 4 Maccabees, a text that glories in the logic of "reason" whenever that virtue is triumphant over the challenge of passion. Although Ignatius was not predisposed to

---

[20] See the parallels as offered by Alan J. P. Garrow, *The Gospel of Matthew's Dependence on the Didache* (JSNTSup 254; London: T&T Clark, 2004), 243.

[21] Though Ignatius makes passing allusion to various Hebrew Scriptures, he actually quotes from them only in three places: Ign. *Eph.* 5.3 (Prov 3:34); Ign. *Magn.* 12 (Prov 18:17 LXX); Ign. *Trall.* 8.2 (Isa 52:5).

[22] See, for example, Ign. *Eph.* 14.2 (Matt 12:33); Ign. *Phld.* 2.2 (Matt 7:15); Ign. *Smyrn.* 1.1 (Matt 3:15).

Jewish traditions and teachings, there is some reason to believe that he envisioned his own trials and persecutions according to the dictates of the Jewish martyr sequence in 4 Maccabees.[23] His language and reflection upon his circumstances, particularly as they are portrayed in the letter to Rome, are highly reminiscent of the phraseology and stories preserved in the Maccabean literary tradition. But most importantly, the bishop has transformed the reason-over-passion philosophy that dominates 4 Maccabees into a discipleship-over-persecution theology that guided his own journey. He successfully redefines an act of pious fidelity that appears in one religious faith and applies it as an expression of faithful devotion within another. As Ignatius sees the situation, the discipline of martyrdom is the ultimate statement of loyalty to Christ. And so this image was adopted and adapted as the basis of the great martyr cults of the late second and third centuries in Near Eastern and North African churches.

The church of Antioch was long recognized as a leader in theological and ecclesiastical issues for numerous centuries. The great school of literal Scripture interpretation that existed in the city stood as a worthy counterbalance to the views of allegory that ruled Alexandrian approaches. At the same time, however, the literature that arose within and around the city had various influences upon the larger church. The text of Matthew was generally recognized as a superior gospel to that of Mark, and the ecclesiastical structure of Ignatius came to dominate most Mediterranean churches. On the other hand, the theology of the *Didache* appears to have disappeared into the great ecclesiastical handbooks of the third and fourth centuries, while the Epistle of James attracted only minimal attention among later patristic authors. Nonetheless, the church of Antioch has provided much for later church tradition that was evidenced in the debates of the great ecumenical councils and remains in our literature from ancient Christian thinkers.

FROM ASIA MINOR TO GREECE

Needless to say, the following segment of materials is not intended to be a systematic survey of the rise of early Christianity in some of the

---

[23] So O. Perler, "Das vierte Makkabäerbuch, Ignatius von Antiochen und die ältesten Märtyrerberichte," *RivAC* 25 (1949): 47–72.

most fertile areas of its first expansion—that is, the whole of Asia Minor and Greece. Instead, I wish to indicate in a single image how much of the early Christian world is absent from the apostolic fathers. We can attribute only the letter of the bishop Polycarp to the Philippians and the *Martyrdom of Polycarp* to this region with certainty. From my own perspective, I would also add the text of *2 Clement* because I believe that it may have derived from Corinthian origins, but this is very much in debate.[24] Of course, one must also include the letters of Ignatius in this survey because they are mostly directed to communities in Asia Minor. However, their author is much more the subject of events in Antioch rather than in Asia Minor per se, and thus his correspondence tells us more about Syrian perceptions of Christianity than about the faith of his audience.

We cannot possibly hope to know all the details of the many scattered churches that existed in Asia Minor and Greece through the end of the second century. The New Testament and apostolic fathers mention numerous faith communities in Asia Minor, including Derbe, Lystra, Colossae, Ephesus, Iconium, Laodicea, Pisidian Antioch, Magnesia, Thyatira, Tralles, Philadelphia, Sardis, Smyrna, Pergamum, and Philomelium as primary examples. In Greece, we hear of well-known communities at Philippi, Thessalonica, Beroea, and Corinth, but surely these represent only the surface of a much broader expansion of the faith. It seems expedient here to make mention of those communities most prominently featured by our authors and to forgo the others.

Ephesus

It is clear both from the literature and from tradition that the church at Ephesus had a powerful impact upon the development of early Christian theology. Paul spent some considerable time in the city,[25] which had also witnessed the preaching of the evangelist Apollos and been visited by Priscilla and Aquila of Rome (see Acts 18:24–28).

---

[24] Corinth is one of two traditional choices, with Rome as the other; see, for example, Karl Paul Donfried, *The Setting of Second Clement in Early Christianity* (NovTSup 38; Leiden: Brill, 1974), 1. A popular third option, particularly in recent decades, is Alexandria; so Robert M. Grant, *Greek Apologists of the Second Century* (Philadelphia: Westminster, 1988), 178–79; Helmut Koester, *History and Literature of Early Christianity* (vol. 2 of *Introduction to the New Testament*; 2d ed.; FF; Philadelphia: Fortress; New York: de Gruyter, 1982), 234–36.

[25] At least according to Acts 19.

The church there has been addressed in three places within our literary records, including the brief letter contained in Rev 2:1–7 (which may have been penned primarily for apologetic purposes), the deutero-pauline New Testament letter to the Ephesians (whose opening address to Ephesus is uncertain and may be a secondary addition to a more general missive), and the letter of Ignatius to the Ephesians, which certainly is based in structure and intention upon its New Testament counterpart.

In addition, tradition attributes the Gospel of John and the texts of 1–3 John to the church of Ephesus, thus to suggest that a specific literary tradition arose within the faith community there. Furthermore, the pious remembrance of the early church also claimed the city as the final home of the mother of Jesus and of the "beloved disciple" (identified as the apostle John), whose presence in the region undoubtedly gave the local faith community a special status among other area churches.

What remains both from the literary records and from tradition portrays a somewhat confusing scenario. Indeed, if our sources may be taken as accurate witnesses to the situation of Christianity in the city, even if only to a limited extent, then the presence of the local church was not without tension or contention.

Let us begin with Acts 18:24–19:24 as an example. In this material we find that Apollos, a Jew of Alexandria, preached to the local church about "the way of the Lord" (ὁδὸς τοῦ κυρίου) in which he had been instructed and about the baptism of John (presumably, John the Baptizer). During that same visit, Priscilla and Aquila confronted him and explained to him more accurately about "the way." Modern editors typically add the phrase "of God" to what Priscilla and Aquila offered, though those words do not appear in any manuscripts. This leaves us with some confusion on the issue. Was there an attempt to offer Apollos more complete training with respect to his Alexandrian instruction? Or, instead, does the use of two different phrases here ("way of the Lord" and "way [of God]") suggest that two different interpretations of the Christian mission had come into conflict? Whatever the circumstances, Apollos afterward was encouraged by the church to cross over to Corinth in Achaia to continue his ministry.

When Paul arrived in Ephesus and discovered that the baptism of John was being practiced, he rebaptized the believers into the baptism of Jesus and laid hands on them so that the Holy Spirit might come into their midst. As the author of Acts attests, the activities of Paul himself eventually led to a riot among the local religious artisans who maintained their livelihood by the creation of statues and souvenirs for the cult of Artemis. Perhaps as a result of the disturbance, Paul found it convenient to leave the city shortly thereafter and to pursue his missionary activities in Macedonia (Acts 20:1). On a subsequent opportunity to pass back through Ephesus, he chose instead to sail past the city without a visit in order to reach Jerusalem more quickly (Acts 20:16).

The testimony of events in Acts is somewhat late, of course, as is our other literary witness to incidents in the city. But the brief framework of events that Acts provides is instructive with respect to our remaining materials.

An earlier New Testament writing, the deuteropauline letter to the Ephesians, even though not likely Pauline, offers a slightly different approach to the situation of the city. The primary themes of this writing address the need for church unity (Eph 2:11–22; 4:1–16), the ministry that the author had conducted among the non-Jewish believers of the city (Eph 3:1–13; 4:17–5:20), matters related to the role of the Holy Spirit (Eph 1:3–14; 3:14–21; 6:10–17), and a desire for order within the community as offered through household codes (Eph 5:21–6:9). It is somewhat curious that these are quite similar to the issues that Acts 18–19 raises: debate among Christians at Ephesus; conflict between Jews/Christians and local pagans; the desire and need for the presence of the Spirit; and a call to orderliness. One must wonder whether the comparison of Ephesians and Acts does not give us a more genuine understanding of the church in the city than our authors would have realized.

From these writings we must turn to the brief letter to Ephesus contained in chapter 2 of the book of Revelation. Here we find commendations for the church at Ephesus, a community that cannot tolerate those who work evil and whose patient endurance in the face of struggle has brought its members to weariness. As the author of Revelation observes, such conflict has caused them to lose their original love for the faith. And so the Christians of the city are called to repent and return to their first works. Most important in the midst of this instruction, however, the Ephesians are credited for their hate of the Nicolaitans, a splinter group whose views of Christianity were deemed to be unsuitable and were known also to have been present at Pergamum (Rev 2:12–17) and perhaps at Thyatira (Rev 2:18–29). This recognition of divergent theological positions at Ephesus is a theme fully recognized elsewhere in the literary record.

When we turn to the letter that Ignatius wrote to the church in Ephesus, our view of a city that is under theological strain is fully confirmed. Ignatius offers a dire warning against the threat of heresies at the very center of his letter (Ign. *Eph.* 6.2–10.3), and he calls for unity in Christ under the authority of the bishop. It seems that he knows of Christians in the city who, though declaring themselves to be representatives of "the name" (presumably, of Christ) (Ign. *Eph.* 7.1), act in a manner that is most unworthy of God. They are malicious and deceitful, "mad dogs that bite in secret" and whose bite can be cured by only one physician, whom Ignatius identifies through a creedal confession: "both flesh and spirit, born and unborn, God in humanity, true life in death, both from Mary and from God, first one to suffer and thus onward, Jesus Christ our Lord" (Ign. *Eph.* 7.2).

It is unfortunate that Ignatius does not give us a very detailed description of the offending party at Ephesus. All that we know from his letter is that their character is highly suspect and that they carry some "evil teaching" (κακὴ διδαχή) (Ign. *Eph.* 9.1) with them. Most important, their actions seem to have disturbed the Ephesian faithful. He offers sage counsel that they should resist their adversaries, persons who are angry, boastful, slanderous, error prone, and cruel (Ign. *Eph.* 10.2).

Most notably, Ignatius does not identify these problem teachers either as Judaizers or docetics, two groups that he specifically castigates elsewhere in his letters. This is particularly significant in light of his experiences at home in Antioch, a city in which we have just seen that conflicting views about the importance of Jewish influence upon the rise of Christianity and debate about gnostic teachings were very much in place. We must assume, then, that if Ignatius had found the Ephesians to be in a struggle with similar groups, he surely would have taken the opportunity to launch an attack against such theological threats.

But this leaves us with an interesting situation with respect to modern reconstructions of the rise of Johannine literature, if such writings can indeed be attributed to the environs of Ephesus. Specifically, it is quite clear that the author of 1 John is violently opposed to the influence of Docetism among the churches, even going so far as to refer to practitioners of this theological bent as "antichrists" (1 John 2:18–27; 4:1–6). In the same way, it seems quite plausible to assume that many of the earliest readers of the Gospel of John interpreted the text to mean that true Christians were living a life of spirituality that removed them from any responsibility for their physical activities. This led the great theologian Heracleon to read the Gospel of John with a gnostic lens, a tendency that continued in full force until the rebuttals of Irenaeus and Origen.

According to the Johannine literature, then, there was a severe theological conflict within the Ephesian church that pitted a more moderate vision of the role of Jesus as the Messiah against a very spiritual understanding of his work. In some respect, one might find this to be identified in the various christological tendencies that appear throughout John's Gospel, specifically between those verses that suggest a certain "agency Christology" as opposed to those that seem to endorse an "incarnational Christology."[26] It is my suspicion that there is no conflict to be found for the author of this gospel, who undoubtedly held both perspectives to be accurate of the Christ. Instead, the theological difficulties of the community most likely began to arise among those hearers of that text who were persuaded in one direction or the other.

It is entirely possible that the complete form of this debate was not fully manifest at the time that Ignatius wrote to the church at Ephesus. Or it is certainly possible that he was unaware of the specific issues involved. But in either case, it is undoubtedly true that he chose to address the personality conflicts that arose as a prelude to the more important theological discussions and ecclesiastical divisions that eventually were destined to challenge the Ephesian church. Indeed, though the city became the center of several later ecumenical councils, ultimately the Ephesian church was doomed to fall and fade away into history in the same way that the city itself would disappear.

Smyrna

We know of the early Christian situation at Smyrna from a variety of sources, many of which have parallels in our materials for Ephesus. For example, Revelation contains a short missive to the church in the city (see Rev 2:8–11), and Ignatius likewise directs a letter there. At the same time, Ignatius sends a second letter to the city, but this one is

---

[26] Compare, for example, John 3:17, 34; 4:34; 5:36, 38; 7:16, 29, 33 (agency) with John 1:1–18 (incarnational).

addressed specifically to the bishop Polycarp, who himself is known from his single letter (or perhaps combination of two letters) to the church in Philippi. Finally, members of the church in Smyrna are responsible for the account of Polycarp's death, recorded in the *Martyrdom of Polycarp*, which ultimately was shaped into a letter that was sent to the church in Philomelium. A number of other texts that lie outside our current purview provide additional information, including the *Acts of Polycarp* and the *Acts of Pionius and His Companions*.

What is clear from our various writings both to and from Smyrna, as well as those that speak about current local events, is that the church in the city was in a state of constant tension. When Ignatius wrote to the Christians there, he found a perfect opportunity to address his traditional concerns about the threat of Docetism. It seems that many in the church had advocated an understanding of Christ that denied his humanity. What is more, Ignatius seems to suggest that these troublemakers had some Jewish background, since he says that they were not convinced either by the prophecies (of Scripture) or the law of Moses (Ign. *Smyrn.* 5.1). This is a particularly interesting observation in the light of his own apparent lack of interest in Jewish traditions and Scriptures. Once again, as Ignatius typically writes within his letters, he calls for unity around the figure of the bishop with the assumption that the theology of Polycarp was in some sense the same as his own.

This assumption may indeed be the reason that we have a second letter from Ignatius, directed to the bishop Polycarp. In one respect, the letter is written as a word of advice on the many trials that a bishop must confront in his duties. At the same time, however, it stands as a warning to avoid those "who teach strange ideas" (ἑτεροδιδασκαλοῦντες) (Ign. *Pol.* 3.1) and engage in wicked practices (Ign. *Pol.* 5.1). Indeed, Ignatius uses a variety of images that he may have drawn from 4 Maccabees, illustrations of struggle and resistance such as those that would describe a worthy athlete or sailor (see Ign. *Pol.* 2.1–3).[27] In conclusion, he chides the Smyrnaeans to respect their bishop and to train together as fellow strugglers, warring against the challenges of temptation and putting on the armor and weapons of baptism, faith, love, and endurance (Ign. *Pol.* 6.1–2).

---

[27] Compare, for athlete, 4 Macc 6:10; 14:5; 15:29; 16:16; 17:15–16; for sailor, 4 Macc 7:1–3.

The troublesome nature of the Jews within the city appears to be supported by the letter in Rev 2. Here the author affirms that the local Christians, though rich (in spirit?), are both impoverished and under affliction. The blame is directed explicitly toward the slanderous activities of the Jews, who form a "synagogue of Satan" (συναγωγὴ τοῦ σατανᾶ) (Rev 2:9). The specific nature of this slander is not identified. And there is no indication that the problem in Smyrna should be associated with false teaching or strife within the churches themselves, unlike what is suggested by Revelation's letter to Ephesus. One must question, however, whether our author has not assumed that some false teaching was involved, particularly since the letter to Smyrna falls immediately between the letters to Ephesus and Pergamum, both of which are warned about such issues. But the situation remains unresolved, and the text of Revelation offers little else about the church at Smyrna.

We turn then to Polycarp's own letter to the Philippians. On the one hand, the letter addresses the needs and concerns of the audience at Philippi, and thus it is necessarily of limited value for our understanding of Smyrna. On the other hand, however, we hear the words of the local bishop himself. And, presumably, the advice that he offers is consistent with the same type of counsel that he offers the church at Smyrna as well. What is most interesting in the letter is that the theology that Polycarp endorses is very much in line with that of Ignatius. He is opposed to the theological interpretations of Docetism and is greatly concerned for harmony and peace within the community.

In many respects, his ideas are highly stylized by Paul before him, a trait paralleled by Ignatius as well. The letter clearly states the bishop's concern for the issue of "righteousness" (δικαιοσύνη) (Pol. *Phil.* 3.1), but then, that was a primary question about which the Philippians had written. Those elements that are associated with righteousness in the mind of the bishop include truth, love and purity, fidelity, and so on (Pol. *Phil.* 2.2–6.3; 9.1–10.2). He employs standard household codes in his description, as we have seen in our discussion elsewhere, as well as traditional virtue-vice lists that were widely employed in the Hellenistic world.

But ultimately, Polycarp agrees with the teachings of 1 John that anyone who "does not confess that Jesus Christ has come in the flesh is an antichrist"; and further, anyone who "does not acknowledge the witness of the cross is of the devil" (Pol. *Phil.* 7.1).[28] This is particularly

---

[28] See 1 John 4:2–3; 3:8.

interesting terminology in the light of the Ignatian correspondence to
Smyrna and the letter to the city in Rev 2. We see here the two elements
of division that these two authors have already identified with Smyrna:
the problem of Docetism (from Ignatius) and the turmoil caused by the
Jews (from Revelation). Of course, Polycarp's comment about the cross
and the devil, having been taken directly from 1 John, need not necessarily be attributed to the Jewish community. One may as easily apply
the situation to anyone who taught against the theology that Polycarp
espoused, much as Irenaeus did in his recollection of the meeting between Polycarp and Marcion, an encounter in which the bishop accused
the great gnostic teacher of having his roots in the devil.[29]

The role of the Jewish antagonists in Smyrna may be further reinforced, however, by a consideration of the *Martyrdom of Polycarp*. We
find the death of the famous bishop portrayed in this work against the
background of the passion of Jesus in the Gospels, with many parallel
elements and names at work. Most significantly for our purposes is the
accusation of the author that the local Jews joined the non-Jewish community in crying out for the bishop's death (*Mart. Pol.* 12.2), and further, that they were swift to gather firewood for the occasion (*Mart. Pol.*
13.1). Finally, the "evil one, the adversary of the race of the righteous"
(πονηρός, ὁ ἀντικείμενος τῷ γένει τῶν δικαίων) (*Mart. Pol.* 17.1)
inspired the Jews to encourage the authorities not to release the body of
Polycarp, for fear that his followers would worship the bones.[30]

Though somewhat tenuous in nature, the combination of sources
that we can associate with the Christians of Smyrna in some reasonable
sense suggests that the city found itself in a continuing struggle of faith,
at least from the end of the first century through the latter half of the
second century. The writings suggest that there were problems with
Docetism and Jewish resistance to the faith within the city. These struggles certainly were not uncommon in Asia Minor in the early stages of
the church's evolution, and it is not surprising to see evidence of them
in Smyrna as well. At the same time, however, undoubtedly it was
through the charismatic efforts of leaders such as Polycarp that the

---

[29] Irenaeus, *Haer.* 3.3.4.
[30] This is a most instructive phrase in consideration of Polycarp's own letter to Philippi, a text in which he focuses upon the need for righteousness as an
essential element of the Christian faith. Presumably, it is his own righteousness
that would motivate his followers to revere his remains.

church of Smyrna became a leading witness to other faith communities throughout the region.

Corinth

The city of Corinth is well known both from the literary record and from archaeological evidence. Its roots in antiquity betray both the spoils and banes of having compiled a reputation as a noteworthy seaport. Its influence as a major political and cultural center was clear.

We have a number of records that inform us about the Corinthian situation, including the witness of Acts, a collection of Paul's own letters to the city now combined into 1–2 Corinthians, the letter from Rome now called *1 Clement*, and, at least as I will assume for the sake of the present discussion, the homily commonly known as *2 Clement* (see chapter 1 above). This final text I will assume to be the single piece of literature that we have from the Corinthian church itself from among our current witnesses.

From the outset, we should not be misled by Paul's various letters to the community in Corinth and our modern standards of propriety to think that Corinthian Christianity was in some special sense out of bounds with respect to the evolution of the ancient church. The circumstances are most likely quite the contrary. Indeed, what we find at Corinth are an awareness of a eucharistic celebration that was more peculiar to the local church than to what Paul had been taught (1 Cor 11:17–34) and various divisions among the leadership of the faith community (1 Cor 1:10–17; *1 Clement*). These peculiarities certainly were reflected among other church communities, particularly with respect to leadership disputes.[31]

At the same time, the list of moral violations and disrespect of common decencies that the Corinthians betray in 1 Corinthians undoubtedly were not unique to that specific setting. On the one hand, their complaints to Paul represent the natural questions that any community of a new faith might have when confronted with a call to depart

---

[31] Indeed, the apparent disparity between the Eucharist that is condoned by *Did.* 9.1–10.7 versus Matt 26:17–30 (following the Gospel of Mark) may suggest that the churches of both Antioch and Corinth may have practiced the common meal in a variety of ways prior to any standardization. As for questions of ecclesiastical authority, the issue is prevalent among most of the writings that appear in both the New Testament and the apostolic fathers.

from traditional value systems. On the other hand, much of the problem seems to have been motivated by non-Jewish value systems that
came into conflict with Paul's own ethical norms, which themselves
were largely shaped by Jewish standards. But to this we must add Paul's
concern for the imminent Parousia, an idea that was popular throughout the early church, which forced him to shape a system of Christian
ethics that took into account a temporal situation—that is, a time in
which the church existed between the teachings of the historical Jesus
and the return of the cosmic Christ. Furthermore, we must recall that
Corinth, as an active seaport, surely attracted a variety of travelers
whose ideas undeniably seemed foreign and disjointed when lumped
together into a single communal setting. We must ask whether any
of these circumstances were so unique to Corinth itself or, instead,
whether we are not simply more acutely aware of the Corinthian
church because of the letters that remain for us from Paul.

What is particularly evident about the Corinthian situation is
that the setting must not have been especially hostile, as is suggested
by the author of Acts, who states that Paul remained there for over a
year and a half (Acts 18:1–18). In certain respects, this stay by the
apostle resembles his time in Ephesus. He actively preached and taught
in the synagogues and public thoroughfares, he mingled with Christian
Jews who were favorable to his work (i.e., Aquila and Priscilla), and
eventually he was encouraged to leave the city because of complaints
from competing religious authorities (in this case, the Jews). It is not
clear whether Paul was readily accepted throughout the churches of the
city, since his personal testimony includes a variety of appeals to his
apostleship and the unique nature of his ministry.[32] The author of Acts
gives little indication either way.

The one fact that is certain about the Corinthian situation from all
of the literature that applies is that there was considerable division concerning leadership. From the writings of Paul we already see the divided
loyalties to Paul, Apollos, Cephas, and Christ (1 Cor 1:10–17). This same
theme is continued in the text of *1 Clement,* a writing that attempts to
provide some modicum of direction for support of traditional authority
within the community in defiance of upstart leaders. Indeed, the homily
of *2 Clement* would seem to betray a parallel concern, particularly with

---

[32] See, for example, 1 Cor 2:1–13; 4:1–21; 9:1–27; 2 Cor 10:1–12:10.

the author's call for obedient living (*2 Clem.* 5.1–7.6) and unification as the body of Christ (*2 Clem.* 14.1–5), not to mention the references to admonishment of the community by the church elders for lack of self-control and worldly desires (*2 Clem.* 17.3–5).

It is most unfortunate that we do not have a letter from Ignatius to provide some further indication of the need for ecclesiastical structure under the rule of a bishop at Corinth! But this is in part the problem with the Corinthian state of affairs—that is, the guidance of the community seems to have been dominated by elders or presbyters instead of a single authority. At least this is what the literary record suggests. Unlike the various communities in Asia Minor to which Ignatius wrote, for Corinth there is no overriding suggestion that a bishop either was, or even should be, in charge.

It is not clear whether the tendency toward plural leadership was a typically Hellenistic penchant that was characteristic around the region, particularly in the light of the various forms of civil governance that appeared in scattered cities around the Greek peninsula. One thinks immediately of Athenian democracy versus the system of kingship that dominated among those city-states that had formed the Spartan confederation. In either case, parallel civic institutions undoubtedly influenced Corinth's problems with respect to church leadership. The Corinthian church's quest for unification was not unique to the struggles of the ancient church in general, but certainly was characteristic of the nature of the local faith community. It seems quite likely that the church's inability to have a profound influence upon Christianity in Greece was to a large degree affected by its continuing struggle to establish a prominent trend of ecclesiastical leadership.

ROME, ITALY

The situation of the early church at Rome, while not quite as clear as many would prefer to see it, certainly is well informed from the perspective of ancient Christian literature. From one viewpoint, one might expect some particularly helpful insight as a result of the fact that Rome stood at the center of the empire both politically and economically. At the same time, the growth of Christianity in the region is well documented for us from a number of different sources, some of which are sympathetic to the Roman cause, and some of which are not.

Among our earliest resources we may count the concluding materials of Acts, which, though not particularly illuminating on the Roman situation itself, at least imply a strong Christian presence in the city by virtue of the support that was offered to Paul. In this same direction we possess Paul's own New Testament letter to the church at Rome, a text that tells us much about the Roman situation as we read between the lines. In many ways, the later letter of Ignatius to Rome serves to reinforce the perspectives that Paul shares some half century earlier, and so we must include the bishop's text in our considerations. From the view of the Romans themselves, we have *1 Clement* and the relevant comments of that author with respect to authority and tradition as those topics are applied to the Corinthian situation. We must also consider the *Shepherd of Hermas,* a text that seems to have been written from a somewhat different perspective from *1 Clement,* but that adds yet another dimension to what was happening in the city.[33]

Further, and somewhat more controversial in nature, I would place 1 Peter, Hebrews, and the Gospel of Mark within the Roman sphere. In the first instance, it seems rather clear that the author of *1 Clement* was aware of the text of 1 Peter, thus to suggest that the two writings may have come from the same milieu, even as the popular tradition suggests.[34] More circumspect is the possibility that Hebrews also comes from Rome. Numerous considerations might be taken into the discussion here, not the least of which being those sections of agreement between *1 Clement* and Hebrews. Traditional scholarly opinion holds that the author of *1 Clement* has made use of Hebrews as a source. This is by no means certain, however, and if we choose to assign *1 Clement* to an earlier date and Hebrews to a later period, then the situation may be quite the reverse. Furthermore, if Hebrews may indeed be attributed to Rome, then we may have an intriguing window into Roman theology that would explain some of the later imagery that appears within

---

[33] It seems that *1 Clement* and the *Shepherd of Hermas* indicate circumstances and theologies that existed in diverse churches throughout the city; see James S. Jeffers, *Conflict at Rome: Social Order and Hierarchy in Early Christianity* (Minneapolis: Fortress, 1991).

[34] Donald Hagner has provided an extensive list of rarely used words that are shared between *1 Clement* and 1 Peter, thus to strengthen the argument of dependence and perhaps geographical proximity; see Donald A. Hagner, *The Use of the Old and New Testaments in Clement of Rome* (NovTSup 34; Leiden: Brill, 1973), 244–46.

Rome's historical insistence upon the sanctity of Christian priesthood and apostolic succession. Finally, a decision to consider that the Gospel of Mark was written in Rome is primarily a nod to the tradition, as there is no sign that later Roman authors made use of this gospel. But to that regard, the text of Mark was not much used by later authors in any case,[35] though the tradition of Mark's apostolic authority continued to dominate Christianity in Egypt and the subsequent Coptic Orthodox Church of Egyptian tradition.

Our sources leave us with a distinct impression of the Roman church. There seems to be clear evidence that the members of the community were vastly mixed in background, some holding roots in Judaism, and others not. This is already clear from Paul's letter to the Romans, a text that can be adequately understood only to the degree that the reader assumes a Jewish-oriented audience for certain portions of the text and a non-Jewish audience for the remainder. This had certain ramifications for subsequent developments within the local church. Concerns for ethical codes and ecclesiastical rites predominate our Roman literature, much of which undoubtedly was influenced by Judaism. Furthermore, Jewish perspectives of divinity and the way that God can be understood to work within history may also have supported the tendency toward Sabellianism that threatened later Roman theology.[36]

We can be reasonably certain that Rome held to high creedal standards from early in its history. Paul suggests this by his opening greetings to the Roman church (Rom 1:1–6), in which he offers a basic creedal confession. This is most unusual for his letter style, and it may represent an attempt to introduce himself to the Romans through an indication that he knows the faith of Rome and is in sympathy with it. Following upon Paul's example some half century later, Ignatius likewise breaks from his normal epistographical standards in a similar fashion. To his own creedal statement at the beginning of his letter to Rome, he adds an effusive series of positive descriptions of the Roman church, a congregation that he deems to be "worthy of God, worthy of

---

[35] This is true apart from its primary importance to the authors of Matthew and Luke, of course, at least for those who follow the so-called Four-Source Hypothesis of gospel origins.

[36] One recalls here the famous Monarchian controversy in Rome among Zephyrinus, Callistus, and Hippolytus in the late second and early third centuries.

honor, worthy of blessing, worthy of praise, worthy of success, worthy of sanctification" (Ign. *Rom.* proem). Such greetings by Paul and Ignatius, two individuals who presumably were not widely known by the Roman church, suggest that the city's reputation for confessional standards and right doctrine were widely recognized by other Christians throughout the empire.

There seems to be some evidence that the church in Rome, much as in other large cities around the Mediterranean, actually was a composite of numerous smaller house churches from around the city. We have seen this view at work already within the context of Antioch in Syria and Ephesus in Asia Minor. It likewise seems true for the capital city itself. Indeed, texts such as *1 Clement* and the *Shepherd of Hermas* offer several indications that their authors worked from divergent storehouses of ancient imagery.

In *1 Clement*, for example, we find a tremendous dependence upon Hebrew Scriptures that have been utilized as source materials. One notes the references to the role of Moses as taken from the Pentateuch's wilderness tradition that serve as the basis for our author's argument that the Corinthians must return to an orderly chain of apostolic succession (see especially chapters 43 and 53). For *1 Clement*, this type of argument is based upon a traditional understanding of authority that is grounded in the divine appointment of leadership within a given faith community. In contrast to this perspective, however, the author of the *Shepherd of Hermas* represents a much more cultic understanding of authority, holding little concern for traditional ecclesiastical offices and more consideration for the role of the Holy Spirit as a guide to the individual's life of faith. In this context, the author of the *Shepherd* employs very little scriptural support, preferring a variety of materials that stem from common early Christian sayings and Hellenistic parable traditions.

This brings us to a second point: the concern for the role of the Spirit. The Spirit is very loosely defined in the *Shepherd* as a gathering of female consorts in a sense (*Herm.* 113.1–5). The place of the Spirit seems to be restricted primarily to the life of the main character, Hermas, and is assumed to be a primary guide for the individual life of faith. At the same time, the Spirit seems to be completely absent in the argument of *1 Clement*. One might have expected the author of *1 Clement* to appeal to such an authority within the argument of the letter, particularly because questions of the Spirit and faith were so prominently considered in Paul's own letters to Corinth. But this does not hold true here. In a certain sense, *1 Clement* reflects the situation of second-century Christian literature in general, which ignored the Spirit because of debates that ensued within the church with respect to the disruption that the Spirit caused in movements that challenged the rise of ecclesiastical offices.[37] At the same time, it may simply be that the role of the Spirit was not considered of primary concern for the church of *1 Clement,* in contrast to the church of the *Shepherd of Hermas.*

If we may truly include the Gospel of Mark as a literary product of the church at Rome, then we must assume that there was a feeling of anxiety and persecution among the Roman Christian population from very early on. During the 60s, Nero had tried to blame the Jews for a variety of local problems, but eventually he was persuaded to shift his charges specifically toward the Christian sect. The text of Mark indicates the fears of such a setting, framing its warnings of coming persecutions within the context of the end of time and the need for a hasty response to the gospel message that Jesus proclaimed in Mark 1:15: "The time is fulfilled, and the kingdom of God has come near; repent, and believe in the good news."[38] Mark's comments about the role of Simon of Cyrene, who carried the cross of Jesus and was the father of Alexander and Rufus (Mark 15:21), often is viewed by students of Scripture as the author's personal knowledge of the Romans Alexander and Rufus, the latter of whom is greeted by Paul in his own letter to the city.[39]

In the same way, *1 Clement* offers a reflection of the troubles for Christians within Rome, making immediate reference to "sudden and repeated misfortunes and reverses" by the church at the very beginning of the letter (*1 Clem.* 1.1). Indeed, it is within this very context of turmoil (whether external or, perhaps, internal) that our author is able to understand the struggles at Corinth. In a similar way, the author of the *Shepherd of Hermas* offers an incredible symbolic vision of the

---

[37] One thinks of the situation of Tertullian and Montanism (the so-called Phrygian heresy), for example, whose focus upon ecstatic prophecy, asceticism, and eschatology forced a wedge between Montanists and evolving Catholicism.

[38] In many respects, this combined theme of suffering and the need for Christian faith is paralleled in the text of 1 Peter.

[39] See Rom 16:13, under the assumption that chapter 16 was not added later by a second hand.

apocalyptic terrors that have confronted the Roman church. This image is offered early in the fourth vision of the *Shepherd* in the figure of a huge beast like a sea monster that rushed toward Hermas as though to destroy a city (*Herm.* 22.1–10). As the author relates, it was "a foreshadowing of the coming persecution" (*Herm.* 22.1). Already, Hermas had been assured that those who suffer "for the sake of the name" would be rewarded by gifts and promises (*Herm.* 10.1), presumably a reference to the history of persecution that Christians had endured in the city. The clear result of such comments is that the church that God builds on the solid rock through the graceful work of Christian virtues is designed to stand as a bulwark against a variety of external threats, whether from the menace of unbelieving religions or from the peril of the civil government.

Much can be said about the churches of Rome in the first and second centuries from the literary materials that remain for us. On the one hand, there was the constant reality of persecution within the local faith community that surely was stabilized to some degree by the apparent participation of various government officials and their families. On the other hand, there was the intermingling of Jewish Christians with non-Jewish believers in the evolving church situation, offering a recipe of internal tension and the grounds for local conflict in the establishment of ecclesiastical authority and roles of governance. At the same time, the sources for such a community clearly were scattered in breadth and scope. We see the use of the Hebrew Scriptures by many authors, placed alongside the incorporation of Hellenistic traditions among others. We find the collection of sayings and parables that undoubtedly were commonly known in the Roman church but indicate little or no parallels among the remaining texts of the New Testament.

Ultimately, what we can know about the church at Rome is varied and elusive. Our materials suggest that the local faith situation was quite diverse in scope and content. They betray the reality that the church at Rome, primarily because of its location at the political and economic center of the empire, was gradually to become a center of gravity for other Christians around the Mediterranean, even as early as the middle of the first century. In many respects, the history of much early Christian literature owes its existence to the authority and influence that Roman faith was to wield among the remaining churches around the empire.

CONCLUSION

Though it is extremely difficult to assign much of ancient Christian literature to specific geographical locations around the Mediterranean basin, efforts to do so can prove to be especially informative in any scholarly attempt to connect certain authors and their ideas within the history of the early church. Indeed, such endeavors are essential if we are ever to understand the nuances of apostolic and postapostolic theology and faith.

In discussions of the New Testament in its relationship to the apostolic fathers, one might break these geographical regions into four primary divisions: Egypt, Syria, Asia Minor and Greece, and Italy. Yet, even here our main considerations are primarily restricted to the principal cities of Alexandria, Antioch, Smyrna, Corinth, and Rome. Much of what we know of the ancient church has been strongly shaped through the views of Christians in these locations, especially via the insights of those who served as leaders for each community. It is their literary production that gives us a glimpse into the mindset of faith in the first and second centuries. Many of these people can be named—Paul and Peter, Ignatius and Polycarp—but the majority of them remain unidentified characters in history.

At the same time, their ideas reflect the theological tendencies of the times. And if we can assume that those tendencies indicate basic movements within specific geographical locales, then often we are able to attribute specific early Christian texts to evolving church communities.

Within the realm of Egyptian Christianity, one finds the heavy influence of Jewish thought and symbols. The blending of Hellenistic philosophy with Jewish wisdom, so typical of the writings of Philo of Alexandria, quickly formed a foundation for similar efforts within both the local and extended Christian community. Thus the focus upon a "logos" theology as found in the Gospel of John might suggest such an influence within the broader sphere of Christianity. But writings such as the *Epistle of Barnabas* and the *Epistle to Diognetus* may be even better examples of the struggle between Greek and Jewish ideas on a local level.

In Syria, we are immediately confronted by the writings of Ignatius, that influential bishop whose reflection of the early Christian experience indicates the influence of a variety of faith witnesses. Included here, without question, are the apostle Paul and the theology of the Gospel of Matthew. So too, one might take account of the *Didache* and the martyr theology of the author of 4 Maccabees. As with Egypt, the influence of Jewish views is evident in Syrian Christianity, though Ignatius himself is loath to accept them as a mainstay of Christian theology.

When we turn to Asia Minor and Greece, our view of the early church situation becomes decidedly broader. We confront the various Christian communities that were addressed by Paul and Ignatius along their journeys. Most notable here is the church in Ephesus, a community that receives the attention of the author of Acts, perhaps Paul, and Ignatius. We hear the voice of one of the leading bishops of the region from the second century, Polycarp, and see evidence of his theology that dominated the church in Smyrna. We witness the testimony of his disciples in the *Martyrdom of Polycarp* about the death that he suffered. We see the rise of the Pauline school at work here, reflected in the theology of Polycarp and Ignatius and in the deuteropauline writings of the New Testament. In Greece, we are able to trace the early rise of the Corinthian situation, known first from Paul, then from the author of *1 Clement* in Rome, and perhaps finally from *2 Clement.*

Finally, the presence of Christianity in Rome, though not fully revealed from our documents, is broadly illustrated from our literature. Again, Paul and Ignatius come into play as outside perspectives, while the authors of *1 Clement* and the *Shepherd of Hermas* suggest an insider's vision of the broad and rich variety of perspectives that the Roman church reflected well into the second century. Though it is difficult to assign New Testament writings such as the Gospel of Mark, 1 Peter, and Hebrews to this same location, either tradition or consistency of theme with known Roman texts might lead us in this direction.

In the final analysis, what we can understand about theological harmony and ideological diversity as reflected among our New Testament authors and the apostolic fathers is shaped by our ability to associate these writings with specific authors and community mindsets. In many cases these sources were broadly accepted into the foundation of early Christian orthodoxy, while in other instances they were relegated to distant shadows of former dimensions of the Christian vision that were either subsumed into or displaced by the larger development of the church. The rise of a dominant ecclesiastical institution throughout the Roman world and the process of canonization have eventually brought us to think of certain texts as primary (the New Testament) and others as distant reflections of our early Christian past (the apostolic fathers). In many respects, however, their authors and traditions reflect the same visions of faith.

FOR FURTHER READING

Most surveys of early Christianity according to geographical boundaries tend to be limited and regional in scope, as with the following:

- Brown, Raymond E., and John P. Meier. *Antioch and Rome: New Testament Cradles of Catholic Christianity.* New York: Paulist Press, 1983.

- Donfried, Karl Paul. *The Setting of Second Clement in Early Christianity.* Supplements to Novum Testamentum 38. Leiden: Brill, 1974.

- Griggs, C. Wilfred. *Early Egyptian Christianity from Its Origins to 451 C.E.* Edited by M. Krause. Coptic Studies 2. Leiden: Brill, 1990.

- Jeffers, James S. *Conflict at Rome: Social Order and Hierarchy in Early Christianity.* Minneapolis: Fortress, 1991.

- Slee, Michelle. *The Church in Antioch in the First Century C.E.: Communion and Conflict.* Journal for the Study of the New Testament: Supplement Series 244. London and New York: Sheffield Academic Press, 2003.

On a more general level, one might consult these works:

- Bauer, Walter. *Orthodoxy and Heresy in Earliest Christianity.* Translated by the Philadelphia Seminar on Christian Origins. Edited by R. A. Kraft and G. Krodel. Philadelphia: Fortress, 1971.

- Brown, Raymond E. *The Churches the Apostles Left Behind.* New York: Paulist Press, 1984.

- Meissner, W. W. *The Cultic Origins of Christianity: The Dynamics of Religious Development.* Collegeville, Minn.: Liturgical Press, 2000.

- Sanders, Jack T. *Schismatics, Sectarians, Dissidents, Deviants: The First One Hundred Years of Jewish-Christian Relations.* Valley Forge, Pa.: Trinity Press International, 1993.

Conclusion

The Significance of the Apostolic Fathers for New Testament Study

The primary difficulty in any attempt to compare the apostolic fathers and the New Testament comes with the recognition that each set of writings represents the culmination of diverse authors and historical contexts within the early church. This situation presents a number of complexities for contemporary research, particularly when we realize that most of the texts in both collections have not been securely anchored with respect to the issues of author, date, and place—the concerns of so-called higher criticism. As a result, scholars who work in the field typically have restricted their research to individual authors and writings, thus to keep the issues under some control. The resulting studies often have been illuminating and serve a central role for our understanding of specific texts within early Christian literature, but they remain limited with respect to observations concerning the larger corpus.

A variety of observations may nevertheless be offered with respect to the overall literary and historical relationship between our two collections, despite the various ambiguities that remain with reference to individual texts. These insights are assisted in large part by the diverse genres that have been preserved, as well as by the witness to scattered geographical regions represented among the writings. The works of the New Testament clearly represent the same faith and theologies shared by the authors of the collected apostolic fathers to some large extent. And the issues and historical situations that the apostolic fathers address add essential testimony to the rise of materials and traditions that now appear within our biblical canon.

First and foremost among our observations is acknowledgment of the early church's struggle to define itself with respect to Jewish tradition and Judaism's standards of theology and ethics. The witness of our collected writings attests to this endeavor as a primary component of churches throughout the Mediterranean world, especially as reflected in the major cities of the Roman Empire. From the Gospel of Matthew to the letters of Ignatius, from the writings of Paul and the deutero-pauline school to the witness of Polycarp, from the polemical language of *Barnabas* and the Gospel of John to the homilies of the Acts of the Apostles and *2 Clement*, it is unequivocal that the church of the apostolic and postapostolic periods was greatly concerned to define itself over against its common roots in Judaism. The earliest witnesses to this process reveal at least two separate approaches. On the one hand, an author such as Paul depicts a concerted effort to define the church within Jewish parameters but beyond Judaism's institutional restraints; on the other hand, leaders such as Ignatius and Polycarp make a concerted effort to reject Jewish tendencies within early Christian theology and institutional structures. Such divergence suggests that there was no unified voice in the early process of faith separation. But by the time of *Diognetus,* under the influence of leaders such as Ignatius and the author of *Barnabas,* a unity of perspective had arisen that ultimately drove the church out of the tumultuous world of Jewish conflict and into a hostile Roman culture that did not embrace Christianity until the rule of Constantine.

At the same time that we see early Christians confronting their Jewish heritage, we also come to recognize the role of Hellenistic roots behind the imagery and theology of ancient church authors. This is immediately evident in the vision of Paul, who, as a Hellenistic Jew from Tarsus, knew and used the philosophical tenets of Stoicism and Cynicism to shape early Christian rhetoric into a model that would appeal to his audiences. And like Paul, the bishops Ignatius and Polycarp drew upon the literary imagery of the Greek and Roman worlds in an effort to pull their listeners into quite specific theological interpretations of the Christian faith. An additional approach is provided by the author of the *Shepherd of Hermas,* who incorporated a variety of parable images whose background is drawn from Hellenistic culture. We are not particularly surprised by these efforts, especially since non-Christian parallels may be found throughout the historical witness of Flavius Josephus and the philosophical machinations of Philo Judaeus. And yet it is enlightening to see that this process of cultural adaptation is somewhat broadly evident throughout the Mediterranean world. As has been remarked so often before, the avenues of the *Pax Romana* provided ample opportunity for Christianity and its preachers to spread a first-century messianic faith that had broad appeal to Jews in the Diaspora and to the non-Jewish "God-fearers" who worshipped with them. Indeed, Virgil's belief that the golden age of Rome had returned with Augustus Caesar certainly held true for the onset of the nascent church. And the influence of Homer and Hellenistic romance literature upon our New Testament and patristic authors gives ample evidence of the importance of contemporary culture for early interpretations of Christian beginnings.

The broad issue of Jewish and Hellenistic influence upon the church as depicted within our literature directs us ultimately to the more specific genres of materials preserved by our authors. On a broader scale, we find that the apostolic fathers, like the New Testament, continued to be dependent primarily upon letters as the vehicle of their literary production. Thus we find that the correspondence of Clement, Ignatius, and Polycarp closely parallels that of the Pauline and deuteropauline letters, 1–3 John and Jude, 1–2 Peter, and the opening chapters of Revelation. Yet, as with the writings of Hebrews and James in the New Testament, texts such as *Barnabas, 2 Clement,* and the *Martyrdom of Polycarp* remain suspended between the genres of letter and homily as productions that are not so easily defined. On a narrower level, we readily detect the use of sayings throughout both sets of writings, primarily (but certainly not exclusively) associated with the teachings of Jesus. And in the same way that the teachings of Jesus in the Gospels often are direct reflections either of traditional or contemporary Jewish ideas, there is a similar portrayal of themes within the apostolic fathers, particularly as seen in the *Didache.* But our authors share other literary forms as well, including household codes, virtue-vice lists, creedal fragments, parables, visions, hymns, prayers, apocalyptic terminology, and miracle stories. All of these forms served as a common foundation upon which early Christian authors wrote about their theological perceptions and shared those convictions with their audiences.

Of particular interest among the collected writings of the New Testament and apostolic fathers is the attention that is continually applied to certain specific issues of church growth and belief. Most prominent here is a general warning against false prophecy and inaccurate teaching. This concern is most prevalent in the Gospels of Matthew and Luke and in the Pastoral Epistles, and it has been addressed quite specifically by the authors of 1 John and Jude. The writer of Revelation also makes use of this theme in the seven letters to the churches of Asia Minor. And as might be expected, later authors such as Ignatius and Polycarp address this issue as well. Their warnings against docetic ideas come through loud and clear. Such a broad response to the problem of false prophecy and false teaching suggests that the predicament was prevalent on a wide scale at the turn of the first century. At the same time, however, if we can accept an early date for the origins of a text such as the *Didache,* then there would appear to be evidence that similar concerns already were manifest in previous decades. It is little wonder that later centuries produced a broad array of literary texts from the great apologists and heresiologists to help frame the theological norms of the evolving church.

Another theme that continually spans the gap between biblical authors and extrabiblical works is the call for unity in the midst of diversity. Paul is a primary witness to this motif from the very beginning of our literature. His teachings, based primarily upon Jewish sensitivities and his recognition of a need for Christian cooperation under the rubric of the body of Christ, served to set a foundation for similar arguments in later years. Indeed, both Ignatius and the author of *1 Clement* offered images that were directed toward the unification of church assemblies. In the view of Ignatius, this effort was marked by theological considerations, ultimately defined by the vision of a single overseer (bishop) who was to direct lesser ecclesiastical functionaries (presbyters and deacons) as the embodiment of God the Father. For *1 Clement,* the figure of Moses, chosen by God alone to lead the people of Israel through the wilderness, served as the prototypical authority behind the ordering of church offices. It is particularly curious that Paul himself never made specific reference to either of these visions of authority in his letters. But then again, his witness to the role of church leadership was much more communal and Jewish in its approach, recognizing the value of elders as the organizers of the early Christian experience. It was only with the development of later ecclesiastical speculation that the offices of the church gained general acceptance among the scattered Christian communities.

A further concern shared among our authors is the role of ethics in the formation of the early Christian lifestyle. Paul serves as the earliest witness for such concerns, particularly as they are manifested in his response to the situation in Corinth, and his ideas became the natural springboard for later speculation. The approaches of the deutero-pauline authors, the text of James, and the letters of 1–3 John and 1–2 Peter all make the ethics of interpersonal relationship the basis of instruction for the church. And such efforts are not restricted to the letter genre, since we find that much of our gospel material is oriented toward matters of religious lifestyle and the attainment of righteousness in the sight of God. By the same token, the apostolic fathers are highly concerned for the lifestyle of early Christians. This is clearly true in the "two ways" segment of the *Didache* and the *Epistle of Barnabas,* and also in the speculation on righteousness that drives Polycarp's letter to Philippi. It is also prominent in the apology contained in the *Epistle to Diognetus* and in the homily preserved in *2 Clement.* Even the *Martyrdom of Polycarp* endorses a less-than-subtle ethic of toleration and discipleship that places love of God and respect for neighbor (= enemy) above concerns for self. The teachings of self-sacrifice that such a witness offered to the late patristic period led to a widely practiced martyr cult that ecclesiastical authorities eventually had to curtail for the good of the church.

Finally, the development of early Christian sacraments and liturgical rites is featured prominently throughout our collected texts. In some writings where this process is evident, the church has become dependent upon our authors as the foundation for later doctrines and practices. Thus the words of institution for the Eucharist that appear in Paul's letter to Corinth and in the passion narratives of the Synoptic Gospels form the foundation of more modern practices. And the teachings about forgiveness after baptism in the *Shepherd of Hermas* and confessional creeds preserved in the letters of Ignatius have helped to shape subsequent sacraments and theological norms. Most recently, various prohibitions against abortion that are found in the two ways materials of the *Epistle of Barnabas* and the *Didache* have been used as the foundation for church teachings with respect to "right to life" issues. Thus we find that the history of theological development within the church often has accepted materials from the New Testament and the apostolic fathers as authoritative for ecclesiastical instruction, regardless of the matter of canonical status. At the same time, early Christian practices from these collected writings likewise have been rejected on an equal basis. The ancient insistence that nonkosher meat be avoided—known from the apostolic decree of Acts, the memory of the *Didache,* and the suggestion of Paul—has hardly affected later church practice. And the paucity of endorsement for specific ecclesiastical offices among our authors has been largely superseded by Ignatius's threefold vision of bishops, presbyters, and deacons. Our texts have been both accepted and rejected by church authorities as the foundation of ecclesiastical practices and interpretations on an equal basis. Despite the process of canonization that came to divide the materials in a formal sense, they have remained ancient contemporaries in practice.

In the final analysis, it is clear that the world, the authors, and the issues that served to frame the structure of the New Testament are essentially the same as those that provided direction to the production of the apostolic fathers. Though it certainly is true that the reach of the latter materials extended perhaps some half a century beyond the scope of the former works, the relationship of the two collections is somewhat analogous to adjoining steps within a staircase: one leads to the next, and they very much resemble each other. They are of the same materials; they are engendered from the same perspective. In the same way that biblical scholars recognized long ago that the New Testament could neither be clearly understood nor accurately interpreted without some direction from the Hebrew Scriptures, so too must Christian historians come to read the church's earliest canonical writings within the light of the generation of ecclesiastical leaders who produced the first responses to that material. Furthermore, due credit must be given to the broad range of authors represented by the apostolic fathers. Those figures, whether their names are known from recognized historical sources or are unspecified by the tradents of Christian history, shared the numerous images and issues that permeate New Testament literature and offer a unique perspective upon the rise of the early church, somewhat apart from the vagaries of ecclesiastical manipulation and pious interpretation. It is often through the eyes of the apostolic fathers that the contexts of the ancient biblical debates are improved and our understanding of the rise of Christianity is greatly enhanced.

Index of Subjects

Tarsus, 11, 124, 147, 248
Tatian, 123, 168, 221
Temple, 18–19, 33–34, 89, 185, 191, 221
Testimonia, 55, 166
Theodosius I, 193
Theophilus of Antioch, 35, 169, 223
Thessalonica, 227
Thyatira, 227, 229
Timothy, 207
Titus, 130
Torah, 83, 90, 104, 127, 161, 181, 215
Trajan, 12–13, 34

Tralles, 10–11, 138, 227
Trinity/Trinitarian, 115, 162, 218
Troas, 10–11
two ways, 46–47, 53, 83, 88–91, 103, 105, 110, 121, 126–27, 161, 189, 216–17, 251

Virgil, 249
virtue-vice list, 80–85, 89, 91, 93, 105, 137, 202, 249
Vulgate, 171

Zechariah, 97

Index of Ancient Sources